DANCE IN SOCIETY

INTERNATIONAL LIBRARY OF SOCIOLOGY
AND SOCIAL RECONSTRUCTION

Founded by Karl Mannheim
Editor: W. J. H. Sprott

A catalogue of books available in the INTERNATIONAL LIBRARY OF
SOCIOLOGY AND SOCIAL RECONSTRUCTION and new books in
preparation for the Library will be found at the end of this volume

DANCE
IN SOCIETY

*An analysis of the relationship
between the social dance and
society in England from the
Middle Ages to the Present Day*

FRANCES RUST

LONDON
ROUTLEDGE & KEGAN PAUL

This edition published 1969
by Routledge & Kegan Paul Limited
Broadway House, 68–74 Carter Lane
London, E.C.4

Printed in Great Britain
by C. Tinling & Co. Ltd
Prescot

SBN 7100 6582 5

To every thing there is a season, and a time to every purpose under the heaven; . . . a time to weep, and a time to laugh; a time to mourn, and a time to dance . . .

Ecclesiastes 3.

TABLE OF CONTENTS

Contents

viii

Contents

ix

Contents

ILLUSTRATIONS

PREFACE

At the outset, I would like to make it clear that this book is, in the main, a small-scale pioneer approach to the sociology of dance, rather than an attempt to establish, on a grand scale, a truly comprehensive social theory of dance in all its aspects. In the first place, one particular category – 'social dance' (or dancing for pleasure and recreation) – has been singled out from a wide spectrum which includes many other important aspects, such as ballet, stage, national, folk, primitive, sacred, and dance in ancient civilizations. In the second place, the main study is scaled down to one particular country (England) and a specific period of history (from the Middle Ages to the present day). Social dance has been singled out because of its very close link with changes in society, and the further limitation in terms of time and place is in order to make possible a detailed and comprehensive sociological investigation.

Other writers may well be able to enlarge the scale by specialist contributions relating to other countries and to other aspects of dance.

A considerable number of people have helped me, directly or indirectly, in the preparation of this book. I would like to thank Professor Fletcher for valuable suggestions in connection with the Ph.D. thesis on which the book is based, and Professor Sprott for advice and help at the publication stage. I would also like to express my gratitude to Drene Dove, whose 'technique' sessions first aroused my interest in the background to the social dances of Latin America. My good friends Marjorie Asquith, Rosemary Mitchell and Fernau Hall have helped me more than they know by their encouragement and sustained interest in the whole project.

The survey would have been impossible without the co-operation of the Principal of Woolwich Polytechnic, the Principal of West London College, and the Principal of Woolwich College for Further Education. It would have been a much longer task without the expert technical advice of Gillian Charman, and the routine operations decidedly more wearisome without the lively help of many Woolwich Polytechnic students, particularly Frank Sealey, John Kay and John Stanmore Smith.

Preface

I am indebted to Dancing Times Ltd for permission to reproduce, in Chapter XIII and Appendix G, the substance of two articles I wrote originally for the *Ballroom Dancing Times*, to *New Society* for permission to reproduce in Chapter XIII part of my article 'The Slavery that bred Jazz', to Herbert Jenkins Ltd for permission to make use of valuable historical material from P. J. S. Richardson's book: *Social Dances of the Nineteenth Century*, to Cyril Beaumont for permission to use his translation of Arbeau's *Orchésographie*, and finally I would like to thank Professor Eysenck for allowing me to reproduce in Appendix L a few sample questions from the Eysenck Personality Inventory.

I
Introduction

(a) Purpose and Plan

Anthropological studies never fail to highlight the significance of dance but, up to the present, there has been no systematic *sociological* investigation of the activity of dancing. The dearth of sociological data compared with the wealth of anthropological has led me to undertake the present study.

My purpose is, firstly, to enquire into the functional aspect of the social dance in society, and secondly, within this general framework, to explore the particular hypothesis that variations in the social dance are never fortuitous or random, but are always closely related to the social structure of society: in particular, to class relationships, ideology and social customs, the attitude to women, and the level of industrialization and technology.

Seen in this light, the social dance is a significant part of the general culture pattern of any society and it is thus not simply by chance that over a period of time some dances disappear, and others – but not all aspirants – take their places. For example, according to this hypothesis, it is no accident that England in the early sixteenth century dances the pavane, in the middle sixteenth century La Volta, in the seventeenth century the gavotte, in the eighteenth century the minuet, in the nineteenth century the waltz, and in the twentieth century the twist. The general underlying argument is that the social dance is very intimately related to human experience, and because of this reflects the spirit of the age in any particular society with great fidelity.

The term 'social dance' is throughout intended to cover all forms of dancing directly for recreation and pleasure. Court dancing and 'true' folk-dancing come, therefore, directly within the scope of the study but professional stage dancing, including ballet, does so only peripherally where it impinges or throws some light on social dance. The Morris and the Sword dance, and other ritual dances of rural England, are not considered true 'social dances' in this sense, and folk-dances, revived and kept alive by minority groups, are not

1

directly relevant except where they can provide information and evidence about the folk-dances of the past.

(b) *Theoretical Framework*

The present study falls into three sections. Part I opens with two background chapters on dance which are intended to supply a certain anthropological and psychological perspective. The first is on the nature and origin of dance and its significance in primitive society, and the second relates to pathological manifestations, in particular, to the dancing-mania of the Middle Ages. Part II contains a detailed historical and sociological analysis of the social dance in England from the thirteenth century to the present day, drawing upon contemporary literary and historical material, where available. Part III consists of a sociological survey of young people's habits and attitudes with relation to dancing, in which particular attention is paid to contemporary teenage solo dancing to beat music.

Appendix A contains a Table of Dates where clear interrelationships can be seen between important dates in the history of social dance, on the one hand, and social and political history on the other. Appendices B to G provide background material of historical and general interest. Appendices H and I illustrate two very different aspects of contemporary social dancing. Appendices J to L contain the survey results and Questionnaires relating to Part III.

The present study has been conceived within the broad framework, or conceptual scheme, provided by a 'structural/functionalist' analysis of society. The functionalist 'school', if it may be so termed, has never lacked critics and detractors[1] but, in spite of opposition, it continues, in my view, to offer the most useful approach to a systematic analysis of social structure, or any element of social structure. This is not to commit oneself to any doctrinaire notion of function, but merely to suggest the utility of the concept for analysis, particularly for the present study. This point of view is succinctly expressed by R. Fletcher: 'Functionalism is not, in the strict sense of the word, a social theory: but rather a systematic mode of analysis, which makes possible the clear enunciation of, the pursuit of, and the elaboration of social theories . . .'[2] It is in this sense that the 'functional' framework is used here – for the analysis of social theories, rather than as a social theory.

The structural/functionalist approach consists, basically, of the assumption that every social system must solve certain functional problems (for if it did not, the system would disintegrate). Following the usage of recent theorists[3] these problems might be termed:

(1) PATTERN MAINTENANCE and TENSION MANAGEMENT

This refers to 'socialization', (the process by which cultural patterns come to be incorporated in the personalities of members of the society) and to the 'management' of potentially disrupting emotional disturbances and distractions.

(2) ADAPTATION

This includes adaptation to the social and non-social environment, division of labour and role differentiation.

(3) SOCIETAL GOALS

This includes all the goals the society sets itself.

(4) INTEGRATION

This includes social control, the co-ordination and successful interrelation of units, solidarity, morale, patterns of authority, and common values.

If any part of the social structure makes a contribution towards solving these problems or meeting these needs, that part of the structure can be said to have a 'function' for the social system. In the words of Radcliffe Brown:

> the function of any recurrent activity, such as the punishment of a crime, or a funeral ceremony, is the part it plays in the social life as a whole, and therefore the contribution it makes to the maintenance of the structural continuity . . .[4]

Implicit in this approach is the view that social structure is a *pattern* of interacting social institutions which exert a mutually determining influence upon each other: hence, from the functionalist point of view, no single institution can be understood in isolation from its context.

From this brief explanation of the structural/functional approach, it is clear that a sociological analysis in functionalist terms of the interrelationship of the social dance and society would ideally have to meet the following requirements:

(a) The basic pre-requisite that the item in question (the social dance) represents a standardized (i.e. a patterned and repetitive) item of social structure (to ensure that it can legitimately be made the subject of functional analysis).

(b) A detailed account of the item (the social dance) and an analysis of its functions, in terms, for example, of the four problems enumerated above together with an account of the way it operates and interacts with other items, and contributes to the functioning of the whole social system.

(c) Observation and analysis of any change in structure and function of the item (the social dance), correlating such change with change in the larger social system of which it forms a part.

The present investigation, although in itself a detailed specific account of the social dance in one society, attempts, none the less, to meet these three requirements. It consists of a two-fold approach:

(1) A detailed analysis, combining a functional and historical approach, of the social dance in England, from the thirteenth century to the present day.

(2) A survey, in order to obtain empirical data about a particular facet of the social dance in contemporary society. (The reason for choosing the 'habits and attitudes of young people' is explained in the preface to Part III.)

The utilization of the historical/functional orientation is not, of course, accidental, but is in line with Dürkheim's insistence that for an adequate explanation of social facts both approaches are necessary. Thus '... The determining cause of a social fact should be sought among the social facts preceding it',[5] and '... to explain a social fact we must [also] show its function in the establishment of social order ...'[6] The value of the sociological survey in Part III (apart from the intrinsic interest of the data) lies in the possibility it provides of subjecting to empirical test many of the hypotheses in Parts I and II.

(c) *Methodological Problems*

A methodological objection that might be raised is one which applies to all forms of analysis of the past in terms of 'period'. As Trevelyan points out: 'In political history one King at a time reigns ... but in social ... history we find in every period several different kinds of social ... organization going on simultaneously. In everything, the old overlaps the new ... there is no single moment when all Englishmen adopt new ways of life and thought.'[7] This overlapping of the old and the new applies very strongly to the social dance and it is a point which must be borne in mind throughout. In order to minimize the too easy generalizations which result from the habit of thinking in terms of historical 'periods', a short summary of significant dates is given at the end in Appendix A. As Trevelyan says: 'dates are facts': periods are not.

A further objection that might be raised to the examination of a general hypothesis of the connection between the social dance and the 'spirit of the age' in the period under review is the fairly rigid social stratification existing in English society until the period of the more fluid class structure of the nineteenth century. If the social dancing of 'nobles' and 'peasants' is utterly different, how can either be taken as representative of the age? It is, of course, true to say that any cleft in society between social strata shows itself in the social dance as in every other aspect of life, and it is not until the twentieth century that dancing becomes 'classless'. A wide gulf between the different social strata, reflected in their social life and hence in their social dancing, is not, however, in itself an argument against the hypothesis. If society is rigidly stratified, the activity of dancing will reflect this stratification in that different social strata will have different dances, and/or different styles of dancing. At the same time, if social dancing reflects the spirit of the age, we would expect to find not only differences, but also common elements in the dances of the different social strata.

This is precisely what happens, albeit with some time lag. History indicates that the generating impulse for new forms of the social dance comes most frequently from the 'people' in that any new folk-dance tends to be taken up by the court. At court, it will be polished and refined almost out of all recognition, but can still be seen to possess certain elements in common with the folk-dance from which it sprang.

One of the best illustrations of this process of 'upgrading' of the folk-dance can be seen in France in the sixteenth century. Part of the entertainment at the French court was the performance of dances by peasants from the various provinces, in national costume. One dance thus introduced was the dance of the Gavots (the inhabitants of Gap in South East France). This dance came to be known as the 'gavotte', underwent various changes in step and style, was taken up by the French court, and arrived in England as a rather stately and formal dance in the early seventeenth century.[8] Other similar examples are the minuet which came from a folk-dance of Poitou, and the waltz which came from the turning-dances of the South German peasants. Similarly, in England, the country-dances of the people in the seventeenth century became popular at court and continued to be danced at State balls until the early years of the nineteenth century. If this common element is admitted between the dancing of 'nobles' and 'folk', the examination of the general interrelationship of the dance and society even in a highly stratified social structure is no longer a methodological problem.

PART I
BACKGROUND

II
Anthropological Perspectives

(a) Nature and Origin of Dancing

An analysis of the nature and origin of dancing involves a consideration of three questions: *What* is dancing? *When* did man first begin to dance, and *Why*? The questions are clear-cut, but the answers can only be described as hazy.

Voss, for example, devotes twelve pages to cited definitions of dancing,[1] and equal confusion reigns over questions of origin and motivation. The following definition of dancing given by A. E. Crawley,[2] however, has the merit of being both simple and non-controversial, and in addition gives a meaningful answer to the question – What is dancing? 'Dancing, in its proper sense, consists in rhythmical movement of any part or all parts of the body in accordance with some scheme of individual or concerted action.' No one knows for certain *when* man first began to dance (in this sense), or *why*. It is not improbable that dancing preceded speech – a theory developed by Langer, who traces the origin of dance to the spontaneous, self-expressive movements and gestures of man which functioned as symbols of communication long before language.[3]

Other theories go even further back in the history of mankind, tracing dance and its basic circle form to man's animal ancestors, particularly the lively, playful circle dances of the apes. Of immense interest here is Köhler's detailed description of a genuine round dance of the anthropoid apes in Teneriffe:

> . . . two of them . . . begin to circle about, using the post as a pivot. One after another the rest of the animals appear, join the circle, and finally the whole group, one behind the other, is marching in orderly fashion around the post. Now their movements change quickly. They are no longer walking but trotting. Stamping with one foot and putting the other down lightly, they beat out what approaches a distinct rhythm, with each of them tending to keep step with the rest. Sometimes they bring their heads into play and bob them up and down, with jaws loose, in time with the stamping

9

of their feet. All the animals appear to take a keen delight in this primitive round dance ... Once I saw an animal, snapping comically at the one behind, walk backwards in the circle. Not infrequently one of them would whirl as he marched about with the rest. When two posts stand close to each other, they like to use these as a centre, and in this case the ring dance around both takes the shape of an ellipse. In these dances the chimpanzee likes to bedeck his body with all sorts of things, especially strings, vines and rags that dangle and swing in the air as he moves about ...[4]

Curt Sachs points out[5] that this description shows a series of completely recognizable motifs: the circle and ellipse as forms: the forward and backward pace: hopping, rhythmical stamping and whirling as movements: and even a form of ornamentation for the dance.

Following this line of thinking, the question of *when* man first began to dance loses some of its meaning, since the origin of dance appears to be traceable back to the very origin of mankind.

The question *why* posed at the beginning of the chapter can similarly be answered only in theoretical terms.

Many theorists[6] take the view that dancing is an instinctive mode of muscular reaction – whose function is either to express feeling or emotion or, at other times, simply to express 'excess energy'. In the latter case, dancing is seen as an aspect or development of physical 'play'. These views are supported by well-observed studies not only of animals (as, for example, the apes observed by Köhler), but also of birds and insects. 'Courtship' dances, where the male dances to attract and rouse the female, are common in the bird and insect kingdoms, and at other times there seem to be clear instances of dances which are simply an expression of play, individual or group. The dance of the argus pheasant, the 'waltz' of the ostrich, and the bowing and scraping of the penguin are well-known, but perhaps no account is more vivid than that of MacLaren[7] describing the dance of the stilt birds in Cape York, North East Australia:

There were some hundreds of them [the birds] and their dance was in the manner of quadrille, but in the matter of rhythm and grace excelling any quadrille that ever was. In groups of a score or more they advanced and retreated, lifting high their long legs and standing on their toes, now and then bowing gracefully one to another, now and then one pair encircling with prancing daintiness a group whose heads moved upwards, downwards and sideways in time to the stepping of the pair. At times they formed into one great, prancing mass ... then suddenly ... they would sway apart, some of them to rise in low, encircling flight . . .; and presently they would form in pairs or sets of pairs, and the prancing and the bowing, and advancing and retreating would begin all over again . . .

It can of course be argued that the 'leap' from the animal world to man is too great, even in terms of activities which are claimed to be biological. If animal studies are to be ruled out, however, one can go to the field of child development for equally convincing support for the 'instinctive' theory of dancing. Most observers report that at about the age of one and a half the majority of children, without training, start some clearly recognizable rhythmical movement such as bouncing or jumping up and down in response to rhythmic music.[8] Abandoning the word 'instinctive' as a relatively unhelpful concept when applied to human beings, one can at any rate claim that the bulk of the available evidence indicates that dancing is basically an unlearned, innate, motor/rhythmic muscular reaction to stimuli, whose function for the individual is either to express feeling or to 'work off' energy.

This view of the dance is well supported by anthropological accounts of the place it holds in primitive societies. To quote Wundt:

> Not the epic song, but the dance . . . constitutes everywhere the most primitive . . . art . . . Whether as a ritual dance, or as a pure emotional expression of the joy in rhythmic bodily movement, it rules the life of primitive men to such a degree that all other forms of art are subordinate to it.[9]

(b) Primitive Dance

At this stage it is possible to leave theorizing behind and build on solid facts. In the life of primitive peoples, nothing approaches the dance in significance. It is no mere pastime, but a very serious activity. It is not a sin but a sacred act. It is not mere 'art' or 'display' divorced from the other institutions of society: on the contrary, it is the very basis of survival of the social system in that it contributes significantly to the fulfilment of all of society's needs. 'Birth, circumcision, and the consecration of maidens, marriage and death, planting and harvest, the celebrations of chieftains, hunting, war and feasts, the changes of the moon, and sickness – for all of these the dance is needed.'[10]

The anthropological data on the subject of the dance in primitive society is, indeed, so extensive that only the most significant facts and illustrations can be presented here, bearing in mind, all the while, that much of this should be put into the 'passing' tense (to use Gorer's phrase) since many primitive societies are now being absorbed by the modern world. The first important fact that strikes the sociologist is that the dance is apparently a universal theme in all primitive cultures, wherever one looks – from the jungles of Central Africa to the Amazon swamps – from the coral islands of the Pacific to the snowy wastes of Siberia.

Secondly, from the sociological point of view, the social functions of the dance in primitive cultures can be seen to fall under the following headings,* all of which can be subsumed under the four main classes of 'functional problems' already listed in Chapter I:

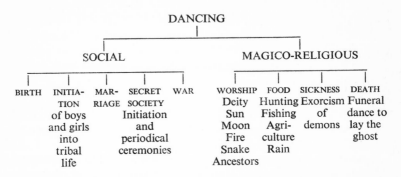

Some examples, drawn almost at random from the wealth of available material, may serve to illustrate each of these.

BIRTH

The Kayans of Sarawak, especially those of the Upper Rejang, perform a dance, the purpose of which is to facilitate delivery. The dancer is usually a female friend or relative of the woman in labour, and her dance includes the dressing of a bundle of cloth to represent an infant. She dances with this dummy and then places it in the type of cradle which Kayan women usually carry on their backs.[11]

INITIATION

Initiation of girls in Africa is always accompanied by dancing. Among the Yao the girls who have reached puberty are anointed with oil, their heads are shaved and they are dressed in bark cloth.

* I am indebted to W. D. Hambly for this method of presentation.

The festivities are opened by drumming in a peculiar and character-istic cadence, in response to which a closely packed body of people form up for the dance. The whole proceeding is called 'being *danced into* womanhood.'[12]

Dancing is indispensable for the initiation of boys, and is resorted to even by very primitive people like the Andamanese, who have no musical instruments. Three men and a young woman all decorated with brightly coloured clay dance round the novice at the ceremonial feasts. The man at the sounding-board sings a song for which he beats time with his foot. The women help by singing the chorus and clapping their hands on their thighs. Each dancer flexes his hips so that his back is nearly horizontal, then with bent knees he leaps from the ground with both feet. At the conclusion of the dance, the novice receives a new name, and henceforth it is considered insulting to use his boyish title.[13]

SEXUAL SELECTION AND MARRIAGE

In Hawaii and other Polynesian islands the daughters of chiefs used to give an exhibition dance designed to attract the attention of eligible young men of rank and station.[14] There were many kinds of dances, says an early missionary – 'all too indelicate or obscene to be noticed.'[15]

Among the Bagesu of Mount Elgon, Uganda, a different method of 'mate selection' occurs. During their harvest festival, generally held at new moon, there is a dancing ceremony which continues throughout the night, accompanied by free beer and free love. It is during these nocturnal dances that men and women customarily arrange their marriages.[16] In this instance it is clear that the harvest festival custom, originally intended to influence the fertility of the soil, has been extended to influence human fecundity. When it comes to celebrating the actual wedding, the role of dancing, along with singing and feasting, is so well known in simple societies that it does not need any special elaboration here.

SECRET SOCIETY

In Torres Strait, youths being initiated into a secret society witness for the first time the sacred dances and learn some of the legends of their tribe. The mask of the first dancer has no eye openings, so the second one has to guide him with a piece of rope. In dancing each foot is raised high before it is brought to the ground, and there are long pauses between the steps. Dancers emerge from a sacred house wearing masks, and dance into the horseshoe group of men, then back again into the house, repeating the performance twice. When returning, the dancers kick out as if trying to drive something away.[17]

WAR

In primitive societies, the war-dance is essential for strengthening communal bonds and for arousing the appropriate mental attitude for battle. Vivid accounts exist of the war dances of the head hunters in Melanesia and Polynesia. In Prince of Wales Island (Muralug), Torres Strait, the dance was performed after dark on a sandy shore fringed with mangrove swamps.

> Near the fire sat the primitive orchestra, beating their drums in rhythmic monotone . . . from the distance, swarthy forms appeared, advancing in sinuous line as if on the warpath, every movement being timed to the throb of the drums . . . each dancer had painted the lower part of his body black and the upper part red, while the ankles were adorned with yellow leaves . . . No incident of the war-path was omitted. There was skipping quickly from cover to cover, stealthy stealing, and a sudden encounter of the foe with a loud 'WAHU!' All the dancers raised their right legs, and with exultant cries went through the movement of decapitating a foe with their bamboo knives. . . .[18]

In one form or another, sometimes more, sometimes less intense, the war-dance can be traced throughout the world. Frequently it takes the form of meetings of warriors and provides a remarkable example of the power of suggestion, imitation and contagious excitement. Everywhere it serves the purpose of preserving social solidarity, and of giving cohesion and unity of purpose either for attack or defence.

An important secondary function of the war-dance is to assist the process of 'mate selection'. When women are spectators, the war-dance of the warriors stimulates sexual feeling, and exhibitions of skill, pugnacity and endurance will influence the women to choose particular dancers as husbands.[19]

WORSHIP

The religious ceremonies of many primitive peoples clearly illustrate the important place held by vocal music and dancing. The Sioux and Blackfeet Indians, for example, have a religious ceremony which is characterized by dances and songs in praise of the spirit counterparts

14

of well-known animals on which tribal existence depends. The dancers circle round in imitation of the movements of beavers when building dams, to the accompaniment of chants and prayers offered up to the beaver spirit. The success of the supplication depends on the detailed accuracy of the ritual: songs, dances, chants and prayers combined.[20]

FOOD

Under this heading come all the dances associated with the 'economic institutional order' of primitive society. In all simple societies there are innumerable examples of dances associated with hunting, fishing, agriculture, and the fertility of the soil.

Hunting dances are very frequently mimetic, the movements of animals being closely imitated either to increase the supply of game or to ensure success in the hunt. Gorer describes a hunting dance which he observed in Yammossoukro, South Ivory Coast:

> There were only three performers – two hunters ... and an 'antelope'. The antelope was danced by a boy of about fifteen ... his knees were permanently bent and his body held forward ... The antelope came forward very timidly, sniffing the air and starting at every sound and shadow ... the scene was repeated several times ... At last greed got the better of caution ... the two hunters pulled their bows. ... The antelope was badly wounded but it was able to stagger a few paces away; then it suddenly collapsed on its side, moved its arms and legs meaninglessly, quivered and lay still ... It seemed spontaneous, but could hardly be so, for the rhythm of the drums and rumba rattles was carefully observed.[21]

Agricultural dances and harvest dances can be found in any part of the world where people depend for their livelihood on the fertility of the soil. Sexual processes are often imitated in these dances in the belief that this assists the fecundity of nature. Thus, the natives of North West Brazil imitate in dance the act of procreation, in order to stimulate the growth of plants.[22]

SICKNESS

In many primitive societies the magician, medicine man or 'shaman' is the most important person in the tribe, since it is he who can bring pressure to bear on the spirit world. In sickness, the medicine man concentrates on overcoming the powers that are trying to seize the patient's soul. In Sarawak, the medicine man chants a dirge and

15

contorts himself in a frenzied dance around the victim, gyrating and miming battle with the spirits who are withdrawing the victim's soul. Sword in hand he strikes in all directions in harmony with the music – frequently the patient is so stimulated by the energetic example of the medicine man that he gets up and actually joins in the dance.[23]

DEATH

So far we have danced through the cycle of life in primitive society: from birth, initiation, marriage, to the closing scene where the medicine man is gyrating round the unconscious body, battling to prevent the soul escaping. If the battle is in vain, there is still an important place for the dance in the interment and funeral ceremonies.

Among the Todas for example, dancing takes place at the funeral of a male within the circular walls of the funeral hut. A buffalo is slaughtered, and on the day after this sacrifice there is more dancing by males only, and a recitative chorus in praise of the dead.[24]

The Veddahs of Ceylon invoke the 'yaka' or spirits to receive a newly-liberated spirit by performing a dance several days after the death. The shaman dances himself into a frenzy in order to approach the spirit world, to ask the 'yaka' of the dead to help those left behind.[25]

Indeed, all over the world from arctic snows to jungle swamps, from fertile islands to arid deserts, the death dance is known to primitive peoples. The ghost has to be 'laid' by ceremonial rites including dancing, the dust has to be shaken out of the house of mourning by means of the dance, and painful emotions have to be 'managed' or relieved by united rhythmic effort.

These traditional ritual dances are typical of unchanging primitive society, but when change comes there will be new dances to mark it. Amongst people who can neither read nor write, the dance is the natural record of historical events. Thus, there are Maori dances which imitate the paddling of canoes setting out from Polynesia to New Zealand, and similarly amongst the Australian Aborigines there are not only shark dances, pelican dances, and buffalo dances, but also vivid dances depicting dog-fights between Japanese zero aircraft and British spitfires.[26]

In terms of the theoretical framework set up in Chapter I, the dance in primitive society can now be seen as a distinctly 'polyfunctional' institution, contributing significantly to solving the functional problems of pattern maintenance and tension management, adaptation, goal attainment and integration.

The foregoing discussion, which has concentrated on the function of dancing for tribal society as a whole, should not be allowed to obscure the fact that dance has also a function for the *individual* in primitive society. Mead, for example,[27] has pointed out how, in Samoa, informal dancing is an influential factor in producing stable, well-adjusted individuals. Society disapproves of precocity and coddles the slow, but for the bright children there is the compensation of the dance which in its 'blatant precocious display of individuality drains off some of the discontent which the bright child feels, [and] prevents any child from becoming too bored.' The occasion is a genuine orgy of 'aggressive individualistic exhibitionism' and thus compensates for the repression of personality in other spheres of life.

Particularly interesting in Mead's account is the fact that every physical defect or handicap was capitalized to the full in this universal exploitation of individual personality. A hunchbacked boy had worked out a most ingenious imitation of a turtle: a little albino boy danced with aggressive facility to much applause: the dumb brother of the high chief of one village utilized his deaf-mute gutturals as a running accompaniment to his dance, and the most precocious girl dancer in Tau was almost blind.[28]

One final example from Mead illustrates very clearly how the dance can sometimes play an important part in socialization, particularly the process of inculcating a particular personality structure in the members of a given society.

In the non-aggressive, non-competitive society of the Arapesh, children are passive, receptive and non-initiatory in their attitudes. The role of 'spectatorship' at adult ceremonies is more engrossing than initiating their own games or activities. This is the role to which they have become reconciled from their earliest years:

> As babies they danced on the shoulders of their mothers and aunts, all through the long night dances. In these dances which celebrated the completion of some piece of work like a yam-harvest or a hunting-trip the women prefer to dance with children on their shoulders and so . . . the little children are handed about from one dancing-woman to another, and so dance the whole night through, bobbing up and down half-asleep on the swaying shoulders of the dancing-women. All of this early experience accustoms them to be part of the whole picture, to prefer a passive part that is integrated with the life of the community.[29]

17

III

Psycho-Pathological Perspectives

(a) Pathogenic Dances in Primitive Societies

The primitive dances that have been considered up to now may, broadly speaking, be regarded as 'normal'. They are sometimes frenzied and frequently ecstatic, but the ecstasy is produced by exaltation and rhythmic movement, not by mortification of the flesh. There is, however, another type of primitive dance – tortured, joyless, convulsive – regarded by Curt Sachs as 'out of harmony with the body'. This tends to be characteristic of shaman cultures, making its appearance where magic power is in the hands of the medicine man and religious experience and cult formation rest on a form of hypnosis.[1]

Such dancing seems to develop involuntarily out of frenzy and extreme neuropathic disturbance as, for instance, the arrow dance of a remote branch of the Veddah in Ceylon:

> ... As the dancers howl and pant a monotonous song and keep time with it, they work themselves ... into a state of extreme nervous excitement. Sweat streams over their bodies. They slap their bellies more and more vigorously and the noise becomes continually louder. Then after a time one after another falls to the ground exhausted. They remain for a while in a prostrate position, panting and gasping out their cries and at the same time trembling convulsively in all their limbs ...[2]

Although such pathogenic dances are limited to certain peoples, they are nevertheless widespread. The Chukchi of North Eastern Asia jump up and down in time, roll their eyes, and throw themselves to left and right with convulsive movements. The members of a secret society in a remote part of Africa

> form a closed circle, in the centre of which three to five drummers and several skilled dancers take their places. ... Suddenly the dancers swing into violent motion. All the parts of their bodies begin to shake, all their muscles play, their shoulder blades roll as

18

if they were no longer a part of their bodies. . . . Their bodies are bathed in sweat from head to foot. Now they stand as though changed to statues. Only the weird jerking of their muscles over their whole body continues. Then when the excitement has reached its highest point, they suddenly collapse as if struck by lightning and remain for a time on the ground as though unconscious . . .[3]

The movements in these dances appear to be in the nature of clonic convulsions – a state in which rigidity and relaxation of the muscles alternate in rapid succession, causing the body to be thrown about in wild paroxysms. The activity is thus not a joy but a suffering.

(b) *The Dancing-Mania in Medieval Europe*

The existence of these tortured, convulsive, 'diseased' dances in primitive societies may well put into better perspective the extraordinary phenomenon of the 'dancing-mania' of medieval Europe. This was an epidemic form of mass hysteria which broke out in Germany, the Low Countries and Italy, principally during the fourteenth and fifteenth centuries, although in Italy it was still reported as late as the eighteenth century. The phenomenon has been described by Hecker, the nineteenth-century German physician and professor as:

a wild, leaping dance performed by people screaming and foaming with fury, having all the appearance of persons 'possessed'. It did not remain confined to particular localities but was propagated in epidemic fashion by the sight of the sufferers over the whole of Germany and the neighbouring countries to the North West.[4]

The outbreaks in Germany are well-documented by contemporary chroniclers. There are, for example, numerous reports that in July 1374 thousands of men and women, who had come to Aachen from various parts of Germany to celebrate the midsummer festival of St John, suddenly began to leap and scream in the streets. Losing all control they danced for hours until overcome by exhaustion. Some saw visions and reported afterwards that they had been trying to leap out of a torrent of blood. Others during the paroxysm saw the Heavens open to reveal the Saviour enthroned with the Virgin Mary. In its fully developed form the attack commenced with epileptic convulsions, those affected falling to the ground senseless, panting and labouring for breath. They would then foam at the mouth and suddenly spring up to begin their strangely contorted dance.[5]

The 'manic' dancers wandered from town to town following well-known pilgrimage routes and in a few months time the frenzy had spread through the Low Countries and into Cologne and Metz. In Cologne[6] the number of those 'possessed' amounted to more than five hundred and about the same time in Metz the streets were filled with eleven hundred dancers.[7] Singly or hand-in-hand, they circled and jumped in hideously distorted choral dances and wherever they raved, the hysteria took hold of spectators who, in turn, quivering and grimacing, succumbed to the fearful compulsion to join in. In Hecker's graphic but guarded prose:

> Peasants left their ploughs, mechanics their workshops, house-wives their domestic duties, to join the wild revels . . . Secret desires were excited and but too often found opportunities for wild enjoyment. . . . Above a hundred unmarried women were seen raving about in consecrated and unconsecrated places and the consequences were soon perceived.[8] . . . Gangs of idle vagabonds who understood how to imitate to the life the gestures and convulsions of those really affected, roved from place to place seeking maintenance and adventures, and thus, wherever they went, spread the spasmodic disease like a plague, since the susceptible are infected as easily by the appearance as by the reality.[9]

A German chronicle of Königshoven reports that Strasbourg was visited by the dancing-mania in the year 1418:

Viel hundert fingen zu Strasburg an Zu tanzen und springen Fray und Mann Am offnen Markt, Gassen und Strassen. Tag und Nacht ihrer viel nicht assen Bis ihn das Wüthen wieder gelag St Vits Tanz ward genannt die Plag.[10]	In Strasburg many hundreds of men and women began to dance and jump in the market-place the lanes and the streets. Many of them went without food for days and nights until their mania subsided. The plague was called St Vitus' dance.

In Strasburg, as elsewhere, the 'manic' dancers attracted to themselves swarms of followers, of whom some were caught up in the general hysteria, some were anxious parents and relatives, and others were rogues and vagabonds out for what they could get. These extraordinary assemblies, were further augmented by musicians playing bagpipes – on the theory that those affected should be helped to dance the disease out of their system. The town council appointed responsible superintendents to conduct them on foot and in carriages to the chapels of St Vitus, the patron saint of afflicted persons. Some, sprinkled with holy water in the name of St Vitus were cured: many were not, and died.

Italy, too, was afflicted by a similar phenomenon from the middle of the fourteenth century to the seventeenth, and, sporadically, even into the eighteenth century. A form of dance-mania called 'tarantism' made its first appearance in Apulia and thence spread over the other provinces of Italy as a great epidemic. The bite of venomous spiders, particularly the tarantula, or, more accurately, the unreasonable fear of the consequences of such a bite provoked this violent nervous disorder which, like the so-called 'St Vitus' dance' in Germany infected onlookers with its own hysteria.[11]

Nicholas Perotti, born in 1430, gives one of the earliest accounts of this strange disorder. Those who were bitten fell into a state of melancholy, and appeared to be stupefied and almost senseless. This condition was in many cases associated with such intense sensitivity to music that at the very first tones of their favourite melodies they sprang up, shouting for joy and danced on without intermission, until they sank to the ground exhausted and almost lifeless. In others the disease took a less cheerful turn: they wept constantly and spent their days in the greatest misery and anxiety. In still other instances, deaths occurred under a paroxysm of either laughing or weeping.[12]

The symptoms enumerated by Perotti coincide very closely with those described by later writers. Matthioli, for example, writing in 1565 describes sufferers as becoming morbidly exhilarated, remaining for a long while without sleep, laughing, dancing and singing in a state of the greatest excitement. Others on the contrary were drowsy. The great majority felt nausea, suffered from vomiting and had constant tremors. Complete mania was no uncommon occurrence, as was also deep depression. Matthioli gives an eye-witness account of how pain-racked patients would spring up at the very first sound of certain melodies – but only tarantellas composed expressly for the purpose. Forgetting their disorder they would dance for hours without fatigue, but if the clarinets and drums ceased for a single moment they would suddenly collapse.[13]

At the close of the fifteenth century tarantism, and with it the morbid fear of being bitten by venomous spiders, had spread far beyond the boundaries of Apulia. At this time there was a general conviction that there was only one way of saving life after being bitten and that was to distribute the poison over the whole body and expel it through the skin. This could be accomplished through dancing, but (as made clear by Matthioli) only by dancing to a particular type of music – the tarantella. It is interesting that alleviation, not complete cure, was expected through participation in the tarantella, thus enabling the patient to get some relief but to keep his symptom.

Tarantism was at its greatest height in Italy in the seventeenth century, long after the St Vitus' dance of Germany had disappeared. Such was the scale of the epidemic that it was considered necessary for whole bands of musicians to scour the land during the summer months, to undertake the cure of the 'tarantati' in towns and villages up and down the country. Subordinate nervous attacks were much more frequent during this century than at any earlier period, taking the form of an extraordinary icy coldness coupled with perspiration, spasms in the stomach, and sometimes loss of voice, blindness, vertigo and complete insanity. Many patients found relief by being placed in swings or rocked in cradles, others had to have the soles of their feet severely beaten to rouse them, and others took to self-flagellation, not with the intention of making a display, but solely for the purpose of allaying the intense nervous irritation which they felt.[14]

There is little doubt that, in Italy as in Germany, the ranks of the 'genuinely' manic dancers were frequently swollen both by spectators who 'caught' the malady and lost control, and also by those who saw the proceedings as a macabre kind of festival and joined in, one is strongly tempted to say, 'for kicks'.

These mass hysterical outbreaks in medieval Europe are usually seen as closely related to the nature of contemporary society, particularly to the turmoil following the Black Death. But, since there is clearly a similarity between the symptoms of these 'manic' dances and the 'diseased' dances of certain primitive societies, it is important to see first whether there can be an explanation in medical, rather than sociological, terms.

'Chorea' is a violent nervous disorder well known to medical science. The layman knows this, generally, as St Vitus' dance, thus indicating a link with the medieval epidemic. It is characterized by 'the ceaseless occurrence of a wide variety of rapid, jerky but well co-ordinated movements, performed involuntarily'.[15] Such a disorder of the nervous system can clearly arise in an individual, without any reference to the nature of his society, as can also convulsions of an epileptic or clonic kind. There is thus no reason to doubt that an explanation in terms of an organic disease of the nervous system can account for some of the 'sufferers' both in primitive society and in medieval Europe.

Another lead given by scientific medicine for the understanding of the phenomenon in Germany is the existence of a disease known as 'ergotism'. This is a form of chronic poisoning, arising from the eating of ergotized grain, and is marked by cerebrospinal symptoms,

22

spasms and cramps.[16] 'Ergot' is a poisonous fungus which in wet weather tends to grow on ears of rye. Of the wet weather there is no doubt, since contemporary chronicles record the overflowing of the rivers Rhine and Maine in February 1374. It is by no means implausible that some of the spasmodic cramps and uncontrolled jerking of the limbs, reported so frequently as symptoms of the dancing-mania, could have been caused, in Germany, by the poisonous fungus 'ergot' and in Italy by the poisonous sting of the tarantula. Further than this, however, in terms of organic causes it is very difficult to go.

It seems clear that in the shaman cultures of primitive society the frenzied, convulsive dancing is much more likely to arise out of hysteria, self-induced or in response to hypnotic stimuli, than from organic causes. There are, indeed, several forms of hysterical or functional chorea known to medical science, of which the most significant in this context are *rhythmic chorea* – 'hysterical chorea in which the patient performs persistent rhythmic movements' and *saltatory chorea* – 'rhythmic chorea associated with dancing movements'.[17]

In medieval and late-medieval Europe the hysterical factor must overwhelmingly have outweighed the organic. For every person genuinely affected with epileptic convulsions or spasmodic cramps arising from poisoning, thousands upon thousands must have 'caught' the nervous disease, to which they added their own delusional disturbances.

The ease and rapidity with which hysterical disorders can spread by means of 'sympathy' is well-known to the student of neuroses: what was so extraordinary about the dancing-mania in Europe was the scale on which it occurred, spreading as it did over large areas of Europe and lasting for more than two centuries. To reach some understanding of this epidemic disorder it is clearly necessary to look closely at the nature of the society in which it occurred.

Firstly, it must be borne in mind that the epidemic arose in Germany and in Italy at a time when these lands were still suffering the effects of the Black Death, the scourge which destroyed so large a proportion of the human race in the fourteenth century, disrupting family units and the stability of society in the process. In the year 1374 there were additional disasters in Germany with the overflowing of the rivers Rhine and Maine in February, causing the collapse of part of the wall surrounding Cologne, and plunging hundreds of villages into the utmost distress. Society was in a state of widespread 'anomie' and disequilibrium, with a consequent breakdown of many social norms and rules. In Western and South

Western Germany bands of people wandered about in conditions of the utmost wretchedness, possibly made even worse by tormenting memories of crimes committed during the Black Death.

Italy, in common with every country in Europe, was visited during the Middle Ages by plagues which followed each other in quick succession and gave the exhausted people scarcely time to recover. Oriental bubo-plague ravaged Italy sixteen times between the years 1119 and 1340. Smallpox, leprosy and other dread diseases were rife, added to which were the incredible ravages of the Black Death during the years 1350 to 1374, spreading misery and devastation over the whole land. Inevitably, at this stage of history many men and women must have been inordinately preoccupied with the horrors of death.

At this juncture in Italy, it was, then, not surprising that the bite of the tarantula spider should produce a violent nervous disorder, probably more through a morbid fear of the consequences than from the actual poison. From this, it was but a step for delusions to arise leading to imagined bites – producing, of course, symptoms of equal virulence. Finally the hysterical disorder spread by 'sympathy' from town to town and increased in severity as it widened its range.

Similarly, in Germany and the Low Countries, as we have seen, some victims may have had compulsive cramps and convulsions arising from ergotism. These were joined by others who, in a high state of delusional disturbance, imitated the actions of the afflicted and took over their symptoms. Spectators were drawn in on the wave of mass insanity and again by 'sympathy' the hysteria spread from town to town. Chroniclers make it clear that during these manifestations sexuality was sometimes heightened and that 'excesses' occurred among the afflicted. This resulted in the maniacs being joined by some of the still sane who looked on the proceedings as a Saturnalia. Inevitably this led to a further breakdown of the social norms, mores and institutions of society.

Other factors which should be borne in mind are the general ignorance and superstition surrounding the masses, coupled with religious fervour strong enough to produce visions, and allied to practices such as flagellation and public penance calculated to inflame morbid imaginings and fancies.

Finally it must be remembered that 'dancing-mania' in a sense was not something entirely without precedent, since it existed in medieval tradition and folklore. As early as the year 1027 tradition has it that near the convent church of Kolbig (Saxony), not far from Bernburg, eighteen peasants (whose names are still recorded) disturbed divine service on Christmas Eve, by dancing and brawling in the churchyard. The priest then inflicted a curse upon them that they should dance and scream for a whole year without ceasing. The story goes that the curse was completely fulfilled, the unfortunate sufferers at length sinking knee-deep into the earth.[18]

Two centuries later it is recorded that in the year 1237 upwards of one hundred children were suddenly seized with a strange compulsion to dance, and proceeded dancing and jumping along the road from Erfurt to Arnstadt. When they arrived at Arnstadt they fell exhausted to the ground. Many of them died after they were taken home by their parents and the rest were affected by a permanent tremor for the rest of their lives.[19]

Whether these stories were partially true and embellished by the priests to ram home a moral, or whether they were entirely fictitious, is a matter of no moment. What is important is that they they formed part of the European folk-heritage, that they were believed, and recounted with fear throughout the Middle Ages. Undoubtedly these stories, centering round an irresistible compulsion to dance, contributed in some way to the particular form of behaviour which the mass psychosis took.

Thus it seems clear that all the social and cultural factors relating to society must be taken into account as well as the more purely psychological and medical factors when trying to understand the phenomenon of the medieval dancing-mania, whether in Germany or in Italy. In terms of social structure, the epidemics must be seen as products of stress, strain and tension. In terms of functional analysis, so far from making for adaptation and adjustment of the social system, they must have lessened its powers to survive and increased the tendency to disequilibrium. Viewed in this light, the medieval dancing-mania must have been 'dysfunctional' to society, using the term in the same sense as Merton.[20]

(c) *The Danse Macabre, or Dance of Death*

The final variety of pathogenic dance to be considered is the *danse macabre*, or dance of death. This was a strange dance which happened, not in reality, but in the minds of medieval writers and artists. It is thought to have been first portrayed by a mural on the wall of a cloister adjoining the Church of the Holy Innocents in Paris, in the year 1424.[21] From France it spread, in the form of paintings and woodcuts, all over Europe and particularly to Germany.

These paintings and woodcuts were allegorical representations, based on the universality of death, equality before death, and the vanity of rank and riches. They often showed Death in the form of a skeleton suddenly appearing in the midst of scenes of joy and splendour, and leading away kings and peasants, young and old, in a choral dance sometimes linked in a long chain and sometimes two by two. Occasionally the fifteenth-century dance of death would portray the dead (usually skeletons) dancing with the living, as a warning of death to come. The general idea is strikingly conveyed by a verse in a volume of woodcuts issued from the famous printing-press of Jacob Meydenbach in Mainz between 1491 and 1495:

> Come along, come along, ye masters and men
> Haste ye thither whate'er ye ben
> Or young or old, or high or low
> Ye all to the dance house must go.[22]

The dance of death had its roots in the late medieval attitude which emphasized the terrifying aspect of death, but none the less looked to the resurrection of the dead and the life to come. Although so essentially a product of its time, representations of the dance of death continued into the Renaissance period, but by this time the old symbols had lost their meaning and the individuality of the artist had come to replace the anonymity of the medieval craftsman. The remarkable woodcut illustrations of Holbein, for example, could have been created by no other hand.

Twentieth-century man might find it strange that the late Middle Ages should choose the choral dance[23] as a medium for portraying certain concepts relating to living and dying, but fifteenth-century man was probably better able to communicate and receive ideas in that way than in any other. In the form of the simple choral dances which he had seen and taken part in since childhood, poets and painters could best convey to him the idea that all must go down the same road to the same goal. In the choral dance the leader seeks out the path for the followers, he opens and closes the chain, and at his will draws all the dancers after him in ever new convolutions of the dance, just as Death draws after him all living things, great or small, rich or poor.

These ideas could almost certainly be conveyed even more readily because many men, women and children of the early fifteenth century had had experience (or had heard tales), not only of the normal choral dance but also of that distorted convulsive dance, in the course of which the 'dancers' were sometimes snatched away at the height of their frenzy by Death the Leveller.

The anthropological data presented in Chapter II leave one in no possible doubt that in primitive societies 'normal' dancing is a functional pre-requisite for tribal survival. The various types of pathogenic dance considered in the present chapter highlight the close relationship of dance, whether 'normal' or 'abnormal', to the structure and climate of society in which it occurs. These two facts taken together are seen as sufficiently significant to warrant an intensive, small-scale, sociological investigation into the functional aspect of dance and society. The historical/sociological enquiry into the social dance in England which follows in Part II is an attempt to meet this need.

PART II
SOCIO-HISTORICAL STUDY

IV
Medieval England:
Thirteenth to Mid-Fifteenth Century

A softe pas they daunce and trede . . .
GOWER: *Confessio Amantis*

No one can say (except, of course, non-historians) when the Middle Ages 'started' and when they 'ended' in England. All that can safely be asserted is that in the thirteenth century English thought and society were medieval, in the nineteenth they were not.[1]

There are abundant general references to dancing in England from the thirteenth to the fifteenth centuries, linked particularly with medieval tournaments and entertainments. In eleventh-century England tournaments were nothing more than crude training grounds for battle but by the thirteenth they had become associated with festive occasions and had been softened by the ideals of knightly chivalry.[2] By the end of the thirteenth century ladies were among the spectators, and music and dancing had become an important feature. At a 'Round Table' (a development of the tournament) at Nefyn, in North Wales, in 1284 the historian notes that there was dancing and that the floor collapsed.[3] Jacques Bretel gives more detail in his account of the tournaments at Chauvenci, which were attended by English knights, in the year 1285:[4]

Apres mangier, en piez leverent.
Tument tables, tument tretel.
Trompent flaiot, tabors, fretel
Eslorent bien en lor saison
Lors comanca une chanson
De chanter chaseuns cuers
          s'avance
'Mal dehait ait qui ne vient
          en la dance'
Qui dont veist dames venir,
Bachelers par les mains tenir,
Bel li samblast et bel li fust
Sans contredit et sans refust
N'i a celui qui ne s'esjoie.

After eating, they rose to their feet and removed the tables and trestles. They played flutes, tabors and flageolets and generally made as merry as could be. Then a song began. Everyone came forward eagerly to sing 'Cursed be he who does not join the dance'. If you had seen the ladies come forward, holding the (young) gentlemen by the hand, you would have thought it a fine and pleasing sight. There is none who does not make merry.

31

The prize-giving ceremony which concluded the tournaments was as elaborate in England as anywhere, taking place in the evening, usually after the second course at dinner.[5] After the prize-giving came dancing: 'Then comys forth a lady . . . and gives the diamonde unto the best juster . . . Then shall hee that the diamount is gave unto take a lady by the hande and begynne the daunce.'[6]

By the fifteenth century the tournament had developed into the '*Pas d'Armes*', a species of mimed heroic drama in which the central action was actual combat. After the jousts came the singing and the dancing, as described, for example, by the author of *The Flower and the Leaf*.

> And so the justes last an houre and more
> But they that crowned were in laurer grene
> Wan the pryse; their dintes were so sore
> Thet ther was non ayesnt hem might sustene;
> And than the justing al was left of clene;
> And fro their hors the nine alight anon;
> And so did al the remnant everichon.
> And forth they yede togider, twain and twain,
> That to behold, it was a worldly sight,
> Toward the ladies on the grene plain,
> That song and daunced, as I sayd now aright.[7]

In the course of time, dancing came to be closely associated with tournaments, 'Round Tables' and '*Pas d'Armes*', and in Glynne Wickham's view it was this factor that eventually drew these outdoor functions indoors, at the close of the fourteenth century, to make an evening entertainment, with ladies dispensing the prizes and leading off the dancing.

Another institution of medieval society in which social dancing played an important part was 'mumming', or, as it came to be known from mid-fifteenth century onwards, 'disguising' – until this, in turn, was superseded by the word 'mask' in the early sixteenth century. A mumming at Kennington, for the entertainment of the young Prince Richard 'in the feast of Christmas' in the year 1377 is described by an anonymous English chronicler, who leaves no doubt that the mumming was followed by music and dancing, the Royal party and the mummers dancing on separate sides of the hall:

> And then ye prince caused to bring ye wyne and they dronk with great joye, commanding ye minstrels to play and ye trompets began to sound and other instruments to pipe . . . and ye prince and ye

lordes dansed on ye one syde, and ye mummers on ye other a great while and then they dronk and tooke their leaue.[8]

Opinions vary as to the origin and purpose of mumming, but if, as many think, the seasonal giving of gifts (dating back to pre-Christian times) was the original object, it seems clear that by the late fourteenth century this had already become fused with another equally important aspect – social dancing.

There is, thus, very little doubt that the social dance was an accepted part of the general life of the upper classes in England in the thirteenth, fourteenth and fifteenth centuries, and that skill in dancing was a social accomplishment on a par with skill in riding, jousting, field sports, harping and singing. Indeed, definite instruction in all these skills formed part of the education of many of the sons of the nobility and 'gentry', whether as squires at the King's court or in the households of great noblemen.

Unfortunately, despite the abundant references to dancing, the chroniclers of these centuries, for some reason, never refer to the names, steps, figures or patterns of the dance. For the first detailed contemporary description of the social dance in England we have to wait until the year 1521.* Before that date, whatever is said must be pieced together from fragments of evidence. Such fragments suggest that 'folk' and 'nobles' in twelfth- and thirteenth-century England danced simple choral dances, called 'rounds', and 'caroles' and that the nobles danced 'estampies'. The rounds (which go further back than the Middle Ages, possibly even to primitive times) are self-explanatory, but the roots of the other two dances have to be sought in the medieval Courts of Provence.

In the early Middle Ages, Provence had one of the most cultured courts in Europe. Until the time of the appearance of the troubadours in the twelfth century, one dance – the Carole – seems to have served the needs of all – folk and nobles alike. The carole was a song-dance in chain formation, the songs usually being sung by the dancers themselves. It had two distinct forms, the farandole – a line of dancers in single file each holding the hand of the next person – and the branle, in which the dancers held hands in a circle.[9] These linked dances were 'a-sexual', in that they could be danced by all men, or all women, or any combination of the sexes.

The troubadours could hardly be expected to favour this impersonal form of dance and it is to them that we owe the earliest form of couple dance, the 'estampie'. This was an 'open couple'

* Robt. Copelande: 'The manner of dauncynge the Bace Daunses after the use of France'.

dance where the only contact was the clasping of hands but in it one gentleman danced with one lady, or (more rarely) with two ladies.[10] Instrumental music had to be developed at this stage since two or three voices were no substitute for the full chorus of the carole.

At this time, close links existed between Provence and England. Richard I, who began his reign in 1189, was himself a Provencal poet (having lived for a long time in Provence and having acquired a taste for its poetry). He was also a 'most magnificent patron of chivalry' and invited to his court many minstrels or troubadours, whom he 'loaded with honours and rewards'.[11] These links were strengthened in 1208 by the flight from Provence of those troubadours who had escaped the massacres of the Albigensian crusade. They fled to various European courts, being welcomed everywhere for their songs and dances, and nowhere more than in England. Some years later, in 1236, Henry III married Eleanor of Provence.

Thus, instead of remaining local Provencal dances, the carole in its various forms, and the couple dance called 'estampie' were transplanted to England and to other European countries. There are several references to the dancing of the carole in the literature of fourteenth-century England:

> He saw a mayden . . . daunsynge in a carrole among
> other maydouns.[12]

> With harp and lute and with citole
> The love dance and the carole
> A softe pas they daunce and trede.[13]

Earlier references are lacking but the known links between England and Provence suggest strongly that the carole was danced in England as early as the thirteenth century.[14]

Contemporary thirteenth century evidence for the existence of the dance known as the estampie is to be found in a manuscript written at Reading Abbey during the reign of Henry III, which contains music for three of these dances.[15] Estampies were essentially dances of the court and polite society, and were danced by one couple at a time with the rest of the company looking on. The persons of highest rank would dance first, followed in turn by those next in order down the social scale.

Apart from the estampies, the patterns of dancing for 'folk' and 'nobles' in thirteenth-century England are thought to have been the same. The style, however, was undoubtedly very different, the folk-dance boisterous and the court dance dignified and restrained. This was the age of courtly chivalry when vigorous wooing was sub-

Plate I Inside medieval castle walls, dancing was restrained and dignified, with bodily contact limited to the clasping of hands

Plate II La Danse Champétre from late 15th century manuscript:
Heures de Charles O'Angouleme

ordinated to the discipline of courtly love. In court and manorial circles, dancing was very disciplined, with restrained movements and gestures, and bodily contact limited to the clasping of hands.*

In the thirteenth and fourteenth centuries, the centre of social activity was the hall: whether the castle hall, manorial hall or the smaller hall in the houses of rich merchants. The typical hall was rectangular in shape, with a platform at one end where the master of the household could sit with his family and special guests. There was a gallery for musicians, trestle tables which could easily be removed after the evening meal, benches round the sides for household retainers, and spluttering wall-torches for illumination. Until well into the fourteenth century or later the hearth was in the centre, with a vent in the roof to let out the smoke.† The master of the household would open the activities, and the dances of the lords and ladies (some of which had originally stemmed from the 'people') would be watched by the household retainers, and later danced out-of-doors, on the village green with much greater vigour.

In this setting, the pattern of indoor dancing had to be in the form of 'rounds' – round the central hearth – but the invention of chimneys in the later part of the fourteenth century made it possible to move the hearth to the side.[16] The greater expanse of floorspace, thus made available, encouraged changes and variations in dance patterns, and the processional form of dance was added to the repertoire. This form of dance was by no means new, since it had existed, out-of-doors, as part of religious processions in much earlier times, but now it could be performed as a social dance, indoors.

This advance in technology made it *possible* for people to perform the processional type of dance indoors, but it was undoubtedly the influence of France which made them want to. Although for the greater part of the century this country was at war with France, English customs were much influenced by the fashions of her enemy. In the early and more successful part of the Hundred Years' War, tribute and plunder from France poured into the more primitive feudal type of English household, and many French nobles were captured and brought back as prisoners of war to England.[17] Until ransoms could be extracted from their peasants, they stayed as honoured guests in the country-houses of their captors where, as Trevelyan tells us, they hunted with the men, made love to the women, and taught Englishmen fashion in clothes and food. There is no doubt that in addition to these activities, or possibly in the course of some of them, the French nobles would have found time to

---

* See Plate I, page 34.
† Penshurst Place in Kent is an example of such a hall, with central hearth.

demonstrate the type of dance which was then evolving in France – a processional dance which was later to find its way into all the courts of Europe as the Basse Danse. As a processional dance it was highly suitable to the hierarchical social structure of the times, since the order of precedence in the dance could exactly match the order of social rank.

French influence could also be seen in the form of dress adopted by the nobility, and this in turn had its influence on the dance. In the course of the fourteenth century, ladies' dresses grew heavier and men's robes ever longer. Ladies of fashion vied with each other in the height and shape of their fantastic head-dresses. This type of dress favoured the dignified processional form of dance, which now became primarily a parade of fashion, with no rapid turns or intricate steps.

In the later fourteenth and early fifteenth century, however, fashion swung in a different direction, again as a result of French influence, notably increased by the marriage of Richard II to Isabella, daughter of the French king, in 1396. Men's dress could now be seen as changing from medieval to modern. The long gown was going out and fashionable young men wore short coats or jackets and tight-fitting 'Hosen' to show off their legs. At the court of Richard II, courtiers wore an extremely colourful costume which might have one leg red and the other blue.[18] Women, on the other hand, appeared throughout the two centuries, no matter what the occasion, in long concealing garments. The men of the court thus had every encouragement to show off in front of the ladies by performing intricate steps and figures. Some of these were probably learnt from the travelling minstrel troupes who, from the beginning of the fourteenth century, could be hired or maintained by the nobles for their entertainment.[19]

In the fifteenth century the custom of 'mumming' underwent some changes and the word was dropped in favour of 'disguising', but there is no evidence to show that this involved any change in dance-forms. In all probability, social dancing in general was much the same in the fifteenth as in the fourteenth century. Historians have noted the slow pace of change in the fifteenth century, an era of consolidation which proved remarkably conservative in most aspects of life and thought. Trevelyan notes that in the gentleman's manor house, the nobleman's castle and the King's court, the culture of the previous century was still alive but in a somewhat faded way. The poems of Chaucer were still being read (and imitated) and the imagination of poets was still bounded by the discipline of medieval love.[20] It is likely, therefore, that in both the fourteenth and fifteenth centuries social dancing for the upper classes consisted of the simple rounds and chain dances already mentioned (performed in rather a stiff and artificial way), enhanced in the later fourteenth, and in the fifteenth century by the addition of the dignified processional Basse Danse, basically simple but yet giving the man plenty of opportunity for showing off intricate steps to his admiring lady. A late fifteenth-century manuscript in Salisbury Cathedral Library, which has Basse Danses noted on the fly-leaf, gives complete support to the theory that the Basse Danse was known in England at this time.[21]

Little enough is known about the dancing of the nobility and 'gentry' in England in the fourteenth and fifteenth centuries, but even less information exists on the subject of peasant-dancing. It is sometimes argued that any peasant living in late medieval England would be so bowed down, in all senses of the word, by his long and arduous hours of labour that dancing would be a notion singularly lacking in appeal. The idea of medieval England being not merrie but miserable, however, is by no means entirely accepted by historians. Much besides toil (admittedly arduous) went on in late medieval England: men rested on Sundays and on a great number of Saints' Days and much money was spent on 'mayegames, wakes and revells'. There seems little doubt that country-dancing would have had its place on these occasions. As Trevelyan points out, there was a 'joyful background' to country life, and medieval England was certainly not wholly miserable, even for the peasants.

Our only information, however, about the dancing of the peasants comes from fifteenth- and sixteenth-century painters and illustrators.* This type of dancing, familiar to many through the paintings of Breughel, can almost certainly be taken as indicative of peasant-dancing in England and shows clearly that (as one would expect) the dances of the peasants were in marked contrast to those of the upper classes – with movements so free that they would be more aptly described as cavorting and skipping, than as stepping solemnly in rounds and processions. In spite of the contrast, however, there is every reason to suppose that the two styles of dancing exerted some influence on each other in the course of time.

Dance historians are agreed, however, that the Morris dance[22] (now taken to be the most characteristic form of rural dance in England in the fourteenth century) was not adopted by the court in any form – possibly because it was a 'ritual' rather than a true social dance, for men only, and possibly because of its vigour. The basic step was a strong forward motion of one leg, with the other maintaining a skipping movement (varied by occasional leaps) accompanied by an energetic swinging of the arms.[23] The 'Moorish

* See Plates II and III, pages 35 and 50.

hypothesis', a theory holding that the Morris dance was of Moorish origin, the word Morris being derived from 'morisco' is now generally rejected in favour of the likelihood that the Morris is a survival of a primitive religious ceremonial.[24]

The historical evidence relating to dancing presented in this chapter is of necessity sparse and circumstantial but, in spite of this, the close relationship of the social dance to society in medieval England has been indicated at several points. For example, the influence of prevailing sentiments and attitudes of artificial courtly love are reflected in the artificial and constrained type of dancing in court circles: the current wish to follow fashionable France brings about the adoption of French forms of dress which, in turn, has a notable influence on the dance: the building technology of the day has a strong influence on the patterns of the dance, and, finally, the cleft in society between upper class and peasant is shown by their contrasting styles of dancing. Above all, the close relationship between dance history and national history is shown by the diffusion of the dances of medieval Provence throughout the courts of Europe.

Apart from these rather wide generalizations, very little can be said, since a detailed sociological study of the dance cannot properly commence without reasonably detailed contemporary records which, in England, do not appear until the year 1521.

V
Early Tudor England: 1485 to 1558

> Dancing or saltation is an art . . . which . . . is
> adapted for the youthful, agreeable to the aged
> and very suitable for all, in so far as it is em-
> ployed in fit place and season without vicious
> abuse . . .
>
> ARBEAU. *Orchésographie*

The year 1501 saw the marriage of Henry VII's eldest son, Prince
Arthur, to Katherine of Aragon, an occasion which was marked by
'disguisings' of the most lavish sort. The first, held in Westminster
Hall, had three spectacular pageants:

> Incontynent cam in the thirde pagent, in likness of a great hill . . .
> in whom were enclosid viii godly Knights with ther banners spred
> and displaied . . . they hastely spede them to the . . . castell, which
> they forthwith assaulted so and in such wise that the ladies,
> yeldying themselves, descendid from the seid castell. The knights
> were right freshly disguised and the ladies also . . . and daunced
> togyder dyvers and many goodly daunces.[1]

The chronicler then tells us that the pageants were removed, after
which the disguiser/dancers departed and the spectators took the
floor, their dances being led by the newly-weds. A personal detail
suddenly lights up the chronicle when we read that the Duke of York
(later Henry VIII) 'perceyvyng himself to be encombred with his
clothes sodenly cast off his gowne and daunced in his jaket.'[2]

In the year 1512, for the first time, the disguised actors 'after the
manner of Italie' were taking their partners from the audience, and
from then on, the Italian title 'Maschera' or Mask gradually came to
be substituted for the English word 'disguisings'.[3] The mask was not
primarily a drama: it was an episode in an 'indoor revel' of dancing.
Masked persons would come, by convention unexpectedly, into the
castle or baronial hall, often bringing gifts, and sometimes accompanied by torch-bearers and musicians. They would dance before the
hosts and principal guests, and then invite them to join in the dance.[4]

This mingling, or 'commoning', of the maskers and the guests
differentiates the mask from 'mummings' and 'disguisings', and, as a

39

corollary, it meant that the performers and spectators had to be of the same social standing. In other words the mask was an amateur, not a professional, performance. For some time the mask and the old-fashioned disguising are traceable side by side at the court of Henry VIII. Ultimately, they became amalgamated, and by the end of the reign, 'mask' or 'masque' was the official name, and 'disguising' had become obsolete.[5]

By this time, 'commoning' between maskers and guests was firmly established. The mask itself could take many different forms, varying from elaborate to simple – from a far-fetched and costly device with speeches, pageants, spectacles and mimic fights to a mere masked dance.

As before, the chroniclers are silent on the question of 'What did they dance?', but in this century there is no need for conjecture. In the year 1521 Robert Copelande published a French grammar with an Appendix: 'Manner of dancynge of bace dances after the use of France'.[6] This provides historical evidence that the Basse Danse was well-known in England by the court and nobles in the early sixteenth century. This dance, in fact, laid the foundations of later social dancing in all the courts of Europe, and its importance warrants a glance backwards in history to Italy and France in the fifteenth century.

This was the century of the Italian Renaissance – a century when the art of dancing, no less than the arts of painting, sculpture and music, flourished as never before. In Italy, the Basse Danse (originally derived from the estampie and farandole) was being developed, and other dances were being created by the dancing-master Domenico of Ferrara, and later by his best pupil, Guglielmo Ebreo (William the Jew), who himself became a composer of dances.[7]

In France, the French Basse Danse (likewise originally derived from the estampie and branle) was taking shape in the 1440s.[8] It is described in the famous 'Golden Manuscript', twenty-five pages of mat black paper ruled in gold entitled: *'Le Manuscrit des Basses Danses de la Biblioteque de Bourgogne'*.[9] The date is uncertain but there is little doubt that it was written in the first half of the fifteenth century. The manuscript gives the theory of the steps and the rules for dancing, and the music and notation of fifty-nine Basses Danses.[10]

The first printed book on the social dance is *'L'art et instruction de bien danser* by Thoulouze, published in France some time between 1490 and 1500, and consisting of five pages of notation and music for forty-nine Basse Danses. The instructions here are almost identical with those given in the Golden Manuscript, and forty-three out of the forty-nine dances are the same in each, indicating that the French

Basse Danse showed little change throughout the fifteenth century.[11] This was clearly the century of the Basse Danse in France and Italy, and there is little doubt that this dance continued to enjoy great popularity in the sixteenth century.

Returning to England – Copeland's 'book' was in fact very brief. It consisted of two pages which formed an appendix to his book on French grammar and pronunciation, probably for the use of English visitors to France. At this time, French manners and customs were very fashionable in England and the combination (to us, highly unusual) of French grammar and French dancing would have aroused considerable interest: particularly so among those English nobles who had attended the ceremonies and watched the French Basse Danses at the Field of the Cloth of Gold the previous year.

Copeland's treatise must have helped to popularize even further the Basse Danse in this country. He did not consider it necessary to go into detail about the performance of the steps, which is itself a good indication that they were well-known to the dancers of the day. He limited himself to describing the order of the steps and the order of the measures with a few comments on style.*

It was, of course, the French version, not the Italian, of the Basse Danse that came to England. At its simplest the dance could be described as in the nature of a procession, often headed by the musicians, moving forward with slow dignified steps, as befitted the heavy dresses and long robes of the period. The steps – reverence, branle,[12] singles, doubles, reprises – each required the same amount of music, four bars of triple time. They were combined into groups called measures by precisely defined rules, and the dancers had to remember the order of steps in each measure and the order of the measures.[13]

Further light is thrown on the dances of early sixteenth-century England by Sir Thomas Elyot's *Boke named the Governour* published in 1531. This was a book on education, the first to be written and printed in the English language. In it were four chapters on dancing. In Chapter 22[14] of the 'first Boke' entitled 'How Dauncing may be an introduction into the first morall vertue, called Prudence', Elyot emphasizes the benefits of dancing:

> Wherfore all they that have their courage stered towards very honour or perfecte nobilitie, let them approche to this passe tyme [dancing] and either them selfes prepare them to daunse, or els at the leste way beholde with watching eien other that can daunse truely, kepynge juste measure and tyme.

* See Appendix B.

Chapter 20 mentions the dances which were being performed in the author's day: '. . . we have nowe base daunsis, bargenettes, pavions, turgions, and roundes.'

The 'base daunsis' would certainly be the French Basse Danses: the 'bargenettes' were caroles in branle form[15] and could be thought of as forming part of the Basse Danse: the 'pavions' are better known to us as the 'pavane' and were probably brought to England by Katherine of Aragon in 1501: the 'Turgions' are considered by Arbeau to be part of the Basse Danse, and the 'roundes' would have been the dances already well-known in medieval England.

The pavane is generally considered to have been a slow and solemn dance, yet Melusine Wood, surprisingly enough, points out that the early pavanes in England were written in galliard rhythm. The dance had, therefore, a certain gaiety, but a gaiety combined with tremendous dignity and restraint. It is the dignity and restraint that are emphasized both by Arbeau (*Orchésographie*) and by Sir John Hawkins, in his *History of Music*. The former gives us this account:

A nobleman can dance the Pavane with cape and sword, and you others dressed in your long gowns, walking decorously with a studied gravity, and the damsel with chaste demeanour and eyes cast down, sometimes glancing at the onlookers with virginal modesty. And as for the Pavane, it is used by Kings, Princes and great lords, to display themselves on some day of solemn festival with their fine mantles and their robes of ceremony: and then the queens and the princesses and the great ladies accompany them with the long trains of their dresses let down trailing behind them . . .[16]

The second writer portrays the atmosphere of the Pavane thus:

It is a grave and majestic dance: the method of dancing it anciently was by gentlemen dressed with capes and swords, by those of the long robe in their gowns, by the peers in their mantles, and by the ladies in gowns with long trains, the motion whereof in dancing resembling that of a peacock.[17]

From all these accounts it seems clear that early sixteenth-century 'upper class' dancing in England could be described as slow, solemn, dignified, with great importance attached to style and posture, the whole being very much influenced by the dancing at the French court. The keen interest that was shown undoubtedly stemmed from the gay court of the (as yet) young, athletic Henry VIII. Surrey,

Henry's courtier poet, describes the tournaments and other court pastimes:

> . . . the ladyes bright of hewe;
> The dances short, long tales of great delight.[18]

Not only was the young Henry an athlete and one of the best archers in the kingdom, but he also delighted in pageants and masques, took a keen interest in dancing (as we have already seen from the chronicler's account of the 'Westminster Disguisings') and frequently danced to his own compositions. Indeed, it was the fashion at court from the King downwards to compose musical tunes and verses to go with them.[19]

It was at this court that the gentlemen of England learnt the intrigue of love and politics, enjoyed the dance, music and poetry, and acquired a taste for scholarship and the arts (influenced by the culture, art and scholarship of the Italian courts of the Renaissance). This was, in fact, the beginning of the ideal of the all-accomplished 'gentleman' of Elizabethan times, and there is no doubt that his accomplishments would have included a mastery of the Basse Dance and the pavane.

Dancing in this period was of course not confined to those of noble birth. John Stow, who was born in London in 1525, recounts how in his youth 'on the Holy dayes . . . the youthes of this Citie, have in the field exercised themselves, in leaping, dauncing, shooting, wrestling, casting of the stone or ball etc.', and 'the Maidens, one of them playing on a Timbrell, in sight of their Maisters and Dames, [used] to daunce for garlandes hanged athwart the streets . . .' and goes on to comment: 'which open pastimes in my youth, being now suppressed, worser practises within doores are to be feared.'[20]

Outside the towns, there is little doubt that peasant dancing continued, as in the previous century, boisterous and uninhibited, in England as on the Continent.

In the reign of Edward VI, Mary and Elizabeth, there was a change in the tone of 'disguisings-cum-Masks'. The mythological allegories of the Renaissance tended to replace the Romance allegories of the fifteenth century, and the cost rose startlingly from the modest £13, which had been usual in Henry VII's reign, to the £400 or more that might be paid in Elizabeth's time.[21] It must, therefore, have been a source of dual satisfaction to Elizabeth, with her reputation for parsimony and her known love of dancing, that in her reign this composite entertainment was to develop into two separate forms: that of drama (with the emphasis on the words, not the spectacle) and the dance, as something to be enjoyed for its own sake.

VI
Elizabethan England: 1558 to 1603

Under the eagle eye of Queen Elizabeth,
Englishmen spun round longer and leaped
higher than the men of other nations.
MELUSINE WOOD: *Historical Dances*

The disturbed reigns of Edward VI and Mary were not conducive to
any development of dancing, but the Elizabethan period is extremely
fertile ground for the student of social dance, not least because the
Queen herself was a talented and enthusiastic dancer who insisted on
the highest standards from her Maids of Honour and her courtiers.

The key to the dances popular in late sixteenth-century England is
given in the poem 'Orchestra' written by Sir John Davies in 1596.
Here[1] he gives an account of 'brawls' (branles), rounds and heys,
ring dances,[2] measures[3] (all of which were 'carry-overs' from earlier
times) and also galliards, courantoes and La Voltas[4] – three dances
which were new to England in this period, although they had long
been known on the Continent.

The galliard is of Italian origin, and is still danced today in parts
of Italy as the 'gagliarda'. Writing in 1523, the dancing master Arena
speaks of: 'the new and graceful Galliarde which is to make our
bodies sweat exceedingly' and he is much amused by the antics of the
dancers who look like 'cocks beating themselves, or cats and monkeys
when they want to scratch'.[5] Something of the atmosphere of the
dance can perhaps be caught from this short extract from Arbeau's
Orchésographie published in 1588:

> The Galliarde is so called because one must be blithe and lively to
> dance it ... It ought to consist of six steps as it contains six
> crotchets played in two bars of triple time, but there are only five
> steps because the sixth note is replaced by a rest.

Air 'Antoinette'

1st step: pied en l'air gauche
2nd step: pied en l'air droit, and so on for 3rd and 4th
On the rest that takes the place of a note, execute a *'saut'*:*
Then change and execute to the right everything that you did
to the left and so till the *congé*.

In Elizabethan England, the galliard had great appeal – both as a dance and as a form of exercise. The Queen herself danced six or seven galliards in the morning for exercise – the equivalent of fifteen minutes with a skipping-rope. She encouraged galliard dancing at court, allowing one pavane at the beginning of the ball for the benefit of 'the most eminent who were no longer young'[6] after which galliards were danced.

Elizabeth's love of galliard dancing endured almost literally to her dying day. In 1599, her share in the Twelfth Night revels was reported to Spain with the caustic comment: 'The Head of the Church of England and Ireland was to be seen in her old age dancing three or four Galliards'. A year or so later she was still dancing *'gayement et de belle disposition'* at the wedding of Anne Russell, and in April 1602 she 'trod two galliards with the Duke of Nevers'.[7]

'Lavolta' or 'La Volta', originating as a folk-dance in Provence, was a very spirited and lively affair, requiring considerable skill.[8] As a court dance it occupied a unique position since, instead of dancing opposite or alongside, in 'open couple' style, the volta dancers turned constantly in close embrace and, without separating, had to leap high in the air.

Sir John Davies gives a poet's impression in 'Orchestra':

> A lofty jumping or a leaping around
>> Where arm in arm two dancers are entwined
> And whirl themselves with strict embracements bound
>> And still their feet an anapaest do sound.

and an extract from Arbeau's *Orchésographie* gives the authentic picture in 1588:

La Volte is a kind of galliarde familiar to the people of Provence: it is danced in triple time . . .

Air for La Volte

* The 'saut' was a kind of limping hop.

When you wish to turn, let go of the damsel's left hand and throw your left arm round her back, seizing and clasping her about the waist. At the same time throw your right hand below her busk* to help her spring when you push her with your left thigh. She, on her part, will place her right hand on your back or collar, and her left on her thigh, to hold her petticoat or kirtle in place, lest the breeze caused by the movement should reveal her chemise or naked thigh. This accomplished, you execute together the turns of the Volte described above. . . .

Many contemporary writers considered La Volta to be bold and indecent, some holding it responsible both for pregnancies and for miscarriages, surely an interesting combination. Arbeau, more moderate and writing after the dance had gained considerable acceptance, says merely: 'I leave you to consider if it be a proper thing for a young girl to make such large steps and separations of the legs: and whether in the Volte both honour and health are not concerned and threatened.' There is not the slightest doubt that Queen Elizabeth – confounding all narrow critics – took a keen delight in La Volta, and fostered enthusiasm for it at court.†

The courantoe (also known as courante and coranto), was, as the name implies, a light running dance. In Elizabethan England it had lost its original artificial pantomimic wooing element and consisted of a swift zigzag pattern of movement[9] which, in the words of a contemporary writer, 'recalls that of a fish when it plunges lightly through the water and returns to the surface'.[10] To quote Arbeau:

The courante differs considerably from the Volte: it is danced to light duple time, consisting of two simples and a double to the left: and the same to the right going forwards or sideways and sometimes backwards. . . . Note that the steps of the Courante must be sauté (jumped) which is not done in the Pavane or the Basse Danse.

Air for the Courante

Another dance which found favour in late sixteenth-century court and aristocratic circles in England was the 'allemande', sometimes

---

* busk: flat front part of corset.
† See Plate IV, page 51.

known as the almaine (also spelt alman and almayne). In Germany, its country of origin, the solemn opening strains were followed by a light, springy movement in triple time. In England and in other countries, the effect of lightening the dance was produced by quickening the tempo and introducing hops between the steps.[11]

A completely different feature of court dancing towards the end of the century was the introduction of English country-dances, 'old and new'. In the year 1591 Queen Elizabeth visited Cowdrey, where she watched Lord and Lady Montagu dancing with their tenants and 'in the evening the countrie people presented themselves to her Majestie in a pleasaunt dance with taber and pipe'.[12]

From this time on, there are references to country-dancing at Elizabeth's court. As she grew older, the Queen became more and more interested in 'English' dances as opposed to those of Continental origin, and on her journeys through the countryside it was customary to bring the country people to dance before her: 'Her Majestie is in very good health and comes much abroad these holidayes; for almost every night she is in the presence to see the ladies daunce the old and the new Country dances, with the taber and pipe'.[13]

The 'old' were the chain, ring and round dances of earlier times, in origin probably traceable back to ancient May-day processions or ritual spring-time round dances of pagan times.[14] The 'new' were probably the more complicated figured dances which were becoming popular among the country people. According to Thomas Nashe, writing in 1596, these new country dances included: Rogero, Turkeyloney, Basilena, All Flowers of the Broom, Peggy Ramsey, Green Sleeves and Pepper is Black –

> 'Who . . . would . . . do as Dick Harvey did that, having preacht against dancing, one Sunday evening, when his Wench or Friskin was footing it aloft on the Greene, with foote out and foote in, and as busie as might be at Rogero, Basilino, Turkeyloney, All the Flowers of the Broom, Pepper is Black, Green Sleeves, Peggy Ramsey, he came sneaking behind a tree and lookt on, and though he was loth to be seene to countenance the sport, having laid Gods word against it so dreadfully, yet . . . he sent her 18 pence, in hugger mugger, to pay the fiddlers.[15]

There are a number of other sixteenth-century references[16] to these country-dances and they were all later included by Playford in his collection in 1651. In two cases, 'Turkeyloney' and 'Basilena' there is contemporary sixteenth-century[17] evidence of the steps and figures used. The manuscript notes which were found fully describe the two dances and look as if they were written by young gentlemen at their dancing lessons. These notes – considered by experts to belong to the 1590s – also record certain current court dances. This piece of evidence, taken together with the extract from Thomas Nashe above, indicate that these two dances were genuine 'village green' dances of the sixteenth century, and also that they were examples of the country-dances now being introduced to the court.

There is no doubt at all that in the reign of Queen Elizabeth, social dancing established itself as an important part of court life and court functions. This was largely because the Queen herself was such a keen and talented dancer, but it must not be forgotten that the central position occupied by the social dance fits easily into the Elizabethan philosophy of the universe. The early Greek doctrine that the creation was an act of music, and the Middle Ages theory that the created universe was itself engaged in one perpetual dance continued into the Elizabethan age.[18]

The perfect epitome of the universe seen as a dance is in Sir John Davies' poem 'Orchestra' – the poem which has already been taken as a source for late sixteenth-century dances. In 'Orchestra' written in 1596, he recounts how Penelope one night is begged by Antinous, one of her suitors, to dance:

> Imitate heaven, whose beauties excellent
> Are in continual motion day and night.

Penelope refuses. There follows a debate on the subject of dancing, Antinous maintaining that as the universe itself is one great dance, we should ourselves join in the cosmic harmony. The various happenings on earth

> Forward and backward rapt and whirled are
> According to the music of the spheres

Even plants are included:

> What makes the vine about the elm to dance?
> . . . .
> Kind nature first doth cause all things to love
> Love makes them dance and in just order move

Penelope herself is full of the dance without knowing it:

> Love in the twinkling of your eyelids danceth
> Love danceth in your pulses and your veins

Then, prompted by the god of love, Antinous gives Penelope a magic mirror to look into. Here she sees first a thousand stars moving

48

around their centre – the moon, followed swiftly by another picture –
the other moon, Elizabeth – surrounded by her courtiers in a dance:

> Her brighter dazzling beams of Majesty
> Were laid aside...........
> ....
> Forward they paced and did their pace apply
> To a most sweet and solemn melody

Davies never finished his long poem but we are entitled to assume
that Penelope would have been persuaded to dance.

There was nothing incongruous to the Elizabethans in the transition from the mystical notion of spherical music and the dancing
of the stars to the realistic notion of actual courtiers dancing with
Queen Elizabeth to the strains of court musicians. Indeed, the idea
that the 'cosmic dance' on one level should be reproduced in the
'body politic' on another level was exactly in accord with their
theories of 'corresponding planes'.[19]

In Elizabethan England, however, the enthusiasm for dancing was
by no means confined to the Queen and her courtiers. The whole
nation seemed to be borne on this wave and in the latter half of the
sixteenth century we earned for ourselves the name 'the dancing
English' and were reputed to leap higher than the dancers of any
other nation. Thus, Shakespeare in Act III of *Henry V* makes the
Duke of Bourbon say:

> They bid us to the English dancing-schools
> And teach La Voltas high, and swift Corantos
> Saying our grace is only in our heels
> And that we are mostly lofty runaways[20]

This is, of course, an anachronism if applied to Henry V's own time,
but is an exact description by Shakespeare of the contemporary
scene in his lifetime. In Shakespeare's day, the English dancing-
schools were one of the sights of London, a source of wonder and
interest to all foreign visitors. Two or three times a week there were
well-conducted assemblies frequented by the wives and daughters of
worthy citizens. When no assembly was in progress, 'there was
always the chance of seeing some young man practising galliard
passages – spinning, leaping and somersaulting'.[21] The days of
medieval jousts and tournaments had gone, the era of 'sport' had not
yet arrived: dancing, it seemed, filled the gap in the lives of athletic
and leisured young men.

The interest of country-folk in dancing is well indicated by the

appearance among them of the 'new' country-dances – those complicated, figured dances which required considerable skill to learn – but
which were danced as enthusiastically as the old, simple medieval
dances.

Two other dances of the English countryside which are mentioned
in contemporary late sixteenth-century English literature are the jig
(or jigg)[22] and the hornpipe. The jig had its origin in Britain, the term
being used to describe certain dances of 'the folk' which were
accompanied by songs.[23] It was something of a generic term for
'dance-with-song' for general groups of young men and girls.[24] Very
little exists by way of actual description of the jig as a dance but
there are frequent literary references to the jig dancer turning like a
top, or like a globe or wheeling until giddy, all emphasizing the rapid
and vigorous nature of the dance. Consider, for example, this
astonishingly up-to-date reference in a seventeenth-century ballad
'The Young-Man's Ramble':

> Priscilla did dance a jig with Tom
> Which made her buttocks quake like a Custard[25]

The jig at this time was not characteristically Scottish or Irish,
although probably there was a Scottish jig which was especially
spectacular. since Shakespeare (as expert on dance technique as any
dancing-master) makes Beatrice, in *Much ado about Nothing* liken
wooing to a 'hot and hasty Scotch jig'. (By contrast, she likens
repentance 'with his bad legs' to a galliard, the 'bad legs' undoubtedly referring to the 'saut' or limping hop specified by Arbeau.)

The jig, a dance of the country people, is thought to have exerted
a strong influence on the courtly galliard. In any event it soon
became established in its own right as one of the social dances of the
upper classes[26] and is well-represented in early musical collections
along with pavanes, galliards, corantoes and other courtly dances.

Little enough is known about the jig as a dance-form, but even less
is known about the early hornpipe. There are, however, many
literary allusions to it as a dance, like the jig, for a number of
participants, in the manner of a country-dance:

> A homely country hornepipe we will dance
> A shepherds pretty jigg to make him sport
>
> . . . .
>
> Take hands take hands our hearts let us advance
> And strive to please his humour with a dance.[27]

There is no evidence to show that it ever became a courtly dance,
and, needless to say, it had no affinity with what today is known as
the 'Sailor's Hornpipe'.

Plate III Peasant Dancing. Extract from 16th Century Flemish
Book of Prayers

Plate IV Queen Elizabeth dancing La Volta with the Earl of Leicester. The illustration clearly brings out the close embrace of partner which La Volta involved in the turns

Comparison with earlier periods of history brings out the threefold nature of the social dance revolution in Elizabethan England. Firstly, there was the tremendous upsurge of enthusiasm for dancing as a pastime. Secondly, the new dances which appeared on the scene (galliards, La Voltas, corantos, allemandes, jigs) were lively, leaping and spirited and in complete contrast to the stiff, artificial posturings of the Basse Danse, in which the feet were kept low and close to the floor.[28] Thirdly, many dances of 'the people', particularly the 'new' country-dances and the jigs were now taken up by court and nobles.

There can be little doubt that the gay and lively dances of the Elizabethan period were a reflection of the adventurous and joyous spirit of the age. This was a period when, according to Trevelyan, England was freed from medieval ways of thinking but was not yet oppressed by Puritan fears and complexes, a period when men rejoiced in nature and the countryside, and were moving forward to agricultural and mercantile prosperity but were not yet over-whelmed by industrial materialism.[29]

In addition, there were the Elizabethan adventurers (Drake, Frobisher, Hawkins, Raleigh and many others) who were sailing the world, and whose exploits were brought to the imagination of all by the writer Hakluyt[30] in 1589. This was the 'Golden Age' of Shakespeare's England. 'Large classes, freed as never before, from poverty felt the uprising of the spirit and expressed it in wit, music and song'.[31] The Elizabethan English were in love with life – small wonder that their joy in living found expression not only in the Elizabethan madrigal and lyric poetry, but also in the zestful and gay dances of the period.

As well as being spirited and lively, one of the dances of the Elizabethan period, La Volta, involved at times a close embrace of partner. This 'hold' contrasts markedly with the distant arm's length style of court dancing in medieval days, and must reflect the difference between the robust Elizabethan attitude to women and the artificial approach of the age of medieval chivalry.

Finally, this was an age of greater harmony and freer mixing of the classes than in earlier or later times. Trevelyan makes the point that this was a period neither of peasants' revolts nor of the snobbery of Jane Austen's day. Class divisions were taken as a matter of course, and Elizabethans, high or low, could consort together without undue self-consciousness or suspicion.[32] The liveliness associated traditionally with peasant dancing now became part of court dancing, an example being set by the Queen herself in her delight in the energetic galliard, the shocking La Volta, and the English country-dances. At the same time, a certain degree of restraint, not to say discipline, entered into country-dancing. It was thus no accident that this was the period when the English country-dances, old and new, and the country-jigs were taken up and danced by courtiers, nobles and Maids of Honour. Earlier in the century the gulf between upper-class and peasant was reflected in their respective type of dance: on the one hand the courtly Basse Danse and pavane, and on the other the rumbustious cavorting of the country-folk. But, by the end of the sixteenth century, with the freer mingling of the classes, peasants and nobles could enter into the spirit, the pattern and even the style of each other's dancing.

VII
Seventeenth-Century England

> Up pretty betimes, but yet I observe how my
> dancing . . . do make me hard to rise as I used
> to do or look after my business as I am wont.
> s. PEPYS: *Diary*. Vol. III.

(a) Stuart England: 1603 to 1649

In the early years of the seventeenth century, social dancing continued to be a popular pastime at court, and in the days of James I it was still very necessary for a courtier to be an expert dancer if he wished to keep in favour with the King. This is clear from a letter written by the Chaplain of the Venetian Ambassador in the time of James I, describing a scene that took place at a masque organized by Prince Charles in 1617:

> The dancers were now getting tired, when the King shouted out: 'Why don't you dance? What did you make me come here for? Devil take you – dance!' Whereupon Buckingham sprang forward and cut a score of lofty and very minute capers with so much grace and agility that the King was delighted.[1]

In the course of the century, however, there was a gradual decline in enthusiasm for the social dance at court. There were three fairly obvious reasons which could account for this. Queen Elizabeth was no longer there with her own keen personal interest. There was now a tremendous enthusiasm for watching spectacular masques which, in that century, could draw on poets such as Milton,[2] Ben Jonson and Chapman and for stage design on the great architect, Inigo Jones. Thirdly, there was the development of ballet.

Ballet did not precede the social dance as is often thought, but on the contrary grew out of it. In the sixteenth century ballet had already begun to develop as an art form in France and Italy, the ballet dancers of the time performing adaptations of such social dances as the pavane, galliard, coranto and allemande. These performances gradually became more and more highly skilled and in the seventeenth century left the court for the stage.

In the latter part of the century, in France, the *Académie Royale de Danse*, founded in 1661 by Louis XIV, began to train professional dancers (women as well as men) in the 'noble' style of dancing, hitherto the preserve of courtly amateurs. In the course of the century, in England as well as in France and Italy, the steps and figures of ballet grew further and further away from the original social forms and, whereas at the beginning of the century the best dancers would have been found at court, at the end of the century the best dancers were undoubtedly professionals.[3]

The social dances which found favour in this period were the brantle[4] (sometimes written 'bransle' and sometimes 'branle'), gavotte, a 'watered-down' version of the galliard, a coranto which had become slow and stately, and the 'country-dances old and new' which had been introduced to the court in the late sixteenth century.

The French branle and the gavotte quickly became popular in the reign of Charles I,[5] France succeeding Italy as the arbiter of fashion, following the marriage of Charles to a sister of the French King Louis XIII. The gavotte was originally a peasant dance of the Gavots (the inhabitants of Gap in the Higher Alps in the province of Dauphine) and was introduced to the French court in the sixteenth century.* At the French court the gavotte underwent various changes until finally it lost practically all resemblance to the original and became rather a formal and stately dance.[6] In the seventeenth-century gavotte each couple in turn took the centre and danced alone. After their solo, the gentleman kissed all the ladies and his partner did the same for the gentlemen.[7] It was in this guise that the gavotte arrived in seventeenth-century England.

The galliard which was now danced had lost nearly all the vitality of the previous century, its 'springs' being reduced to mere instep movements, and it was soon to be forgotten.[8]

The coranto, or courante, was a dance which was characteristic of the seventeenth century, but this had now become slow and dignified, with pauses as the dancers progressed round the hall.[9] The only exception to the slow and stately nature of seventeenth-century court dancing in England was the 'country-dance' which will later be treated in more detail.

(b) Commonwealth and Restoration England: 1649 to 1700

In the year 1642, England was plunged into the civil wars of Charles I and Cromwell, a struggle leading eventually to the beheading of the

* See Introduction, page 5.

King, and the establishment of the Commonwealth in the year 1649.

It is well known that under the Commonwealth masques and mixed dancing* were frowned on, Richard Baxter, for example, complaining that the sound of pipe and tabor and maypole dancing disturbed his study of the Bible. Maypoles were certainly pulled down but there is ample evidence to show that dancing continued. The date of publication (1651) and the popularity of Playford's book of country-dances shows that dancing by no means suffered a total eclipse under the Commonwealth. Further evidence is given in the detailed accounts of the expenditure of that 'seventeenth-century country gentleman' Sir Francis Throckmorton. Going up to Cambridge in 1654, and later to Oxford in 1658, he made immediate arrangements with a dancing-master for instruction at the dancing-school (£1 5s. 0d. per quarter). Student days over, on his return to London in 1659 he arranged for more lessons at the fencing and dancing-schools.[10] Finally, there is the remarkable fact that Oliver Cromwell gave a grand ball at Whitehall to celebrate his daughter's wedding in 1657, where the guests danced till 5 a.m. to the music of forty-eight violins and fifty trumpets.[11]

None the less, it cannot be denied that social dancing in England suffered severe setbacks under the Puritan regime and the disturbed conditions of the civil war which preceded it. No longer could we merit the title of the 'dancing English' with a reputation for leaping higher and spinning faster than the dancers of any other nation.

With the restoration of the monarchy in 1660, however, social dancing in England received a decided fillip. Charles II, who had grown up on the Continent, had a great love of music and dancing and was himself a talented dancer. This interest in dancing continued after his return to England as King, as shown, for example, by a letter written by him on 18 August 1655 to Henry Bennett, afterwards Earl of Arlington: 'Pray get me pricked down as many Corants and Sarabands,[12] and other little dances as you can, and bring them with you, for I have a small fidler that does not play ill on the fiddle.[13] Three years earlier Pepys records the King's participation in a New Year's Eve Ball at White Hall: 'After that [the bransle] the King led a lady a single Coranto; and then the rest of the lords, one after another, other ladies; very noble it was, and great pleasure to see. Then to country dances, the King leading the first, which he called for which was: "Cuckolds all awry" . . .'[14]

These country dances which Pepys was watching were the dances, rooted in the English countryside, which had been brought to Queen

* It was quite permissible, however, for men to dance together in one room and women in another.

Elizabeth's court towards the end of the sixteenth century. In the year 1651 they were to be immortalized in the manual: *The English Dancing Master or Plaine and Basic Rules of Country Dances* written by John Playford, a composer and publisher who kept a music shop in London near the Temple.

The date – 1651 – which was two years after the execution of Charles I and the establishment of the Commonwealth, is regarded by some as extremely odd, in view of the Puritan attitude to dancing, but, as has been pointed out, dancing was not officially banned during this period. In the prevailing conditions, when wise men kept out of trouble and stayed at home, cut off from dancing-schools, a book such as Playford's, which could be circulated throughout the country, made complete sense. The preface, interestingly enough, is apologetic, including as it does an acknowledgment 'that these Times and the nature of it [the dance] do not agree' and a highly convenient excuse that he would not have published 'this Worke . . . but that there was a false and surrepticious Copy at the Printing Presse, which if it had been published, would have been a disparagement to the quality and the Professors thereof, and a hinderance to the Learner . . .' In the event, Playford's book enjoyed immense popularity and was reprinted seventeen times between 1651 and 1728. Samuel Pepys bought a copy and met the author in November 1662.[15]

An enormous variety of dance-forms is shown in the Dancing Master, including 'rounds', 'longs' and 'squares'. All these dances belonged, originally, in the open air, but at court they came indoors and during the disturbed years of the seventeenth century dancing, generally, was an indoor domestic affair. For this reason, 'rounds for as many as will' which were open-air dances tended to die out and were replaced by, for example, 'long for eight', 'long for six', 'square for eight or four' all of which fitted comfortably into reasonably-sized rooms. 'Longways for as many as will' fitted the long gallery, a feature of most seventeenth-century country-houses.

John Playford's book was published about one hundred years after the first traceable reference to English country-dancing and about sixty years after Queen Elizabeth's Maids of Honour first began to dance country-dances at court. This must inevitably raise the question: to what extent were Playford's dances really 'English' or 'country'? In Douglas Kennedy's opinion, the dances contained in the early editions (1651–70) were basically both.[16] Later editions show that dancing-masters and composers of the day were inventing dances and dance-tunes on the 'Folk-model' to satisfy the growing market. Some of the names clearly indicate 'town life' rather than country: 'The New Exchange', 'Mayden Lane', 'Hide Park'; others commemorate the names of dancing-masters of the day: 'Parson's farewell' while others clearly indicate that they were composed for special occasions or personages: 'Graies Inn Maske', 'My Lady Foster's Delight', etc. Still others indicate anything but English influence: 'The Spanish Jeepsie' and *'A La Mode de France'*. These were the fashionable country-dances. Without doubt, the folk in the countryside went on with their own local versions of their country-dances as before, including jigs and hornpipes.

In this century there are many links, historical and sociological, between the nature of society and the social dance. Historians indicate that the first forty years of the seventeenth century were largely an uneventful prolongation of the Elizabethan era, under conditions of peace and safety instead of domestic danger and war. Few industrial, social or agricultural changes of importance took place in England in those forty years.[17] One might therefore expect the social dancing of the period to be a less exuberant version of what went before, and, indeed, the most significant difference between the dancing of Elizabethan and seventeenth-century England is the difference in speed, vitality and enthusiasm.

In addition to the reasons already indicated or the waning of interest in dancing, there was the additional factor that in this century great enthusiasm began to be shown for recreations of an intellectual, rather than a fashionable, nature. In the first forty years of the seventeenth century, the learning of the time, classical as well as Christian, was very widespread and political and religious controversies were avidly read by a wide public.

The troubled times of the civil war and the Puritan background to the Commonwealth meant a setback to the social dance but, as already made clear, by no means a total eclipse. Charles II, as we have seen, did much to revive the popularity of social dancing but in this 'new age' (an age of experimental science and the founding of the Royal Society under the patronage of the King) it is most unlikely that the dance was ever restored at court to the place it had enjoyed under Elizabeth.

It might be wondered whether the scandal and licentiousness of Charles II's court, so effectively portrayed in early Restoration drama, had any reflection in the social dancing of the time. Apart from the fact that the King's favourite country-dance was named: 'Cuckolds all awry' there is no evidence of this. It is certain that Samuel Pepys, that outspoken observer of dancing at court functions, would have recorded any such trend, had it existed. The theatre, of course, had been suppressed by the Puritans; dancing had merely been discouraged and in fact continued to flourish, especially at indoor functions. Hence after the Restoration, there was less reason to expect any violent reaction in the social dance.

Throughout this era distinctions between the social strata continued to be rigid but, as in the Elizabethan period, the different social classes could still mix relatively freely, without feelings of self-conscious discomfort. Both 'gentry' and villagers, for example, shared in common enjoyment of country pursuits such as the hunting of fox, deer, and hare – the 'gentleman' on horseback and the 'common folk' running alongside.[18] This relatively free mixing of members of different social classes with each, of course, keeping to his 'appointed station', fits in exactly with the general popularity from highest to lowest of the country-dance. With the exception of a few 'kissing-dances' the English country-dances were very impersonal, depending for their effect on the teamwork of 'figure-dancing'. All classes could mix freely on this level and the servants were frequently brought in to 'make up a set'. As long as each person 'knew his place' and 'kept it' all went well.

VIII
Eighteenth-Century England

No more the well-taught feet shall tread
The figure of the mazy Zed.

C. M. FANSHAWE: *Memorials*

From the beginning of the eighteenth century onwards, the influence of the court in general began to decline. None of the monarchs of this century – stern, asthmatic William, invalid Anne, the German Georges – had any wish to keep up a court like, for example, Queen Elizabeth's.[1] Alongside the declining influence of court life there arose the growing influence of Parliament, politicians and the country-houses of the nobility and 'gentry'.

The court, however, continued to exert a great deal of influence on dancing in Georgian England, particularly through the institution known as the 'King's Birthnight Ball'. A new dance was always composed for this occasion by the court dancing-master: it was printed in stenochoreographic notation* for circulation to other dancing-masters and for sale to the public. Those people hoping to attend, or wishing to give the impression that they were going to attend, had to know the new dance. It must be stressed that a particular feature of dancing in the eighteenth century was this individual creation of dances to fit one particular piece of music: one bourrée, for example, could not be danced to the music of another. Sometimes a dance would take on a multiple form, a combination of several dances in one, for example, sarabande-bourrée.[2] The dances in general use in the first half of the eighteenth century were the bourrée, passepied, loure, rigadoon, the still popular gavotte and country-dances, and the minuet.[3] Later, in the course of the century, the allemande, contredanse and cotillon were to become popular dances.

Of all these, the minuet must stand alone. Unlike the specially composed individual dances each requiring a particular piece of music, there was but one 'minuet' and this could be danced to any minuet air. The origin of the dance is to be found in a French folk-

---

* Feuillet's system of dance-notation, invented by him and explained in *Choreographie* published in 1701.

59

dance, the *'branle de poitou'*.[4] In the year 1650 it was adopted and adapted by the French court and for over one hundred and fifty years was to be the opening dance of practically every State ball in Europe. In England, by the early years of the eighteenth century, it had displaced the coranto and held pride of place at court and in the Assembly Rooms at Bath and many other fashionable spas and watering-places.

The name derives from the French 'menu' and the Latin 'minutus': small and neat. Originally, the 'floor pattern' of the minuet was a figure 8, then an 'S', still later a '2' and about the year 1700 it became a letter 'Z'.[5] In its developed form the minuet was an 'open-couple' dance performed with tiny precise steps and a dainty mannered air. 'With dainty little steps and glides, to the right and to the left, forward and backward, in quarter turns, approaching and retreating hand in hand, searching and evading, now side by side, now facing, now gliding past one another, the ancient dance play of courtship appears here in a last and almost unrecognisable stylization and refinement.'[6] It is not difficult to see that the minuet was essentially a product of its age. In a period when the correct method of offering snuff or of doffing one's hat were actions ruled by certain definite formulae and could be mastered only after years of practice, the tiny precise steps, the stylized and mannered charm and constrained movements of the minuet suited the ladies and gentlemen of the Georgian age as nothing else could have.

Reginald St Johnston is of the opinion that the minuet can hardly be called a dance at all, but rather one of the finest schools of courtesy and deportment ever invented.[7] This was certainly true for the eighteenth-century débutante who, at her first ball, had to take the floor with a partner and dance an exhibition minuet before the assembled company.[8] In England the minuet was still danced at court and at the 'St. James's Palace Birthnight Balls' until the early years of the nineteenth century. When George III became ill and unable to attend, the minuets gradually died away and after his death in 1820 they never returned to our ballrooms. To quote from the 'Elegy on the abrogation of the Birthnight Ball and consequent final subversion of the Minuet':

> In vain, these eyes with tears of horror wet
> Read its death warrant in the Court Gazette.
> 'No Ball tonight' Lord Chamberlain proclaims;
> 'No Ball tonight shall grace thy roof, St. James!'
> 'No Ball!' The Globe, the Sun, the Star repeat,
> The Morning paper and the evening sheet;

Through all the land the tragic news has spread
And all the land has mourned the Minuet dead.[9]

Throughout the eighteenth century, the 'country-dances' more than held their own. In this period the nobility and gentry were country-dwellers rather than townsfolk, tending to come to London only for their parliamentary and court duties. Their roots were in their landed estates and their big country-houses. Here, gentry and tenants would mingle in the periodical celebrations to mark weddings, births and comings-of-age celebrations where country-dancing for 'high and low' was the accepted form of communal enjoyment.

Country-dances were also popular at the aristocratic eighteenth-century open-air pleasure gardens of Vauxhall and Ranelagh, and at the fashionable Assembly Rooms in London and Bath. The 'compact' form of country-dance (such as square for four, or square for eight) so appropriate for the 'domestic' indoor dancing of the previous century was now dropped in favour of the 'Longways Progressive, for as many as will' in the large and sumptuous Assembly Rooms.[10]

Towards the end of the eighteenth century a steady decline in the standard of English country-dancing set in, the depths being plumbed by a dance called 'Grave and Gay'. In it the top couple began by dancing slowly down the set to the strains of 'God Save the King'. At each reference to His Majesty the lady made a very deep curtsey and her partner bowed. On a sudden change of music to 'Polly, put the kettle on' the couple skipped briskly to the bottom of the set.[11]

As early as the turn of the seventeenth century, English country-dancing 'proper' had crossed the Channel and been taken up enthusiastically in many European countries, particularly France. In France, the English country-dance was introduced to the French court and called the '*contredanse anglaise*'. After the year 1725 or so the 'contredanse anglaise' was replaced by the 'contredanse francaise' and became known simply as the 'contredanse'. By this time, the 'contredanse' had a technical meaning of its own which had no rural connections, either French or English.[12] In 1706 Feuillet asks in the introduction to *Recueil de Contredanse*: 'What is a contredanse?' and gives the answer: 'It is the repetition of a figure by two or more couples.' The French contredanse in its turn crossed the Channel and, under the name 'contredanse', was danced in England in the latter part of the eighteenth and early years of the nineteenth century.

The 'cotillon' (a 'square for eight' figure dance) is an example of one specific French contredanse which came to England[13] and enjoyed great popularity in the second half of the century. The name 'cotillon' comes from the beginning of a popular song which accompanied the dance in France:

> Ma commère, quand je danse
> Mon cotillon [petticoat], va-t-il bien?[14]

Various cotillons were named after the airs to which they were danced. One exists with the unlikely name of 'Les Plaisirs de Tooting',[15] a title which does at least acknowledge a distant English origin.

The allemande also came to England from France. Originally derived from a sixteenth-century German dance, and already known in sixteenth-century England as the almayne or alman, it is said to have been adopted by the court of Louis XIV following the annexation of Alsace. The basic step seems to have been the *chassée*, the changing step to the side, and its particular charm lay in 'the fine carriage of the torso and in the graceful interlacing of the arms'.[16]

The cotillon, allemande and contredanse gradually came to oust the minuet from popularity in the second half of the eighteenth century, a fact that accords well with the gradual decline in the standard of dancing. The first quarter of the century – the heyday of the minuet – is sometimes regarded as the peak of technical perfection in the social dance. After that, 'social' dancers gave up the unequal struggle to reach the standard of excellence attained by the professional dancers, trained by the Academie Royale, and tended to relax with their cotillons, country-dances and contredanses. The minuet, of course, remained for quite a long time because it had become something of a ritual.

No relaxation or decline in standards was permitted, however – particularly at the fashionable Assembly Rooms at Bath – as long as Beau Nash held sway as Master of Ceremonies, a position which he occupied for over half a century. He compelled the fashionable world to lay aside their swords when entering the evening assemblies and dances, and forbade top boots and coarse language. The rules of Beau Nash were that the balls were to begin at six. Each ball was to open with a minuet danced by the two persons of the highest distinction present. After the minuets, which generally lasted two hours, the country-dances began, with the ladies of the highest rank standing up first. At nine, came a short interval for rest and tea. Country-dances were then resumed until the clock struck eleven when, even in the middle of a dance, the ball ended.[17]

The rise of Bath as a fashionable spa in the first half of the eighteenth century is of considerable sociological interest. The firm regulation by Beau Nash of the balls and assemblies meant some standardization of social manners for Georgian England, and the spreading of a polished social pattern among the upper- and 'aspiring to be upper-' class patrons of the spa. Provincial and local barriers were loosened. People of the upper- and middle-classes were brought together as never before, from all parts of the country. The higher aristocracy already knew each other through court life and the House of Lords, but up to now there had been no process whereby the 'middling gentry' – the rising professional and commercial classes and their womenfolk – could meet each other socially.

Bath, now accessible as a consequence of improved communications, was the national resort where the squires of Wessex, with their ladies and marriageable sons and daughters could meet and dance and flirt with the small gentry of East Anglia and possibly even with the higher aristocracy, who flocked there as soon as the London season was over. Intermarriage thus followed between families from widely separated parts of the country, and England's local dialects began to give way to a more standard accent. Polite manners could be diffused more readily at Bath than at London, so seldom frequented by the smaller gentry.[18] In sociological terms, the manners and customs of the 'reference group' could now be assimilated by aspirants to that group, with the result that the 'upper class' (formerly a small élite clustering around the court) was now widening to include a great many smaller landowners, down to the 'squires' at the lower end of the scale.

No picture of social dancing in the eighteenth century would be complete without a reference to a number of extremely sumptuous Assembly Rooms which were opened in the heart of London in the second half of the century, no doubt to cater for those who did not wish to make the journey to the Open-Air Pleasure Gardens of Vauxhall and Ranelagh. These were Carlisle House in Soho Square (1763), Almack's in King Street, St James's (1765), the Pantheon in Oxford Street (1772) and the Argyll Rooms in Regent Street. Of these, the most important and the most interesting is undoubtedly Almack's, which governed fashionable dancing from 1765 when first opened until about 1840.[19]

Contemporary announcements for these Assemblies confirm that by the second half of the eighteenth century the minuet was gradually being ousted by the livelier and more warmblooded contredanse, cotillon and allemande. An announcement in the *Daily Press* in 1769 runs:

On Friday next, the 10th instant, at ALMACK's Assembly Room in King Street, St. James's, will be the First of the Two Nights

Subscription for Minuets and Cotillons, or French Country Dances. The Doors will be open at Eight. No Person admitted without their Name wrote on the Back of the Ticket.[20]

From further announcements of the day we can read that at the then fashionable Carlisle House in Soho Square, 'a new gallery for the dancing of Cotillons and Allemandes, and a suite of new rooms adjoining' were opened in January 1769. Two years later an announcement in a London newspaper dated 19 March 1771 referring to the annual ball to be given by Mr Yates (a well-known dancing teacher) at Carlisle House ran as follows:

After the Minuet, Cotillions and Allemands are danced by his scholars, there will be a Ball for the Company. There will be refreshments of Tea, Coffe, Lemonade, Orgeat, Biscuits etc. and music in a different room for those who choose to make sets for Cotillions etc. before the scholars have finished.[21]

From this review of social dancing in the eighteenth century it seems clear that the minuet was the significant dance of the earlier years, and the country-dance, contredanse and cotillon of the later. The parallel between the movements of the minuet and the exquisite manners of the upper class Georgians is obvious and has already been drawn. It is, however, possible to see in the harmony, grace and stylization of the minuet a reflection of certain facets of early eighteenth-century life which go deeper than the mannerisms of the day. This age appears to have had a certain peace and harmony which was reflected in many different aspects of life; in, for instance, the balance between town and country and, artistically, in eighteenth-century landscape gardening, in Georgian architecture, in artists such as Hogarth, Gainsborough, Reynolds, Romney and the Adam brothers, and in literary figures such as Gray, Goldsmith, Cowper, Johnson, Boswell and Burke. The works of these writers and artists were not so much 'works of protest' but rather the result of processes of supply and demand in a period where the level of taste and of production were both remarkably high.[22] The point that is being emphasized here is that the balanced, stylized, graceful minuet was a dance eminently suited not only to the early eighteenth-century exquisites but also to the general spirit of the age.

After the 1760s considerable changes began to make themselves felt. The year 1769 saw the patenting of mechanical power both in cotton and in engineering: agricultural and industrial innovations were on the way, and the face of rural England was becoming altered by the ever-increasing number of enclosures. In short, the pace and manner of life was becoming less and less suitable for a dance such as the minuet. It did, however, continue to be included in court balls and fashionable assemblies until the early years of the nineteenth century. In France the minuet and the other stately court dances were killed outright by the French Revolution but in England the life of the minuet was prolonged, somewhat artificially, owing to the influx of numerous French aristocrats after the Revolution, many of whom sought to gain a living by teaching dancing, particularly in girls' schools.[23]

IX
Nineteenth-Century England

These sort of boobies think that people come
to balls to do nothing but dance; whereas
everyone knows that the real business of a ball
is either to look out for a wife, to look after a
wife, or to look after somebody else's wife.

ROBERT SMITH SURTEES:
Mr. Facey Romford's Hounds

(a) 1800–1837

Following the relatively settled 'classical' period, England entered upon more restless times, already foreshadowed by the closing years of the eighteenth century. The war with Napoleonic France formed a background for the very rapid industrial and social changes in the early years of the century. This was indeed the era of the 'Two Nations'. The poor suffered from wars, unemployment and high prices but the landed gentry pursued, undisturbed, their prosperous and peaceful lives in the country. The Navy provided complete protection from foreign invasion and, while in Europe the Napoleonic wars were at their height, at home the elegant extravagance of the dandy reached a peak in the days of Beau Brummel.

Factory conditions, lack of sanitation, and the new slum dwellings were, as yet, no concern of the aristocratic ruling class who continued to enjoy (until the influence of evangelism) their pleasant life in town- and country-house. This enjoyment included a high appreciation of the poetry and painting of the age and, of course, a keen participation in dancing.

In the early years of the nineteenth century the fashionable dances were the English country-dance, the French contredanse, the cotillon, the minuet (its life, as already indicated, somewhat artificially prolonged in England), the French quadrille, the waltz, Scottish reels and the ecossaise.[1]

The country-dance remained a great favourite until about 1850 when (with one exception: 'Sir Roger de Coverley' or 'Virginia Reel') it was swept off the floor by the increasing popularity of the quadrille, waltz and polka. Until then, it was danced at State balls, at Almack's and at all public assemblies.[2] At State balls it was customarily the concluding dance until, after the Queen's marriage to Albert, it was replaced by the polka.[3]

The minuet continued to be danced at the leading assembly rooms and, until the death of George III in 1820, remained the ceremonial dance at court.[4] The minuet was frequently followed by the quadrille, or, to give it its full name, the quadrille de contredanse. At first it consisted of four figures (all popular contredanses); Le Pantalon, L'Été, La Poule and La Trenise.[5] Later on a fifth figure, derived from the cotillon, called Le Final, was added.

There are two theories about the introduction of the quadrille into England. The most widespread is that it was not danced in England until it was brought over to Almack's from Paris in 1815 by Lady Jersey (one of the Lady Patrons who ruled these assembly rooms).[6] The other belief, held by Reginald St Johnston, is that it was introduced into England by a Miss Berry and then taken up by the Duke of Devonshire and made fashionable about 1813.[7]

The French quadrille was for two, four or any number of couples but four seems to have been the usual number in England. Each pair of dancers remained *vis-à-vis* and danced only with each other, except for a variation allowed in the fifth figure which involved a continuous change of partners. This variation was sometimes called the Saint-Simonienne,[8] after Saint Simon the French philosopher and child of the Enlightenment whose aim was the total reconstruction of society and who held unorthodox views on the exchange of marriage partners. Sometimes, more harmlessly, it was simply called the 'Flirtation'.[9]

As the quadrille was made up by combining contredanses and cotillons it was possible to form a great many different sets. There were in fact sixteen different sets and in order to help him remember the order of the figures the Master of Ceremonies used to carry a small set of cards concealed in the palm of his hand. When first introduced into England in 1815, some extremely difficult steps were used but gradually these came to be ignored by all except the most accomplished dancers, and the less gifted were content to dance the quadrille with much simpler steps.

In complete contrast to the waltz to come, the quadrille was welcomed by London society with open arms and by the time Queen Victoria came to the throne it had been established as the ceremonial court dance. During Victoria's reign the State balls at Buckingham Palace always began with a set of quadrilles in which the Queen would partner her most important guest.[10] The quadrille was of course a livelier dance than the minuet and, indeed, in its later years the dance would frequently be rounded off by a 'galop'. The liveliness of the quadrille must surely have helped to pave the way in England for the greatest revolution in social dancing – the waltz.

Although there is some controversy about the origin of the waltz (many French writers claiming 'La Volta' as its ancestor) Curt Sachs and other leading authorities accept the view that the waltz, as danced in Europe in the eighteenth and nineteenth centuries, was derived from some of the 'turning-dances' which were prevalent in Germany.[11] There is further controversy about precisely which turning-dances it is derived from, but the probability is that it comes from the 'Weller' and the 'Ländler' which came from the 'Ländl' or little country lying to the west of Austria, abutting on Switzerland and Alsace. As an urban dance it was born in Vienna. Here, it lost the lifting of the feet and the hopping made necessary by heavy peasant shoes, and by 1805 it had become a gliding dance suitable for light footwear on polished floors.[12]

In England, in 'allemande' form (i.e. with intertwining arms held up at shoulder level but no close hold) a type of waltz probably formed part of the contredanse and cotillon at the end of the eighteenth century. At any rate, waltz music was well-known in England then, but the real waltz, danced as a 'closed couple', was first introduced to Almack's around 1812 – probably by travelled aristocrats who had seen it on the Continent.[13] This was the first time the 'close hold' had ever been seen in an English ballroom (apart from La Volta which had long been forgotten) and the supposed indelicacies of the waltz profoundly shocked Regency England.

Even Lord Byron expressed his outrage at the 'promiscuous' element in the 'voluptuous' waltz in his satirical poem: 'The Waltz – an apostrophic hymn'

> Say – would you wish to make those beauties quite so cheap?
> Hot from the hands promiscuously applied,
> Round the slight waist or down the glowing side . . .[14]

and again in *English Bards and Scotch Reviewers*

> Now round the room the circling dow'gers sweep
> Now in loose waltz the thin-clad daughters leap
> . . . .
> Those after husbands wing their eager flight
> Nor leave much mystery for the nuptial night . . .[15]

The Times, ever the guardian of the nation's morals, conducted several fierce attacks on the waltz, but in spite of this the dance captured England, and indeed the whole of Europe. At the Congress of Vienna in 1815 there was an outbreak of what contemporaries called 'dance mania' when, to the tune of '*Ach, du lieber Augustin*' the 'Congress danced but did not take a step forward.'[16]

On 12 July 1816 the waltz was included in a ball given by the Prince Regent – the Regent's Fête at Carlton House.[17] Although none of the Royal Family danced on that occasion, the stamp of official approval had undoubtedly been given to the waltz. In spite of this sanction from the highest quarter, *The Times* a few days later, on 16 July, launched this devastating tirade:

> We remarked with pain that the indecent foreign dance called the 'Waltz' was introduced (we believe for the first time) at the English court on Friday last. This is a circumstance which ought not to be passed over in silence. National morals depend on national habits: and it is quite sufficient to cast one's eyes on the voluptuous intertwining of the limbs, and close compressure on the bodies, in their dance, to see that it is indeed far removed from the modest reserve which has hitherto been considered distinctive of English females. So long as this obscene display was confined to prostitutes and adultresses we did not think it deserving of notice; but now that it is attempted to be forced on the respectable classes of society by the evil example of their superiors, we feel it a duty to warn every parent against exposing his daughter to so fatal a contagion. '*Amicus plato sed magis amica veritas*'. We owe a due deference to superiors in rank, but we owe a higher duty to morality. We know not how it has happened (probably by the recommendation of some worthless and ignorant French dancing-master) that so indecent a dance has now for the first time been exhibited at the English Court; but the novelty is one deserving of severe reprobation, and we trust it will never again be tolerated in any moral English society.

But *The Times* was fighting a losing battle. From 1825 onwards the growing popularity of the waltz was fostered by the compositions of Joseph Lanner, Johann Strauss the elder and Johann Strauss, his son – the 'Waltz King'. In England, by the time of the accession of the Queen in 1837, all opposition was overcome and the waltz was firmly established. The 'closed couple' dance, as opposed to the more impersonal country-dance and quadrille, had come to stay.

At various times and in different places the dance took on a different tempo, sometimes fast, sometimes slow. From 1865 onwards, at more aristocratic functions the 'Deux Temps Valse'*

* See Appendix D.

was much in evidence, whereas at more popular places the older 'Trois Temps Valse' never lost its hold. Sometimes the form changed, but the essential rotary movement remained.[18] In effect, the waltz overcame all opposition so successfully that it became entrenched as part of life in Europe generally, wherever music and dancing were to be found. In the dancing world of England in, say, the middle and the latter half of the nineteenth century it would have been unthinkable to imagine life without the waltz, and ludicrous to think in terms of the minuet.[19] A late nineteenth-century book on etiquette equally at home with Instructions on How to Cut the Toe-nails, Carve a Sucking-Pig, Arrange the Honeymoon Tour or Dance the Polka, declares:

> Valses form the staple commodity of the modern dance-programme, and the announcement of 'square' is the usual signal for all the young couples to fly from the ballroom. The hostess should be careful, however, to include a few quadrilles or lancers in the programme for the benefit of those who do not valse . . . The waltz is the favourite dance of modern times and has held its own for the last fifty years. Good waltzing means good dancing, and you cannot be said to dance unless you waltz.[20]

What, then, was the appeal of the waltz? The first waltzes were probably played at the Austrian court in the second half of the seventeenth century, but the true period of the waltz did not open until round about 1780. In France, there is no doubt that the French revolution killed the minuet and put an end generally to the formalism and artificiality of court manners. In Europe the Romantic Revival was taking place and the trend of the time was towards naturalism and spontaneity. It is not to be wondered at that the stilted minuet, with mannered play of finger-tips, affected courtesies and tender but insincere glances, should give way to the waltz with its hearty grasp, vitality and more natural movement. One can see the same difference between the romantic, rhythmic and full-blooded waltz and the dainty, mannered minuet as one can see between the wild, sweeping, primitive lines of Shelley and Wordsworth, and the careful, polished, urbane couplets of Pope. Although Lord Byron rails (to what extent with tongue in cheek?) against the new freedom of the waltz, it is just as much a product of the age as his own poetry.

Arthur Franks[21] has put forward an hypothesis which he himself terms 'unlikely' to account for the popularity of the waltz in the late nineteenth century. He sees it in terms of an 'unconscious obeisance' to the rotary power of the steam-engine. At this time, society is being transformed by the industrial revolution for which the motive power is provided by the steam-engine. Can one, he wonders, see the rotary movement of the waltz as an unconscious attempt to subordinate, by imitation, the new techniques of society – along the lines of 'sympathetic magic' in primitive societies, where hunters imitate, in the dance, the movements of the animals they wish to capture.

To call this theory 'far-fetched' is no valid criticism. It is, indeed, no more far-fetched than many other widely-accepted and fruitful psycho-analytic theories. A much more telling argument against it is, surely, the fact that the waltz derives from the 'turning-dances' of rural, mountainous Austria. The turning element in the 'Weller' and the 'Ländler' is necessary because of the twisting paths and mountainous terrain, and owes nothing whatsoever to the rotary movement of the steam-engine. Urban society, reaching out towards naturalism, is captivated by modified versions of this peasant dance. Soon, its free, lyrical, rhythmical movements sweep away the last remnants of the mincing elegance of the minuet. Then gay, enchanting melodies come to enhance the delight. It is to these factors, and not to the industrial revolution, that we must look for an explanation of the appeal of the waltz, particularly as those who waltzed, and those who operated power-driven machinery, were by no means the same.

Almack's, at which both the quadrille and the waltz were originally introduced into England, were the sumptuous assembly rooms which had opened in 1765. Almack's were 'snobbish' from the outset, but at the beginning of the nineteenth century their exclusiveness was a by-word. The fee, or 'subscription' was not the important consideration. A ticket for Almack's was one of the most difficult things in the world to obtain – especially around 1814, when Lady Jersey was Chairman of the Committee which had to approve all applications. Of the three hundred officers of the Foot Guards, it is said that only six ever obtained admission. On two occasions, the Duke of Wellington was refused admission, once because he arrived after midnight and once because he was wearing trousers instead of knee-breeches.[22] The other assembly rooms similarly tended to be extremely exclusive (in the real meaning of the word) in the early part of the nineteenth century. The Cheltenham Assembly Room, for example, had the following rule: 'That no clerk, hired or otherwise, in this town or neighbourhood; no person concerned in retail trade, no theatrical or other public performers by profession be admitted.'[23] This 'exclusiveness' persisted up to the first half of the nineteenth century.

In addition to the two dances already discussed, Scottish reels were in vogue in England during the early nineteenth century. In 1813, the Prince Regent gave a ball to celebrate the Battle of Vittorio in the Peninsular War, at which, according to Captain Gronow,[24] his sixteen-year-old daughter, Princess Charlotte, 'asked for the then fashionable Scotch dances'. The interest in Scottish dancing (both in Scotland and in England) at this time might be explained by the repealing in 1781, of the 1746 Act of Proscription, an Act which had forbidden, amongst other things, the wearing of the kilt. Additional factors were the influence of the poems and novels of Scott and the enthusiasm for the Scottish soldiers who did so well in the Napoleonic campaigns. Almack's was at this time owned by a Scot, and 'Neil Gow's', the famous Scottish band played there.[25]

The Ecossaise, in spite of its name, is thought to be of French, not Scottish origin, but was danced to Scottish music. It was lively and spirited, in 2/4 time, partly a reel and partly a country-dance, and was popular at Almack's and elsewhere between 1801 and 1815.[26]

The 'galop' or 'la gallopade' is perhaps the simplest dance there has ever been. It is in quick 2/4 time and consists of chassés with occasional turning-movements.[27] J. S. Pollock, writing in 1830, tells us that the dance was 'first introduced into this country at H.M. Ball, St. James's Palace, on 11th June, 1829, when the Princess Esterhazy, the Earl of Clanwilliam, the Duke of Devonshire and some of the foreign Ministers exerted themselves in teaching its novel movements to the company, and was danced alternately with Quadrilles and Waltzing during the whole of the evening.'[28]

(b) *Early Victorian England: 1837 to 1860*

Dancing was immensely popular in fashionable England in the period following Queen Victoria's accession to the throne in 1837. The celebrations surrounding her marriage in 1840 highlighted this general enthusiasm and may well have paved the way for the coming of a new 'closed couple' dance – the polka.

This was a dance from Bohemia which captured first France, then the whole dancing world. A great deal of mystery and myth surround the birth of the polka and the meaning of the name[29] but many authorities agree that it was originally a folk-dance of Bohemia, probably called 'Polka' or 'Polish girl' by the Czechs as a compliment to Poland, and to express admiration for the Polish revolution of 1831.[30]

In 1840, the polka was danced in Paris, on the stage,[31] and a few years later it was feverishly welcomed by the Parisians as a fashionable ballroom dance. On Thursday, 14 March 1844 *The Times* Paris correspondent comments:

The Paris papers of Monday are destitute of news. Our private letters state, that politics are for the moment suspended in public regard by the new and all-absorbing pursuit – the polka – a dance recently imported from Bohemia, and which embraces in its qualities the intimacy of the waltz, with the vivacity of the Irish jig. You may conceive how completely is 'the Polka' the rage from the (I am assured) fact that the lady of a celebrated ex-minister desiring to figure in it at a *soirée dansante,* monopolized the professor par excellence of that *specialité,* for three hours on Wednesday, at 200f. the hour . . .[32]

Allen Dodsworth, an American dancing-master writing in retrospect in 1885, is of the opinion that the Parisian craze for the polka caused a general decline in moral standards.

In Paris the rage to learn this dance became so general that Cellarius was compelled to employ many ballet-girls to assist in teaching. . . . Subsequently, places were opened in New York, multiplying rapidly in many of our largest cities. . . . Small rooms were generally used . . . with surroundings not conducive to delicacy, to say the least. Many young men became very expert . . . but in gaining skill they lost the modesty and innocence that should accompany the pleasure.[33]

In March 1844 polka music was beginning to become known in England. *The Times* of 26 March 1844 carried the following advertisement (indicating, incidentally, that confusion about the polka's country of origin existed from the very start):

The new Dance, la Polka, for the Pianoforte. By Labitzsky: The Prague or Vienna Polkas 3/–; Narcissen Polka 2/–; Heitzer Sinn, three Polkas 2/6; and Hyacinthen Polka 2/–. . . . In Paris and Vienna the above Hungarian country dances are all the rage . . .

Shortly afterwards came the dance craze. Monsieur Coulon, a French dancing-master resident in London, visited Paris for the express purpose of learning it from the great Cellarius, and was one of the first to teach it in England.[34] A contemporary of Coulon's wrote a small book in 1844 (with Coulon's help) giving authoritative instructions and advice for the fashionable dances of the day. In it, he expresses disapproval for what he considers to be the excessive popularity of the polka:

At the last ball given at Apsley House by the Duke of Wellington in commemoration of Her Majesty's birthday the polka furore rose to such a pitch as to be danced, we are told, six times during the evening. Now this will not do. In our opinion, the Polka . . . stands certainly without parallel; still, it ought by no means to detract from the usual amusements, by superseding all other dances. Were the spirit of a Nash to rule once more over the arrangements of our ballrooms, it would no doubt resist such an encroachment, no matter how high the quarter . . .[35]

The controversial polka inspired several articles in the *Illustrated London News*. First, in April 1844, comes criticism and ridicule:

... the same weathercock heads of the Parisians have been delighted always by any innovation, but they never imported anything more ridiculous or ungraceful than this Polka. It is a hybrid confusion of Scotch Lilt, Irish Jig and Bohemian Waltz, and needs only to be seen once to be avoided for ever.

But one month later, in May of the same year, this paper reports the first polka at Almack's as follows: '. . . the polka as danced in Paris, and now adopted by us, is elegant, graceful and fascinating in the extreme . . .'

The polka craze was comparable to the tango, charleston and twist crazes in later years, and all kinds of things, from hats to puddings, were named after the new dance. In its wake, it brought the 'Tea Dance' which came into vogue in England in 1845. In England and in France the polka stayed popular until well into the 1880s, George Grossmith's song 'See me dance the polka' being published as late as 1886. By the close of the century, however (except at court balls, where it was included until 1914), the furore had subsided and the polka had become a museum piece.[36]

What sort of a dance was this and why should it have generated such tremendous enthusiasm at this particular time? Nationalistic movements, and the sympathy existing in France and England for peoples under foreign domination can go a long way to explaining the diffusion and acceptance of foreign 'national dances' but part of the explanation of the appeal of the polka must be sought in the nature of the dance itself. The rhythm – 2/4 time, like a military march[37]

with an obvious and emphatic beat, and the physical movements, involving as they did hops and jumps, could hardly have been more different from the gliding ballroom waltz. This contrast is important since, undoubtedly, people were ready to transfer their enthusiasm from the romantic waltz to a dance more in keeping with the quickening tempo of social change. In Paris, the time was certainly ripe for just such a dance. Shortly before the advent of the polka, dancing in Parisian dance halls had already become extremely energetic and vital, with accelerated waltzes, exuberant galops and can cans, involving robust whizzing, twirling and leg-kicking. According to A. H. Franks the polka came just at the right moment to harness this energy and direct it into a less unseemly direction. The world of fashion, at this time, tended to be languid on the ballroom floor[38] but even they were galvanized by the polka, although never quite permitting themselves the stamps and exaggerated movements of the 'masses'.

During this period, the polka of course, had its rivals in English ballrooms and dance halls. The small book, already referred to, written in 1844 with the co-operation of Coulon describes the following fashionable dances of the day: polka, polka cotillon, valse a deux temps, quadrilles, galopades, mazourkas, circassian circle, polonaise, waltz cotillon, Scotch reel. A few years later, in 1852, Thomas Wilson, dancing-master, cites as currently popular dances: quadrilles, valse a deux temps, cellarius waltz, redowa waltz, polka, schottische, sauterelle, circassian circle, gavotte quadrille and Sir Roger de Coverley.[39]

Some of these other dances – notably the polonaise, mazurka and redowa – were Polish or Bohemian dances, for which the success of the polka had paved the way. The polonaise, a stately processional march to a lively tempo, was useful as an opening at a fancy-dress ball. The Costume Ball given by Queen Victoria in 1856, for example, opened with a polonaise, led by the Queen and the Prince Consort.[40] The mazurka became known in England about 1845 but was more important for its influence on other dances than in its own right. A contemporary writer likens it to a 'Russian Cotillon' reporting that it was introduced into England by the Duke of Devonshire on his return from Russia after residence there as British Ambassador.[41] The redowa had some popularity in Paris and in London about the year 1845 but in England it was more talked about than danced.[42]

The schottische, a dance with music similar to the polka but slower, was popular from about 1848 to 1880. Earlier than this, it had been danced in Bavaria under the name 'Rheinländer'.[43] Although the name 'scottische' might seem to indicate that it came from Scotland, Routledge's Ballroom Companion of 1860 states firmly that it was essentially German both in music and in character.[44]

From about 1850 onwards, a variation of the quadrille – which became known as the 'lancers' – became popular in England.

According to Reginald St Johnston they were introduced in France by M. Laborde in 1836, and made their first appearance in England in 1850.[45] As with the quadrille, the steps were at first extremely complicated and difficult, but soon society 'walks' both the quadrille and the lancers, instead of labouring after the intricacies of the 'correct' style.

This change of style was not confined to England. Heine, at that time acting as Paris correspondent for the *Allgemeine Zeitung*, commented in February 1842 that

> formal balls are becoming more boring than they have any conceivable right to be, on account of the prevalent fashion of only seeming to dance, of 'walking' the prescribed figures and moving the feet in an indifferent and almost sulky manner. Nobody wants to please others any more and this selfishness manifests itself in society dancing today.[46]

Cellarius, the famous Parisian dancing-master, on the other hand commented favourably on the change in *Fashionable Dancing* in 1847.[47]

As people became more and more familiar with the waltz, waltz steps came to be used in figures instead of the correct steps. This gave rise to the boisterous sets known as the 'Kitchen Lancers' in which the ladies were swung off their feet in the third figure.[48] It now became customary for the music to be based on popular musical comedies, operettas and even operas of the day. Slowly but surely the lancers rose in favour at fashionable dances and at popular assemblies. By about 1875 they had almost eclipsed the quadrille as the principal square dance, and continued to be the most popular square dance until the close of the century. Thereafter, they suffered a rapid decline. The lancers had had their day and since 1918 they have been confined to 'Old Time' dances.

During this period, from about 1840 onwards, the 'assemblies' gradually grew less exclusive and less fashionable. As this happened (whether cause or effect it is difficult to say) society hostesses began to give lavish private parties and to organize balls in their town houses. Gradually a number of other buildings appeared which were given the name of 'Assembly Rooms', chief among them being Laurent's Casino on the site of what afterwards became Gatti's Adelaide Gallery in the Strand, the New Argyll Rooms in Windmill Street, Mott's in Foley Street, and the Casino de Venise in High Holborn, on the site subsequently occupied by the Holborn Restaurant.[49] In the 1840s it had been the National Baths: in the 50s it 'blossomed forth as the Casino de Venise and finally was christened the National Assembly Rooms but to its gay patrons it remained "The Casino" until it finally disappeared in the early 70s.' Its marble ballroom and magnificent band of fifty were among the sights of London.[50] Despite the splendour of 'The Casino', these assembly rooms did not have the sumptuous furnishings and the noble architecture of their predecessors, and were built to cater for a much more popular demand – an early foreshadowing of the modern 'Palais de Danse'. The clientele of these popular assemblies were 'men-about-town', Guards Officers, ballet girls and *'demi-mondaines'*. The 'toasts of the town' – 'Skittles' and Mabel Grey were constantly to be seen at these assemblies, and Mabel Grey was the acknowledged Queen of the Casino de Venise, usually partnered by a leading young-man-about-town. A nostalgic article on 'Round the Town: Old and New Night Clubs' in the *Era* for February 1895 comments that beautiful Mabel Grey used sometimes to lead the dance for a fee, adding 'Harlotry has no such acknowledged queen today'.[51]

(c) *Late Victorian England: 1860–1900*

In the last forty years or so of the nineteenth century, dancing was much neglected in England. With the death of the Prince Consort in 1861 and the retirement from public life of Queen Victoria, mid-century enthusiasm for dancing waned and died. In the closing years of Victoria's reign, dancing in the fashionable world was at its lowest ebb and for the first time it became 'bad form' to dance well. Society took no interest in any new dance with the exception of the barn dance and (briefly) the Washington post or 'twostep' and the cakewalk.[52]

The barn dance, or to give it its correct title, the 'military schottische' arrived from America about 1888. It was first danced to the tune: 'Dancing in the Barn' and hence came to be known as the barn dance. It was quickly taken up by all grades of society and except for State balls, it was found on every programme up to about the year 1910.[53]

In 1891, John Philip Sousa composed the Washington post march. The music was lively and different, with a new kind of beat, and caught on immediately in America. The 'two-step' which was danced to it was a simple dance, not much more than a double-quick march, with a skip in each step, done as rapidly as a couple could go forward, backward and turn.[54] Three years later, in 1894, the 'Washington Post' or 'two-step' came to England, and was danced everywhere for one season.[55]

The 'cakewalk' came into popularity in America around 1880 – especially in the southern States. It gained some popularity in England at the end of the nineteenth century, particularly in Lancashire, but its main importance lies in the fact that it gave an inkling of the coming of ragtime.[56]

From the point of view of the history and sociology of the dance, the hundred years of the nineteenth century are crammed full of interest. Throughout the century, dances had a tendency to be lively and spirited – ranging from quadrilles, reels and waltzes to lancers, polkas and two-steps. In this period, social and industrial change was inescapable: society was no longer semi-static, and the quickening tempo was reflected in the vitality and diversity of the dance.

Until the latter decades of the century, dancing is held in high esteem and carries great social prestige. There are at least three historically-authenticated occasions when new dances were introduced with great enthusiasm by statesmen or members of the aristocracy: the quadrille by Lady Jersey, the galop by Princess Esterhazy, the Earl of Clanwilliam, the Duke of Devonshire and some of the foreign ministers, and the mazurka by the Duke of Devonshire, ex-British Ambassador to Russia. Indeed, until the late nineteenth century there is no break in the continuous social attitude originating with the courtiers of the thirteenth century or even earlier, that it is a social accomplishment and the mark of a gentleman to dance well. In the late nineteenth century and continuing into the twentieth century, not only does this cease to be true but the opposite appears – it becomes the mark of a gentleman not to be able to dance and 'bad form' to be a good dancer.

The reason for this curious reversal of social attitude will be explored more fully in the next chapter, in the course of the discussion of the 'democratization' of the social dance in the twentieth century. Suffice it to say here that it stems from the time that Queen Victoria went into retirement after the death of the Prince Consort in 1861. Then, and for some time to come, it was clear that there would be no enthusiasm for dancing, at any rate, in those circles closest to the court. Added to this, there was the influence of evangelical religion steadily infiltrating into all classes of society, including the highest, and changing many habits of life and thought. The late Victorians were certainly not gay and spontaneous. To quote the Kinneys: 'Self expression was in bad taste, respectability standardized conduct. The resulting caution of movement sterilized the dance, and sterility all but killed it.'[57]

One particularly important basic change in this century was the passing of the era of the open-couple dance, as typified by the minuet, and the coming of the closed-couple dance, as typified by the waltz and polka. Much of the opposition to the waltz had arisen from the allegedly close contact between the partners, but by the time the polka appears this is taken for granted. This reflects to some extent the gradual relaxing of the conventions of social etiquette governing the relations between the sexes, in particular the loosening of some of the shackles binding the early Victorian female. This flicker in the direction of emancipation becomes a steady beam in late Victorian times when, after 1869, the professional and social emancipation of women went forward assisted by such works as John Stuart Mill's *The Subjection of Women* written 'to prove that the legal subjection of women to men is wrong, and should give way to perfect equality.'[58]

From the point of view of social structure the great gulf that separated the different social strata in this century has already been mentioned. *This* period of history, rather than medieval times, was the period when dancing was unlikely to have played much part in the lives of the underprivileged, except, possibly, those who were attached to the households of the rich. The countryside was losing its vitality and fast becoming a backwater of national life – an appendage to the towns – and it is only the sentimentalist who can persuade himself that dancing on the village green played much part in rustic life. The men and women who worked in the fields under the new capitalistic methods of agriculture would certainly have been too tired to dance. The same would have been true of the army of workers – men and women – attracted, or driven, into the towns to play their part in the developing factory system, even had there been any dancing facilities available.

A final point of interest in the nineteenth century might be termed a new kind of 'cultural diffusion'. Throughout the centuries, we have seen that dances have come to England from Italy, Spain, France, Germany, Poland and Bohemia. Now, at the end of the nineteenth century, England turns for the first time to the New World – particularly the U.S.A. – for sources of inspiration for new dances and new rhythms.

X

Twentieth-Century England

> The most popular of all dances is the One-Step
> ... It can be learned in a very little time by
> any one, young or old, who is able to walk in
> time to music – and, I might say, by many who
> cannot.
>
> I. AND V. CASTLE: *Modern Dancing*, 1914.

(a) Edwardian England: 1901 to 1910

Edwardian society, like late Victorian, retained a certain aristocratic flavour, but the class structure was gradually becoming less rigid and most sections of the community were coming to share in a measure of increased prosperity and improved conditions. As might be expected in such circumstances, the 'democratization' of ballroom dancing, which had begun in mid-nineteenth century with the building of the 'popular assembly rooms', continued into the twentieth. The 'popular assemblies' now included 'shilling assemblies' run every Saturday in big towns at the town hall, or in rural areas at the village hall, often in connection with a particular dancing academy.[1]

P. J. S. Richardson[2] gives an excellent picture of the dances in vogue in 1910, by quoting from typical programmes:

State Balls	Three quadrilles, three polkas, fifteen waltzes and final galop.
'Society' Private Dances	About sixteen waltzes and four two-steps.
Hunt and County Balls	About fifteen waltzes, one or two lancers and two or three two-steps.
Popular Assemblies	Lancers, quadrilles, d'Alberts, Valse cotillon, sequence dances such as Veleta, and four or five slow waltzes.*

* At the popular assemblies the waltz was played much more slowly than anywhere else – thirty-two bars compared with fifty bars to the minute.

80

The popular assembly programme offered a greater variety of dances, but, by and large, the *same* dances (with the exception of sequence dances[3] like the veleta) were now being danced by all strata of society, the class distinction being shown more by *where*, and to a certain extent *how*, they danced than by what they danced. Distinctions between rural and urban had also disappeared as might be expected, in an era of urbanization where town and country were becoming assimilated and local traditions were vanishing. Writing in 1906, a dance historian[4] reports: 'I cannot now find even among the rural population any traces of what might be called a national dance . . . the country-folk dance the waltz, polka and lancers just as the upper classes – albeit, generally, with more abandon and fun.'

A further point that emerges from these programmes of 1910 is that apart from the two-step, the form of dancing in England had altered little since mid-nineteenth century. The Edwardian era appeared secure, comfortable and stable, and the Edwardians took pleasure in orderly participation in set and sequence dances. Of the individualism and upheaval to come, in music, dance and society there was as yet no hint.

(b) *The War-time Decade: 1910 to 1920*

Perhaps one of the simplest ways to see the difference between dancing in England in the first ten years of the century, and dancing in later decades, is to realize that ballroom dancing in the first decade consisted mainly of what is now termed 'Old Time Dancing': lancers, quadrilles, sequence dances and fast rotary waltzes – all based on the five positions of the feet as used in ballet.

After the year 1910 or 1911, however, ballroom dancing in England presented such a different spectacle from the preceding years that dance historians are prone to use such terms as the 'dance revolution'. The first revolt was against what was now felt to be the artificial turned-out position of the feet. The fast waltz, almost completely rotary, had been admirably suited to the turned-out position, but younger dancers were now finding lateral positions more to their liking, since the amount of turn was not so great and the feet did not need to be turned out as in ballet. This led to the widespread adoption of the 'Boston' type of waltz – a dance which had been introduced into Britain from the U.S.A. some years previously without much success. The Boston is important in the history of the social dance since it was the first example of the smooth flow and natural walking movement which came to be developed as the 'English style'.[5]

In the years 1910 to 1911 the Boston enjoyed great popularity in England. The timing of the dance allowed a leisurely movement to fast music, for a full turn occupied four bars of music instead of the two required for the waltz. Six steps went to the turn, which allowed a more natural foot movement, and there was a great deal of forward and backward movement – or 'natural walk' – in the dance. After enjoying great favour in Britain for a few years and playing an important part in the formation of 'English style' the Boston virtually faded away about the time of the outbreak of war in 1914.[6]

In the years 1910 to 1911 people were clearly ready for new styles of movement and for new dances. One answer to both these needs was the 'Argentine tango',* a dance which arrived in England via France and played a big part in English ballrooms between 1911 and 1914. In the season following the summer of 1911, English people who had seen the tango danced at Dinard, Deauville and other Casino towns began to ask for it in London, and 'tango teas' came into fashion. From then on, for nearly two seasons, London (in common with all the great cities in Europe) went 'tango mad'. In 1913 and 1914 nearly every hotel and restaurant in which the public could dance held tango teas, publicized as *'Thés Tangos'*, and private tango teas became a prominent feature of many strata of social life.[7]

In the early months of 1914, the general craze for the tango in England helped to popularize another South American dance – the Brazilian maxixe. This was the first urban dance of true Brazilian creation, and was itself a mixture both musically and choreographically. The European polka determined the movement, the Cuban habanera gave the rhythm, African styles contributed the syncopation and Brazil set the manner of playing.[8] In its original form it was sensual and lively, with many exaggerated movements, but after some modification it gained widespread acceptance in Brazil as a ballroom dance. In England however, unlike the tango, it faded into complete oblivion during the troubled months preceding the outbreak of war in August 1914. Some forty years later, however, some of the movements of the maxixe were to be revived in the ballroom version of the Brazilian samba.† The tango has never disappeared entirely from the dancing scene, but the craze for it evaporated in mid-1914, dispelled partly by the outbreak of war and partly by that other aspect of the 'dance revolution' of the post-1910

* See Appendix G.
† See page 105.

years, namely, the revolution in dance-music, or the coming of 'ragtime'. (In the mid 1920s, however, when England was 'dancing mad' the tango enjoyed a second boom, under the name of the new French tango.)*

Ragtime was the other answer to people's need for new styles of movement and new dances. It came, of course, from the U.S.A. and, indeed, from now on new dances came to England from New York rather than from Paris. In America, as the Sousa marches began to pall, ragtime suddenly captured the people with its syncopated spell. This type of music has been described by Dannett and Rachel[9] as distinctively American music, made by Negroes primarily for Negroes, and it differed from all previous dance music by being 'syncopated' throughout. The syncopation becomes the rhythm, rather than a device for varying the rhythm. Music in ragtime contains two, four or six beats to the bar. Without syncopation, the main stress would fall on the first beat of the bar, with a subsidiary accent on the third beat, but in ragtime the accents fall on the second or fourth beats. The principle of syncopation can be applied in a number of ways, the commonest being by tying the second beat to the third in the bar, and the fourth to the first beat of the next bar, thus lengthening the stress on the tied notes (second and fourth) and eliminating the stress on the 'normal' first and third beats. Whatever principle of syncopation is applied, the result is always the same: the duration of each bar remains constant but the rhythm becomes irregular, jumping here, hesitating there and constantly displacing the normal beat.[10]

The new syncopated music brought about an urge for more freedom in dancing, and for new dance forms. Thus, in U.S.A. at and after the turn of the century (though not yet in England) a host of new dances – many with fantastic animal names (Bunny Hug, Grizzly Bear, Turkey Trot – later to be known as the one-step – Crab step, Kangaroo Dip, Horse Trot) all became tremendously, though briefly, popular. These new dances were all part of the reaction against the inhibited and restricted movements of the past and were, for the most part, frenzied and crude. All were made up of the same elements and were very simple in design. Couples walked in a rocking, swooping, manner, swaying outwards with each step in a 'go as you please' style, and true to the name of one of the dances, the embrace of the partners often resembled the clinch of the Californian Grizzly Bear.[11] The Bunny Hug was considered indecent and for this reason was banned for a time in the States. To defeat the ban girls took to wearing 'bumpers'.†

* See page 89
† See Plate V, page 98.

But, of all this, nothing had as yet reached England. The 'Boston' was still the newest dance and, indeed, the March 1911 *Dancing Times* published a description of the Boston, with an introductory note from the editor, explaining that he had been requested to do so by readers in the country, where the dance was not so well-known as in London. The waltz (a world removed from the current American contortions) continued its supremacy in all kinds of ballrooms, from the highest to the lowest. Indeed, it might be said that many dances and balls, particularly the 'upper-class' ones, were becoming boring through lack of variety – but all this was soon to change.

In the United States a further stimulus had been given to the new music in 1911, when Irving Berlin incorporated the jerky rhythm of ragtime into the hit 'Alexander's Ragtime Band' which was to rocket round the world. This was very probably the first form of ragtime music to reach England. At any rate, around 1911 to 1912 ragtime music came to England and with it, the 'Turkey Trot' or 'one-step' or, as it later came to be called, the 'rag'.[12] This dance – immensely appropriate to ragtime – became tremendously popular. 'The waltz is beautiful, the tango is graceful, the Brazilian maxixe is unique. One can sit quietly and listen with pleasure to them all; but when a good orchestra plays a 'rag' one has simply got to move. The one-step is the dance for ragtime music . . .'[13]

Irene and Vernon Castle have described the style of movement and the various figures of the one-step in *Modern Dancing*, stressing that the main point to be borne in mind is the extreme simplicity of the dance: '. . . when I say *walk*, that is all it is. Do not shuffle, do not bob up and down or trot. Simply *walk* as softly and smoothly as possible, taking a step to every count of the music . . . It is simply one step – hence its name.'[14]

The steps in fact were of no importance and could be learnt by anyone, young or old, able to walk in time with the music. Here, according to A. H. Franks,[15] lies the fundamental difference between pre-1910 and post-1910 social dancing. Up to 1910, no matter what the dance, the main attraction lay in the actual steps, and in some cases, the exhilarating movement. After 1910, the main attraction was unquestionably the rhythm: and from now on, rhythm was to inject all our dance forms with an entirely new force.

After the one-step came the fishwalk and the horsetrot – of ephemeral interest only – and then came the foxtrot. This was the dance which was to push all the others into the background and remain (albeit with many modifications) an essential part of the dancing scene to the present day. The foxtrot made its first appearance in the States in the summer of 1914 and was described by a contemporary as 'very rollicking, and has a tendency to put everyone in a good humour.'[16] It was the direct offspring of the one-step or 'rag' in that the 'trotting movements' were danced to ragtime rhythm. Many people are of the opinion that its name derives from Harry Fox, an American music-hall artist who danced the new fast but simple trotting step to ragtime music in one of the hit musical shows of the year. This strange kind of movement became known as Fox's Trot and, with the incorporation of a few walking steps to make the trotting motion less tiring, it became a ballroom dance, popularized and given definite form by a group of New York dance teachers. In the same year, 1914, Mr Oscar Duryea, a well-known U.S. dancer and dance teacher demonstrated and taught this foxtrot to members of the Imperial Society of Teachers of Dancing (ISTD) in London.[17] It had a great success in England and was danced indefatigably for the next few years.

During the first few months of the 1914–18 war, dance halls, ballrooms and other places of public entertainment were closed down but gradually they all re-opened in response to public demand from soldiers on leave and war-weary civilians. London, in fact, was ragtime mad all through the war, but not many English musicians were able to adapt themselves to this new type of dance music. The older type of string orchestra which had excelled in the graceful tunes of an earlier age could not deal with this new 'hiccupping' ragtime music. Ragtime bands, many from America, consisting of piano, banjo, saxophone and drums came into prominence and, in 1915, the Savoy Hotel thought this new musical craze sufficiently important to instal a ragtime band (Murray's Savoy Quartette) consisting of banjo, banjo and vocalist, piano and drums.[18]

The terms 'ragtime' and 'jazz' are today often used albeit inaccurately as if they were synonymous but it was not until the end of 1917 that people in England first heard of jazz, although they had been familiar with ragtime since around 1911 or 1912. For quite some time, according to Philip Richardson, the term 'jazz' was thought in England to be the name of a new dance, or a new routine of steps, and for some years the modern dances, as opposed to the old, were referred to as 'jazz dances'.[19] The January *Bystander* in the year 1919, for example, reported that 'there was morning dancing in country houses and town mansions for the "newest jazzes and the latest rags" had to be learnt without delay'. Mrs Vernon Castle, in London in 1918, was asked for her opinion: 'It is difficult to define jazz . . . they [jazz bands] slur the notes, they syncopate, and each instrument puts in a number of fancy bits of its own.'[20] An American paper at the time described jazz in this way:

Strict rhythm without melody. The jazz bands take popular tunes and rag them to death to make jazz. Beats are added as often as the delicacy of the player's ear will permit. There are many half-notes or less, and many long-drawn wavering notes. It is an attempt to reproduce the marvellous syncopation of the African jungle.[21]

Towards the end of 1917, the great wave of enthusiasm for dancing in England was beginning to ebb. In the final months of the war, however, the arrival of American soldiers bringing with them the latest thing in American dances led to another dancing craze in England which lasted after the Armistice and into the post-war years.

In this period, the process of 'democratization' of dancing was immensely speeded up. The popular assemblies of the nineteenth and early twentieth centuries had offered programmes consisting mainly of the set and sequence type of dance, with music provided by the old-type string orchestra. At the end of the First World War everyone wanted to dance – but not to string orchestras playing veletas and lancers. They wanted to step out to jazz bands playing the latest rags and foxtrots. These modern dance bands were to be found in fashionable hotels and restaurants, but such establishments were far beyond the means of the thousands of young men and women who wanted to take up the new dancing. For them the coming of the Palais de Danse (a straightforward question of demand and supply) was to be the answer.

The first was the Hammersmith Palais de Danse opened in 1919 by Messrs Booker and Mitchell. This was soon followed by the Palais de Danse in Birmingham under the same management.[22] These, and others which followed, differed from the old popular assemblies in their size, their perfectly sprung floors, and their top-quality modern orchestras featuring the new sound and the new rhythm. In 1920, for example, Dominic la Rocca and the famous 'Original Dixieland Jazz Band' appeared at the Hammersmith Palais.[23] This was the outstanding white American ragtime band of the period and the one chosen by the Savoy Hotel to play at their Victory Ball to celebrate the signing of the Versailles Treaty.[24] It is difficult to overestimate the sensation they created, both at the Savoy and at the Hammersmith Palais and, after this, jazz bands, playing ragtime music, began to spring up on all sides.

Thus, in the second decade of the twentieth century, the decade including the war and the immediate post-war years, it was evident that the settled way of life of the Edwardian era had gone for ever. New styles of behaviour, attitudes and dress were all becoming apparent and the seeds of great social changes were being sown: changes which will be discussed more fully in the next section.

These changes, all in the direction of greater freedom and individualism, were reflected in the revolution that had overtaken the social dance. The new 'go-as-you-please' dancing to jerky, jazz rhythms, was completely ousting the formal and 'set' dances with their accompanying smooth melodies. By 1918, the waltz had become almost extinct, since, apart from being out of tune with the times, the war had put an end to the German and Austrian orchestras which had specialized in this kind of music. The orderly quadrilles, lancers and polkas of yesteryear had already been relegated to history, their place now taken by the free and easy ragtime one-step and the early rollicking foxtrot. As always in restless times, there were those who equated change with degeneracy, and in 1919 a clergyman was writing:[25] 'If these up-to-date dances, described as the "latest craze" are within a hundred miles of all I hear about them, I should say that the morals of a pig-sty would be respectable in comparison.'

XI
The Twenties: 1920 to 1930

I am New York aware of Africa and something lost:
Two exiles, Judah and the jungle, Broadway-crossed.
A. S. J. TESSIMOND: *Dance Band*

In the twenties, the foxtrot and the one-step or 'rag' continued to be popular, and were danced – indefatigably – to 'Kitten on the Keys', 'Tea for Two', 'Crazy Rhythms', 'Limehouse Blues', 'St Louis Blues' on trumpet and saxophone. In addition, many new dances, such as the Twinkle, the Jog Trot, the Vampire, and the Camel Walk[1] arrived from America. All were to prove ephemeral, with one exception, the famous 'shimmy'.

This dance, by no means easy, became popular in England after being danced on the stage by Mae Murray in 1921. It was characterized by the turning-in of the knees and toes, followed by the '*frisson*' or shake of the bottom, considered by some to be rather vulgar.[2] The shimmy and the other 'jazz dances' as they were called were by no means confined to night-clubs in large towns. On the contrary, the dancing-craze was very widespread and, as one newspaper put it: 'The Shimmy is Shaking Suburbia!'

The alleged degradation of the early twenties' dancing brought forth widespread protests. *The Times* of January 1920, for example, made it clear that the Church's strictures were interfering with life at the highest social level: '. . . several projects for charity dances have been abandoned . . . The tango and the foxtrot come under his [the Archbishop's] stricture – [namely] . . . the dances may be harmless but the manner of dancing them has degenerated'.[3]

At a less lofty level the Leyton Urban District Council, in allowing the Municipal Hall to be hired for a dance, expressly prohibited the 'one-step and jazz dances in any form'.

Newspapers and 'letters to the Editor' continued the campaign. An anonymous surgeon pointed out the 'great degradation and demoralization of these wild dances'. Analogies were drawn between the 'discords' of jazz music and 'discordant' jazz minds and girls who 'sacrificed their nerves and beauty' to the foxtrot were warned that 'old age would claim them'.[4] Journalists wrote sensational articles on such themes as 'Nights in the Jazz Jungle' and the *Daily Mail* featured an article 'Jazzmania' describing a scene remarkably similar to a 'psychedelic happening' of 1967: 'Frantic noises and occasional cries of ecstasy from half a dozen Negro players. Dim lights, drowsy odours and futuristic drawings on walls and ceilings . . .'

The wild, go-as-you-please early twenties' dancing did not last more than a year or so in England, and as the exhibitionism died out, dancing itself became ever more popular. According to the *Daily Mail* in February 1922 'some hundreds of dance schools have reduced the shortage of dancing men. For every man who danced two years ago, eight or nine dance now. Freak steps . . . have gone out, and easy straightforward steps are the rule'. So popular was dancing in the mid-twenties that it was even to interfere with English football. In October 1926, the new Brighton football club found it necessary to issue a ban on late night dancing. Commenting on the ban, Crystal Palace admitted 'A few seasons ago two men had a period of bad play, and it was found to be due to too much dancing'.[5]

This widespread popularity of dancing led to another tango craze in 1925. This time it was the 'new French tango', an easier dance than the 1911 version and one suitable to small floors in restaurants or private houses. The craze spread from London to the provinces and some pupils of West End dance teachers came 100 miles for a weekly tango lesson. This new tango, easy to dance but with the authentic haunting melodies played on the bandoneon (a large concertina with a keyboard at each end, capable of sighing like a heart-sick lover) and the syncopated jazzy foxtrot consolidated the popularity of mid-twenties 'tea-dancing'. As the *Daily Mail* correspondent put it in Autumn 1926:

> Tea dances used to be considered . . . even a bore. People said: 'If we are going to dance let's dance in the evening. Who wants to dance at 4 o'clock?' The answer today is that any number of people want to dance at 4 o'clock, irrespective of what they are doing in the evening.
>
> A business man I met at one the other day explained that once or twice a week he got away early for these affairs. They put him in a good humour, cleared his brain, gave him needed exercise.

The relatively quiet phase of dancing did not last long. Jerks, kicks and frantic speed were soon to return with the Charleston and the Black Bottom. The Charleston was originally a Negro round dance which was discovered in 1923 among Negro dock-workers in Charleston, South Carolina.[6] In October 1923 the Ziegfield follies introduced it at the New Amsterdam Theatre and afterwards it became part of a coloured show 'Runnin' Wild' which toured the States. Teachers of dancing saw the possibilities of a ballroom hit and modified the stage Charleston, combining the 'winging and lifting' steps with the foxtrot walk and the two-step. It soon became the rage in the U.S.A. and in July 1925 it was introduced to English dancing teachers at a special tea dance arranged by the *Dancing Times*.[7]

It reached the height of its popularity in England in late 1925, and early 1926, but even at its peak, the Charleston was regarded by many people with extreme suspicion and distaste. By the Spring of 1926, the press in London was uniformly and violently hostile – using such adjectives as 'freakish', 'degenerate', 'negroid'. The *Daily Mail* featured the dance under such headlines as 'A Vulgar Dance' and denounced it as 'a series of contortions without a vestige of grace or charm, reminiscent only of negro orgies', without of course making it clear how many 'negro orgies' the correspondent had attended. Health hazards were made much of, up and down the country. At Walsall, the School Medical Officer reported that 'children of all ages now seem unable to keep their feet still' and 'foresaw a development of a new form of St Vitus' dance – "Charleston Chorea".'[8] A Harley Street specialist warned the public that dancing the Charleston would lead to a permanent distortion of the ankles, and other doctors warned that 'the shocks to the body may displace the heart and other organs . . .' and that 'Charleston knee, paralysis and total collapse due to the contortions, shocks, jolts and jars of the Charleston are quite common'.[9]

But all to no avail. The Prince of Wales became an enthusiastic and accomplished Charleston dancer,[10] and the dance became even more popular with the general public. Self-appointed censors continued the opposition, the Rev. E. W. Rogers, vicar of St Aidan's, Bristol, asserting: 'Any lover of the beautiful will die rather than be associated with the Charleston. It is neurotic! It is rotten! It stinks! Phew, open the windows', but the Bishop of Coventry, disagreeing, said mildly: 'It is a very nice dance'.

The masses ignored the vicar and agreed with the Bishop, and by the beginning of 1927, the Charleston was an element in Newcastle's traffic problems. The police in that city complained of the obstruction caused by hundreds of young people (not yet known as 'teenagers') who were in the habit of dancing the Charleston on a public highway on Sunday evenings.[11]

Some of the strictures on the Charleston in the early days were well-deserved, because of the dangerous side-kicks and exaggerated movements indulged in when the dance first became popular. For this reason, the Piccadilly Hotel and, at the other social extreme, the Hammersmith Palais each had notices 'You are earnestly requested not to dance the Charleston' and in many other dance halls the notice: 'P.C.Q.' (Please Charleston quietly) became familiar.[12]

In the course of time, however, the better dancers came to leave out the dangerous kicks, and the drop and rise gave way to an almost flat movement, with slight 'play' at the knees.[13] The Charleston proper* was a rigidly defined dance with one basic step demanding supple knees and perfect co-operation between partners, plus a few established variations. The Charleston rhythm remains utterly compulsive and is probably timeless in its appeal, as can be seen by the revival of the dance in the fifties and sixties, and also by the incorporation of the rhythm in the modern quickstep.

The 'Black Bottom', like the Charleston, appeared in a Broadway hit, as did another contemporary dance, the 'varsity drag'.[14] Both of these dances became popular in England during the late twenties, after the movement and steps had been made more suitable for ballroom dancing. The 'Black Bottom' was a dance of stamps, knee-sways and shuffle steps, described by Curt Sachs as 'a lively mixture of side-turns, stamps, skating-glides, skips and leaps'.[15]

The 'jazz dances' described in this section were all in that 'glittering rhythm of syncopated four/four measure' called ragtime. This hiccuping music on brass instruments differed as much from the sugary strains of stringed orchestras as did the accompanying unorthodox, jerky dancing from the standardized glides, turns and bows of waltz and quadrille. These dances were a peculiarly apt reflection of the spirit of their age, a point which will emerge from a consideration of the social history of the period.

Popularly, England in the twenties has been portrayed in various and often contradictory ways, as for example: 'The Age of the Flapper', 'The Gay Twenties', 'The Age of Speed' and finally the 'Age of Mass Unemployment and the General Strike'.

It is always misleading to try to sum up a decade in a short, journalistic phrase, as though it were utterly different from any other period of ten years. None the less, there is some justification for regarding the twenties, that decade between the end of the Great War and the onset of the Great Depression, as *sui generis*, and characterized not, of course, by any *one* of these phrases but by a fusion of all of them.

The feature of the period that is most closely linked with the social dance is without doubt, the first: the age of the 'flapper' or newly emancipated young woman. This movement towards greater freedom
* See Plate VI, page 99.

for women in the twenties was only a continuation of the trend which started during the 1914–18 war. While on war work, women had cut their hair short, worn trousers and smoked cigarettes. In 1919, skirts were six inches from the ground: in 1920 twelve inches.[16] Hair (bobbed during the war) became progressively shorter, culminating in the shingle of 1924 and the Eton crop of 1925. Similarly 'twenties dancing' was itself a continuation and development of the style and form adopted earlier.

In 1918, women had been given the vote at the age of thirty, and in the following year they became eligible to enter many hitherto exclusively male professions. In the 1923 General Election there were thirty-four women candidates. In 1928, the Equal Franchise Bill or 'flappers' vote', proposing to give women the vote at the age of twenty-one became law in October. Important as all these measures were, however, it is highly probable that Dr Marie Stopes, the pioneer of birth control in the twenties, was responsible for a more radical change in the life of everyday women than any of the legislation of the day.

In any event, relations between the sexes were easier and freer from the war years onwards, whether in terms of sexual freedom or of friendly comradeship. These new attitudes found expression in the casual, informal, more intimate kind of dancing, the permissible frequent change of partner and, in the early years, the close embrace and wild go-as-you-please dancing frowned on by respectable and solid citizens.

The 'Gay Twenties' label is a convenient way of highlighting certain aspects of the decade. In Autumn 1921 the Licensing Laws were relaxed, allowing drinks to be served in certain circumstances, until 12.30 a.m. In London, restaurants flourished, cabaret began and Mrs Meyrick opened the first of her night clubs, the '43, in Gerrard Street. Cocktail parties became popular about the same time. The 'Bright Young Things' of the late twenties also helped to give the decade its future label of 'gay' through their highly-publicized gate-crashing antics, pyjama parties and such 'flings' as the 'Babies' Ball' where guests 'arrived in prams and got drunk in rompers'.[17]

It would be a great mistake, however, to think of the 'gaiety' of the twenties only in terms of an extended Noel Coward comedy. All classes of society shared to some extent in the freer and lighter spirit of the times, provided they were employed. Mass-production techniques began to take some of the toil – as well as some of the skill – out of daily tasks, and allowed most people greater leisure. The coming of the cheap, light car revolutionized transport and increased the scope of weekend enjoyment. Finally, some gaiety, colour and variety at last entered the life of the working-class woman with the invention, in 1921, of artificial silk or 'rayon'. This – the first of the man-made fibres – was soon to mean the end of the traditional working-class black cotton dress and stockings. The coming of films (developing into the 'talkies' around 1929) meant the beginning of an era of amusement for all classes. Crazes like the pogo-stick (to the tune of 'Oh! the Ogo-Pogo') the 'put and take' gambling toy and 'Mah-Jong' swept the country.

In this context, dancing – to the 'new American jazz' as it was called – quickly became 'all the rage' in town and village throughout the country. The process of 'democratization', or provision of inexpensive facilities for dancing, went on apace throughout the twenties. In 1921, Cricklewood Dance Hall was opened. In 1925, even the Royal Opera House, Covent Garden, was to some extent 'taken over.'[18] A dance floor was constructed to cover the whole of the stalls and the stage, and thereafter, popular dancing alternated, for some years, with opera and ballet. 1927 saw the opening of the Astoria dance hall, and gradually all large urban centres and holiday towns came to have excellent facilities for social dancing. There is no suggestion, however, that the different social strata danced with each other. All classes now enjoyed the same dances and the same rhythms, but the upper and upper-middle classes would tend to find these in clubs, hotels and restaurants (usually with minute dance-floors) while working-class and lower-middle-class dancing enthusiasts would go to the local dance hall or palais (generally with superb facilities for dancing). In the course of time, this factor undoubtedly contributed to the situation where skill and grace in ballroom dancing came to be in inverse proportion to social status.

The transformation of work and leisure, discussed above, was largely the result of advances in technology. The view of the twenties as the 'Age of Speed' particularly the 'Age of Speed Records' highlights another aspect of technological progress. In 1927, Malcolm Campbell broke his own 1925 world land speed record and in October of the same year Flight Lt Webster set up a new air speed record. In 1929, Major Segrave raised the land speed record to 231 m.p.h. and in the same year Britain again won the Schneider Trophy, setting up an air speed record of over 335 m.p.h.

Technological progress can account for the achievement of speed records, but it does not explain the urge to set them up. The craze for speed, so typical of the twenties, can probably best be seen as one manifestation of the general restlessness and recklessness of the decade – features which showed themselves markedly in the works of many of the young artists and intellectuals of the time. If the Bright

Young Things were challenging convention and breaking with the past in a superficial way, the writers, artists and thinkers of the twenties were doing the same in a more profound way.

Thus, the year 1921 saw the publication of R. H. Tawney's *Acquisitive Society* and 1922 T. S. Eliot's *The Waste Land*, Joyce's *Ulysses* and D. H. Lawrence's *Women in Love*. A few years later came Aldous Huxley's *Antic Hay* to be followed by *Those Barren Leaves*. These works, of course, did not appeal to more than the educated minority, but Michael Arlen's *The Green Hat* and Margaret Kennedy's *The Constant Nymph* each in its own way strongly contested conventional values, and each became a best-seller when published in 1924.

On the stage in 1923, the public saw Noel Coward's *The Vortex*, a play about a young drug addict with a promiscuous mother, and in 1925 his *Fallen Angels* caused disgust and fury, the *Daily Express* describing his characters as 'suburban sluts'. In 1927, Miles Malleson's play *The Fanatics* discussed birth control and trial marriage, and attacked militarism, capitalism and the church.

In the field of art, physics, and psychology, Epstein, Einstein, and Freud respectively administered shocks and contributed to the general process of upheaval and uncertainty. The theory of relativity was doubtless as little understood, generally, as was psycho-analysis, but, intelligible or not, both theories meant to the man in the street that the established order was being shaken, and that nothing was quite the same any more.

The craze for speed, the feelings of restlessness and the urge to defy convention were all clearly shown in the social dancing of the decade. Throughout the period, new dances, usually fast and jerky, were taken up avidly and dropped again with astonishing rapidity, and the general style of dancing challenged older, formal conventions in almost every conceivable way. Indeed, so great was the anarchy, improvization and individualism in the social dance, that a number of conferences had to be called in the early twenties, to try to bring some element of order and standardization into the dancing scene.*

Much emphasis has been laid on the change and instability of the twenties. One feature, however, remained remarkably constant – large-scale unemployment. The immediate post-war boom collapsed in midsummer 1920. In the early Autumn of that year there were only 250,000 unemployed, but by Christmas 6·1% of the insured population was out of work.[19] During the following year, 1921, the percentage unemployment rate for Great Britain shot up to 16·6.[20] An angry, revolutionary spirit was abroad, showing itself in riots of

* See Appendix F.

the unemployed and in miners' strikes. In 1926, the Samuel Commission (appointed to enquire into the mining industry) recommended a reduction in miners' wages or longer hours of work. The Commission's findings were rejected by the miners, their views summed up by the slogan of their leader, A. J. Cook – 'Not a penny off the pay, not a minute on the day'. Negotiations broke down, the General Council of the T.U.C. called for a general strike in support of the miners, the Government declared a state of emergency, and on Monday, 3 May the stoppage was complete. By Wednesday, 12 May the strike was over, with nothing solved. In the severe winter of 1928, the unemployed numbered well over one million,[21] and in his Christmas Day broadcast the Prince of Wales spoke eloquently of the plight of the unemployed miners in Durham and the Rhondda Valley. That Christmas, the most popular toy in the shops was the dog – 'Dismal Desmond'.

In 1929, wages and salaries remained steady and, as prices had fallen, life for the employed was fuller and better. The problem of unemployment, however, seemed no nearer a solution and the May 1929 election was fought on this issue. At the end of the year neither the Government nor the general public had any inkling of the approaching crisis and *The Times Review* of the year described the course of events as 'tranquil'. But, as everyone now knows, the collapse of the Wall Street Stock Exchange on 29 October 1929 had the most disastrous consequences, first for America and later for all Europe. Thus – in Britain – the decade ended in the shadow of the Great Depression, and unemployment – the most pressing problem of the twenties – was carried forward and greatly magnified in the decade to come.

This view of the twenties does not fit in well with the picture of free-and-easy dancing to catchy, ragtime rhythms, any more than it fits in with the idea of the New Woman, the Gay Twenties, or the Age of Speed. It is evident that the lightening of the burden of work, the transformation of leisure, and the adoption of new and up-to-date attitudes and values were luxuries which were not for the unemployed and their families. This contradiction of unemployment and misery for some and rising standards of work and play for others, however, was all part of the paradoxical, 'bitter-sweet' atmosphere of the twenties. In such an age, one of the functions of social dancing may well have been to shut out harsh economic and social realities. If so, what better medium could there be than brassy jazz?

Swim with the stream! Sleep as you swim! Let the wave take you!
However loud they play, these saxophones will never wake you

. . . .
This stream's the moving shadow of your thigh.
Dance and forget to die, forget to die![22]

The twenties have been analysed in some detail because they are
of such extraordinary interest: politically colourful, socially restless,
feverishly gay yet hopelessly miserable. With hindsight, one could
say that the casual one-step or rag, the rollicking foxtrot, the shame-
less shimmy, the free and easy Vampire and Jog Trot of the early
twenties followed by the fast, energetic, shocking Charleston and
Black Bottom were so appropriate to the age that it is difficult, in
retrospect, to imagine the twenties without these dances and their
accompanying ragtime rhythms.

XII
The Thirties: 1930 to 1940

When you go down Lambeth Way
Any evening, any day
You'll see them all
Doing the Lambeth Walk. Oi!
(By permission of
Cinephonic Music Co. Ltd.)

By the end of the twenties, the dancing fever had cooled off considerably and, around that time, many of the halls built for dancing came
to be converted into skating-rinks. The decade which followed was
not (at any rate, until the closing years) a fertile or an enthusiastic
period for the social dance.

No one could claim that the thirties were 'gay'. The Wall Street
Stock Exchange crash in October 1929 ushered in a period of
prolonged economic depression and severe unemployment in
Britain: the period of the 'distressed areas' and the hunger-marchers
from Jarrow. The unemployment figures speak for themselves. In
1932, the worst year, the percentage unemployed among the insured
population was 21·9, representing almost three million. In 1937, the
percentage, although still high, had dropped to 10·6,[1] an alleviation
due in part to the first stage of re-arming for the war everyone hoped
to avoid.

Sociologically, it is interesting that at the close of the twenties the
'flapper' virtually disappeared. Perhaps there was no longer any need
for women to proclaim their emancipation quite so shrilly: at any
rate, Eton crops and very short skirts gave way to longer hair and
lower hems.

Social change was paralleled by changes that were overtaking
music and dancing. The 'red-hot baby' rhythm so completely suited
to the Charleston, Black Bottom and similar dances of the twenties
went right out of fashion and 'sweet music' came in.[2] The wild dances
of the twenties were seen no more and, until the latter half of the
thirties, ballroom dancing was sedate, consisting mostly of the
'modern' waltz,* the quickstep and a sober version of the foxtrot,

* See Appendix F.

97

then called the 'slow foxtrot'. The thirties (and later) versions of these ballroom dances were much influenced by the ballroom-dancing teachers' conferences of the twenties, which 'rescued' and modernized the waltz and 'standardized' the quickstep and foxtrot. These conferences* laid down 'official' styles and tempos for all these dances, and in the thirties and forties Victor Silvester played his part by providing unlimited smooth, sweet, strict-tempo dance music.

In the latter half of this decade, however, came a development which was to disturb the tranquillity of the dancing scene, and so far as the young were concerned, to transform it completely. This was the new vogue for 'swing' music, a development of jazz, which came to England from the U.S.A.

The name 'swing' was the musician's description of the new sound and two explanations by musicians may help to convey the general picture. Mr Sigmund Spaeth, quoted by Philip Richardson,[3] writes: 'Take any melody, begin and end with the original note, but between these break up the melodic line with improvisation, returning to the original melody only now and then so as to *suggest* it rather than follow it exactly.' Mr Stanley Nelson writing in the *Dancing Times* puts it this way: 'Swing consists of complex polyrhythm made up of (a) four basic beats to the bar; (b) the natural rhythms of the melody; (c) additional rhythms added by the arranger or by improvisation of the players.' Unlike the original jazz band players, musicians in swing bands follow written arrangements and any improvization is left to instrumental soloists.

New rhythms call for new dances. Young dancers in New York, and particularly in Harlem, found that they could not give free expression to these complex rhythms without the use of complex movements. In this way, American swing dancing, first under the name of 'Lindy Hop'[4] then as 'jitterbug' was born.[5] And with 'jitterbug' came the 'hep-cat' or avid follower of swing music.

In England, in the latter half of the thirties, the increased popularity of swing music made swing dancing a necessity. Young dancers in this country tried to evolve some movements – often indescribable – to express the new rhythm. Tempos could vary from very slow American blues, suiting the mood of the depression, to the excitement of very fast swing (up to sixty bars a minute). In the early days of this dance, young people in England danced in a frenzied way, with bad style, using acrobatic and highly dangerous movements.[6] Added to this was the fact that it was an 'on the spot' dance which did not mix with the older type of English 'moving' or progressive dancing. Jitterbug eventually came to be barred in some halls (as was the

* See Appendix F.

98

Plate V To defeat the ban on The Bunny Hug, girls took to wearing 'Bumpers'

Plate VI The Charleston: 1926

Charleston in the twenties) and might have died out as a result of the general opposition, had it not been for the influx of the American G.I.s in the early days of the war. When the Americans came over in their thousands, the dance took on a new lease of life and was much better performed.

In the meantime, there was another straw in the wind. In the U.S.A. in the thirties, an entirely new rhythm and dance from Cuba was becoming known – the so-called Rumba. The true rumba is of Afro-Cuban origin, deriving from the days of Negro slavery[7] in Cuba, and is an erotic[8] dance with violent and sinuous movements of hip, shoulder and torso. Melody and words are either non-existent or of little importance, the outstanding feature being the percussion rhythm. This uninhibited rumba is the dance of the bawdy dive or shady night-club in Cuba and is rarely seen in respectable society. The Cubans, however, also have a ballroom dance, the 'son' which is a slower and more refined version of the rumba. This ballroom dance lacks the wild freedom of the true rumba and may be accompanied by a romantic and sentimental melody and text. 'The rumba flaunts, the son insinuates.'[9] When played at a fast tempo, the 'son' is the dance generally known outside Cuba as the 'rumba'.

In England the rumba was the first Latin-American dance to attract attention. It was first heard of in the thirties, probably when a famous Cuban band, under the leadership of 'Don Aspiazu' played for some weeks in London. The public was not yet responsive to Cuban music and gave only a lukewarm reception to this band.[10] In the thirties, there were many arguments in the ballroom profession about the counting of the steps to this new rhythm, but the dancing public in general remained quite uninterested in the rumba until the next decade.

Another interesting feature towards the end of the thirties (and, as with the rumba, one which was to be developed in the forties) was the appearance of what might be called 'participation social dances'. These novelty dances, such as the Conga, the Lambeth Walk, the Chestnut Tree and the Hokey-Cokey, were all 'social' dances in the real meaning of the word, since they called for the participation of a group.

The 'conga' – a simple dance in march rhythm consisting of a chain of people performing steps which might be described as 'one, two, three, kick' – came to England from the Riviera but, according to Lekis,[11] it was originally an Afro-Cuban dance, the name being derived from the African Congo. In Cuba, it is essentially a street dance, the best examples being seen during carnival or fiesta time, where the conga 'cumparzas' roam the streets, attracting hordes of followers who march and dance with the typical one, two, three, kick pattern. Sensibly, the Cuban revolution has taken this in its stride. The carnival in Havana now has, it is true, the somewhat solemn title of the 'Havana Carnival of Solidarity' but, according to *The Times* Latin American correspondent: 'The dancers are traditional enough and the proceedings ended with the usual mass conga line, with the onlookers joining in. Cuba's ideology still has the big beat . . .'[12]

In England the conga was a 'fun dance' performed during the war, to keep spirits up and it is still popular as a novelty dance for appropriate occasions. The other 'participation dances' all involved actions and the singing of one particular song. Not one of these novelty dances was an isolated 'couple-dance' and therein, no doubt, lay their appeal to young and old in the days and months of mounting tension and ever-increasing fear of war. In times of anxiety and danger people discover anew the age-old truth that fears can be alleviated by rhythmic group activity.

XIII

The Forties: 1940 to 1950
World War II and Aftermath

And round and round old Hitler's grave
Round and round we go;
Gonna lay that poor boy down
He won't get up no mo'.

Almanac Singers

During the forties the whole of British life was affected by World War II and its aftermath. The five years of war and, to a certain extent, the five years of austerity peace were years of hardship – but hardship tempered by a certain idealism, a great deal of sentimentality and much gregarious gaiety.

In entertainment, the highlights were the sentimental voice of Frank Sinatra, ousting the jollier style of Bing Crosby, the singing of Vera Lynn, the 'Forces' Sweetheart' and the sound, jazz or sweet, of the big dance bands, ranging from the American Glenn Miller's A.E.F. band, and British service bands like the Squadronnaires and the Sky-rockets, to the civilian or part-civilian bands of Geraldo, Joe Loss, Ambrose, Billy Cotton and, from 1945, Ted Heath.

Social dancing in this decade, as in all others, reflects the values and attitudes of the period. One interesting feature during the war years was the prevalence of various kinds of group or participation dances. These included 'novelty dances' such as the Conga, Lambeth Walk, Boomps-a-Daisy, Palais Glide, Hokey-Cokey and Chestnut Tree first seen in the late thirties, and also 'Old Time', Country and Square dancing. 'Old Time' might be defined as the kind of social dancing in vogue around 1910. It had a remarkable revival* during the war years, with Old Time clubs springing up all over the country, in which, broadly speaking, two different styles of Old Time dancing were taught. One was the 'traditional' based on the five foot positions of the ballet, and the other was the twentieth-century sequence style,

---

* Contrary to the expectations of most people, the revival of Old Time in the forties has proved lasting. The Old Time clubs now number thousands. For a typical dance-programme, see Appendix H.

based on earlier versions of the foxtrot, one-step and tango.[1] During the war years, country-dancing shared in the general revival of interest in communal dancing. The English Folk Song and Dance Society remained in their London headquarters in spite of enemy air-raids, and found that there was growing interest in the meeting of small groups to learn country dancing. The prejudice against 'folk-dancing' as something rather cranky or old-fashioned disappeared almost entirely during this period.[2] 'Square dancing', itself based on old country-dances which English settlers had taken with them to America, but with a 'caller'[3] for the figures, became a craze in the U.S.A. in the forties, even in the big cities.[4] In England, the popularity of square dancing, already considerable, received a decided boost with the arrival of the American G.I.s in the early years of the war.

The 'jitterbug' dancing to swing music, already popular in England in the late thirties, continued to be danced in the early war years, still characterized by acrobatic and eccentric movements.[5] About a year after the outbreak of war, this dance became even more complicated by the introduction of a new rhythm known as 'Boogie-Woogie' – a constantly recurring rhythm of eight beats to the bar in the bass.[6] The presence of U.S. troops in England greatly increased the popularity of jitterbug and at the same time helped to produce a more polished version of the dance. In many dance halls, however, jitterbug was still unpopular because of the danger to other dancers and because of the interference with 'progressive' dancing. But, as time went on, in the course of this decade there developed a dance, known as jive, which expressed the rhythm of modern swing music, retained some of the essential characteristics of jitterbug, but eliminated the dangerous acrobatics. Some people still objected to jive, however, because it interfered with 'traditional' couples dancing a quickstep, and as late as the 1950s many 'No Jive' notices were still displayed. Eventually it was realized that jive and quickstep could not be danced on the same floor at the same time.

In 1946 the rumba which, in the thirties, had come to the notice of a minority of dancers was 'recognized' by the ballroom-dancing profession. At that time, the rumba taught was the American or 'square' rumba, based on the 'rumba box'.[7] This is still the rumba of the U.S.A. and the Continent, but in England, as we shall see, it came to be superseded in the fifties by a different style. In England, generally, interest in Cuban music increased greatly after the war, and since about 1948 the rumba has been firmly established as a ballroom dance in London and the provinces.

The Brazilian samba was another Latin-American dance which

became known in England about the end of the war. It was introduced to London teachers by some American teachers,[8] and the tune 'Tico-Tico' helped to make it known. Princess Margaret became an enthusiastic samba dancer and the dance soon became extremely popular both in London and in provincial cities.

One interesting general feature about dancing and popular entertainment in Britain in the late 1940s was the decline of the big dance bands. In the 1930s and early 1940s the dance bands, then at the height of their popularity, played most acceptably for dancing. After 1945, however, the big bands seemed increasingly not to want to bother with dancers, and many disappeared from the scene. The demise of the big bands was, of course, considerably hastened by two events which occurred in the U.S.A. in the mid-forties and in England in the late forties. One was the 'new sound' or 'bop'[9] revolution which shaped a style that has lasted for twenty years, and the other was the New Orleans revival, which touched off the 'trad. – modern' jazz war, still a feature of the sixties. The only point of agreement between the two schools was that small groups were economic and big bands were not. In the Palais and other large dance halls, the 'Silvester-style' public still danced of course to the big dance bands, but already the 'jivers' (soon to become the 'rock-and-rollers') and the Latin-American dancers were turning to the small group.

Such, then was the dancing scene in England in the forties, during the war and the post-war years – a wealth of choice to suit all tastes and ages. In addition to the established ballroom dances (foxtrot, quickstep, waltz and, occasionally, tango) and the newer ballroom dances (jive and Latin American) there was now a profusion of 'communal type' dances (Old Time, novelty, country and square).

The vastly increased enthusiasm for social dancing in the forties, as compared with the thirties, with the popularity of the 'group-participation' dances during the war and the post-war years is not difficult to understand. Evacuation mixed up the population and tended to spread knowledge of different kinds of dances throughout the country, the 'black-out' and the absence of transport facilities meant an increased emphasis on the 'locality' and on the provision of one's own amusements and, finally, the greater feeling of diffused warmth and friendliness always manifested in times of war and danger could be much better expressed in the group dance-forms than in the isolated 'couple dance'.

If the forties are compared, not with the thirties, but with the twenties, an interesting contrast can be seen between the ordered, even in some cases disciplined, dancing at the end of the second war and the frenetic individualistic dances at the end of the first. The contrast is as marked as that between the long skirts (almost ankle-length) of the 'New Look' of spring 1947 and the 'flapper's' short skirt (twelve inches from the ground) in 1920. The mood of the two eras was completely different. The optimism, exhilaration, and throwing of bonnets over windmills that followed the end of the First World War was remarkably absent in the late 1940s. Gone, too, was the urge on the part of women for ever greater emancipation and, in its place came a swing in the direction of greater femininity.

The contrast between the two eras is reflected in the specific social dance innovations which 'caught on' in each period: in the 1920s 'jazz dances', to use the idiom of that day, and in the 1940s Latin American dancing. The two phenomena are by no means strictly comparable since the former became a craze and the latter remained a minority interest, but the fact that each took root and developed at different periods is sufficiently interesting to warrant a closer look at their similarities and differences.

Jazz and Latin American music and dancing have in common a background of negro slavery but there the similarity ends. In the Southern states of the U.S.A. jazz was explosive and revolutionary. It burst upon the world as recognizable early jazz around the 1890s, played by Negroes who had not personally known slavery, but who were not far removed from it, psychologically and chronologically. Jazz orchestration broke every tradition of European music. The white man's music was turned over, shaken up and completely transformed. Strings were ousted by brass; the European tone-system was ignored; 'sweet' harmony gave way to strange new sounds; old systems of rhythm were mocked by syncopation, and an element of caricature entered in with the 'dirty' tone, or imitation of the human voice. To crown everything, a new feature appeared on the musical scene – improvization, necessary because the Negro musician lacked musical education and background, and was unable to acquire any, being virtually excluded from society, even after emancipation. Seen in this light, jazz is the music of protest, the music of a people who have lost their own background but are denied access to the new, a music which stems from Negro slaves, but has very little of Africa in it.[10]

In Latin America, Negro slavery was equally prevalent, and was not abolished until 1888, but the effect on music and dancing, particularly in Brazil and in the Spanish West Indies, was one of fusion and evolution rather than explosion and revolution. There is not the slightest doubt about the African influence on such music and dances as the samba, rumba, son, bolero, conga, beguine and danzon, for instance,[11] but these dances and accompanying music are a product of the gradual blending and fusion of traditions, races and cultures over a period of 450 years; they existed probably 100 years before jazz, and are still evolving. The samba and the rumba may be taken as illustrations.

The word 'samba' is used in Brazil not for a specific dance, but, rather, as a generic term to indicate dances of African origin. Since the word indicates a style of dance, the number of varieties must obviously be great: as, for example, the Samba of Sao Paulo, the Samba Bahiana (from Bahia), the Samba de Morro (from Rio de Janeiro) and the Samba Carioca (the favourite dance at Carnival time in Rio). All these forms of samba are known as rural sambas or, sometimes, as 'batuques' and they are accompanied by percussion instruments only, the bomba drum being the most prominent, closely rivalled by the 'noise-makers' beating on iron, glass and wood. The urban ballroom samba (which, unlike the rural is a 'couple' and not a 'group' dance) derives its rhythms and musical style from this rural samba, but its patterns and movements are thought to have developed more from the Brazilian maxixe and the African lundu. Evidence of this complicated line of development can be seen, quite specifically, in certain figures and movements of the modern ballroom samba: for example – the 'Samba Walk' (sometimes termed 'Copacabana' which is the typical step of the Rio Carnival; the 'body rolls' and sways, which have been taken from the maxixe and the lundu; and the 'Cuidado' and 'Plait' figures, which show distinct African influence in the hip movements.

The origin of rumba (and son) rhythms similarly has to be sought in the institution of African slavery – this time in the West Indies, particularly Cuba. In that country the influence of Africa was so strong that in many instances the Spanish musical and dance forms were completely transformed, particularly by the syncopated Afro beats. In the course of time, a new music, termed Afro-Cuban, gradually emerged, and travelled north to the U.S.A., across the sea to Western Europe, and also throughout Latin America itself. This Afro-Cuban music (somewhat diluted and toned down) became accepted everywhere as the new 'Latin' rhythm.[12]

The ballroom rumba, has, of course, as mentioned in the chapter on the thirties, come a long way from the original uninhibited Cuban dance, and is more like the Cuban 'son', but even this 'son-type'of ballroom rumba still shows many African features: for example, foot movements, hip movements, and the keeping still of shoulders (a relic of slave days when burdens had to be carried). These African elements are fused with features of Cuban life in certain parts of the dance: for instance, those figures which represent stamping on cockroaches, and the 'spot turns' which represent an attempt to walk round the rim of old cart-wheels, which used to lie around the countryside.

Musically speaking, although characterized by a steady pulsating beat and syncopation associated with African rhythms, Latin American music provides a strong contrast with jazz music. Its smoothness and subtlety are a world removed from the harsh vitality of jazz and clearly call for entirely different dance-forms.

The reasons why Negro slavery led eventually to the upsurge of jazz in the U.S.A. but not in Latin America are immensely complicated and cannot be explored here. Suffice it to say that the fusion characteristic of Latin American music and dance is paralleled by countless examples of ethnic and cultural fusion in Latin American countries, particularly of African elements, whilst the explosive element of American jazz has its counterpart in the rejection of the Negro as a full human being both during slavery and after emancipation.

The point of greatest interest in the present study is that, whereas dancers in the 1920s in England found the new wild 'jazz dances' greatly to their liking, in the 1940s, in the aftermath of the Second World War, the innovation which had most appeal was the smooth, subtle and sensuous Latin American sound.

XIV
The Fifties: 1950 to 1960

One, two, three o'clock, four o'clock ROCK
. . . .
We're gonna rock
Around the clock tonight
We're gonna rock, rock, rock
Till broad daylight.

BILL HALEY

The most striking features of social dancing in the fifties were, firstly the development of Latin American dancing, and secondly the coming of 'rock and roll'.

The samba, already widely danced in the forties, continued to boom in the fifties, along with the ever-growing popularity of Latin American bands such as those of Edmundo Ros and Roberto Ingles. The rumba of the forties continued to be popular, but very soon a new style of playing Cuban music began to be noticed. Cuban orchestras in the fifties were being influenced by American jazz and swing and were accentuating the off-beats. This combination of American jazz and Afro-Cuban music resulted in a different exciting rhythm that suggested a new dance, rather than simply a variation of the rumba. Thus, in Latin America, the U.S.A. and countries taking their lead from the U.S.A. a new dance – the mambo[1] – came into being: a dance with one beat in every bar on which no step is taken.

In the U.S.A. and on the Continent the mambo became important in the world of dancing, but a great complication arose in English Latin-American dancing-circles when this new-type Cuban music was presented. The American and Continental type of rumba, based on the 'rumba box' as danced in the forties, was now dropped by most of the English dance-schools[2] and a completely new type of rumba was developed. This was danced both to the new-style 'jazzed-up' Cuban 'mambo' music and also to the older style Cuban 'rumba' music. Thus, in England, the mambo is not generally taught as a separate dance, and the rumba as taught in England (by schools interested in competitive dancing) is very different from the rumba danced in America and on the Continent.

Meanwhile, during the fifties, mambo music was itself developing,

107

and America was now using three rhythms; single mambo, double mambo and triple mambo. As always, when music develops, the dance develops accordingly. Triple mambo, involving five movements to one bar of music, became the basis of the 'cha-cha'.[3] The first form of this dance to reach England was called the 'cha-cha-cha', taught by most teachers to a count of 'one, two, cha cha cha' and indeed many of the commercial recordings stress this beat. With the arrival of authentic Cuban music played by Cuban bands, however, it was realized that the essential beat was being missed, and the count of 'one, two, three, cha-cha' (or five steps to one bar of music) came to be accepted, fairly widely, as being correct.[4] The other version, however, is still taught and is a competition style.

Latin-American dancing in England, inevitably, is in the nature of a minority interest, since these dances have to be learned, but the other development of the decade – 'rock and roll' – was more in the nature of a mass phenomenon, at any rate for teenage dancers. In the forties, jitterbug had been tamed into jive, a dance suitable for the ballroom. In the fifties, however, things began to happen to the music, particularly with the release in 1955 of the film 'Rock around the Clock', featuring Bill Haley and the Comets.

This film created tremendous public interest in the 'rock and roll' type of dancing and large numbers of teenagers – to the accompaniment of unlimited press publicity – danced in the cinema aisles, wherever the film was shown. Early rock and roll was like early jitterbug, wild, dangerous and acrobatic, but before very long a form of rock and roll more suitable to the dance hall emerged. This later rock and roll can be thought of as a simplified form of jive, four steps being danced to the basic figure instead of six steps or eight, as in jive. The rocking (and sometimes rolling) action of the body is typical, but the style is flexible and it is not possible to standardize the figures.[5]

In the fifties, 'rock', as it came to be called, continued to develop, associated with changes in tempo. Bands were now playing rock music over a range of tempos: twenty or less to sixty or more bars to the minute. Some adaptation was necessary for the fast 'rock' and the new feature was a tendency to simplify even further. The basic movement kept its fundamental design but the rhythm of SSSS or QQQQ came to be adopted instead of QQSS.[6]

Dancing schools wrongly considered that rock was too simple to teach. Frank Borrows considers that any teacher of dancing would take quite a long time before he could master and perform rock at the level of good teenage exponents, and that when well-practised and performed, it is an exceedingly rhythmic and satisfying dance.[7]

The Fifties: 1950 to 1960

One very significant feature of the fifties, so far as popular music and dancing are concerned, was the foreshadowing of the teenage 'population explosion' of the sixties. The birth-rate for England and Wales for the years 1941–50 was 17·4 per thousand, compared with 14·8 per thousand for the years 1931–40.[8] This increase is mostly accounted for by the 'delayed births' at the end of the war, the net reproductive index rate for 1947 being 1·2 compared with 0·75 in 1935.[9] In the late fifties, the 'bulge' as it is so often inelegantly called, was reaching its teens, and older people, helped by the publicity attending 'rock and roll' began to notice the phenomenon of the teenager in their midst.

Another interesting feature, also to reach its peak in the next decade, was the advent of cheap, unbreakable, easily portable records. In 1949, the first light and bendable long-playing records came out in America. In June 1950 Decca issued Britain's first L.P.'s and in the Autumn of 1952 the E.M.I. group brought out L.P.'s and 45 r.p.m. records. From the mid-1950s, pop music appeared on 45s – this type of cheap, unbreakable, easily obtainable record being ideally suited for quick and widespread commercial success.

The developments of the fifties – whether Latin American or rock and roll – show clearly that even minor changes in rhythms can produce major changes in dance forms. Equally clear is the fact that neither the music nor the dance can be understood in isolation from the rest of society. Rock and roll, and rock, were teenage crazes in the fifties, continuing into the sixties, because the new type of music – exciting, rhythmic, with a pounding beat – calling for an uninhibited but basically simple dance, fitted in with the mood of the affluent, independent teenagers, now coming to regard themselves as a class apart, with safety in numbers, having their 'own' music and their 'own' dancing.

XV
The Sixties: 1960 to 1969

You can express how you feel when you dance
modern.

'Day Release' girl

You let off steam, and meet the best of the
females.

'Business Studies' boy

The Latin American dances of the fifties have continued in popularity
in the present decade, an innovation in the early sixties being the
'Bossa Nova'. As the mambo is to the Cuban rumba, so is the Bossa
Nova to the Brazilian samba. It represents a fusion of American jazz
or swing with Brazilian folk-music, a particularly happy combination
being the jazz saxophone of Stan Getz blending unforgettably with
traditional samba sounds and rhythms. The music was very popular
in England[1] but the dance never really gained a firm hold in this
country.[2] The Latin American musical idiom in general has had a
considerable effect on pop music and singers in the present decade,
and from time to time many of the 'top twenty' provide pleasant
rumba-type or cha-cha-type music, complete with bongoes and
claves but, of course, the authentic Latin American rhythm is not
to be found in English or American pop music.

Rock and roll, or rock, continuing from the fifties became a
progressively simplified dance in which a simple one, two, one, two,
count was used, with both partners using either their right or their
left feet at any one time (instead of, say, the man using the right and
the girl the left). It was thus difficult to say who was leading and who
following, and there was a tendency for this to change during the
dance.[3]

Early in the sixties came the 'twist' craze. Here the tendency to
simplify the expression of the body to music is carried still further.
There are no standardized steps and no hold – indeed, a partner is
not strictly necessary. All that is called for is the rhythmic movements
of the body to music. The twist is undoubtedly the most important
development in the social dance since the advent of the waltz. The
waltz ushered in the era of the 'closed couple dance' and spelt the

doom (except for 'Old Time') of 'open couple' set and sequence dances. The twist, in its turn, ushered in the era of 'solo' or 'partner-less' dancing, now accepted as completely normal amongst the young, but still regarded as a rather startling phemomenon by the middle-aged.

This dance has inspired a considerable number of articles in journals and newspapers, but none of them throws any light on the actual origin of the twist. Where did the rhythmic hip and arm movements come from in the first place, who first performed them, and why? The answers to these questions will probably never be known for certain, but my theory is that the movements of the twist probably originated with singers not dancers. Long before the days of the gyrations of Elvis Presley, it was the custom for American popular singers (very often coloured) to emphasize the rhythm of the music by a subtle hip-movement. English singers would be more inclined to use their arms for this. It is possible, therefore, that the hip movements of the twist originated with vocalists, not dancers, performing exaggerated versions of their normal hip-swaying to the very strong beat of the early Chubby Checker records in 1960. These exaggerated rhythmic hip-movements might then have been imitated by dancers on tiny floors, in clubs such as the Peppermint Lounge, New York's 'Twist Centre'. The twist, of course, needed less floor space than any previous dance ever recorded.

Whatever the actual origin, there seems no doubt that the twist was born in America. Indeed, so apparently alien was it to Britain in the beginning that an intensive public campaign was necessary before it really 'caught on' with the British public. In this campaign, the large commercial interests spared no effort. By the summer of 1961, the twist had become popular in Parisian night clubs, and from there it spread to the 'exclusive' night-clubs in London's West End. By Autumn 1961 it was taken up by the Mecca and Arthur Rank dance hall chain, by Arthur Murray's London dance studios, and by the record companies. Towards the end of 1961, the American film companies joined in the campaign. Paramount produced a twist feature called: 'Hey, let's Twist' which had been shot in New York's Peppermint Lounge, and Columbia made 'Twist Around the Clock' deliberately echoing 'Rock Around the Clock'. Columbia's publicity manager in Britain summoned seven hundred teenagers at forty-eight hours' notice to a special preview. Within ten minutes the teenagers were twisting in the foyer and the aisles: thus encouraged, Columbia started on a £7,500 publicity campaign.[4]

The collaboration and synchronization of the different commercial elements is of great interest. For example, when the London run of

Paramount's 'Hey, let's Twist' started, the Arthur Murray School of Dancing in Leicester Square staged a demonstration of the twist in the foyer and distributed complimentary tickets for the film. As the film had been shot in the Peppermint Lounge, E.M.I. then weighed in with a record called 'The Peppermint Twist'. When the Columbia film went to the provinces the provincial Rank ballrooms were ready to back any stunts the film company cared to arrange. Local cinema managers were instructed to get in touch with as many stores as possible so that they might all give their goods a 'twist' angle. Thus, hairdressers produced 'The Twist – a spiral upsweep coiffure', dress manufacturers displayed dresses with flared skirts or pleats below the knee – 'The Twist Dress' – and shoe manufacturers did their bit with 'Twisties'.[5]

In spite of all this ingenuity, the teenage market showed itself very reluctant to be converted from rock and roll, and in 1961 they still tended to 'rock' to the twist. In financial terms, the publicity campaigns for the Paramount and Columbia films were comparative failures, especially if compared with the success of Columbia's predecessor: 'Rock Around the Clock'. But although the film companies did not reap the expected financial benefits, they sowed the seeds of the mass craze for the dance. Within a few weeks the twist had soared to national popularity and the record boom began in earnest. The first twist long-playing disc appeared at Christmas 1961 and sold as fast as it could be produced. Now, everyone tried to jump on the band-wagon. 'Dance the Twist' by Normie Dwyer appeared as a paperback on 20 January at 2/6d. and a first print of 125,000 was sold out in ten days. Shopkeepers everywhere, with no promptings now from cinema managers, tried their hardest to cash in on the twist craze by linking their products, wherever possible, to the new dance. Schools of dancing and teachers of dancing (many of whom had refused to have anything to do with the twist earlier) now vied with one another in advertising lessons in the twist.[6]

Although it took such an intensive public campaign to popularize the twist (in striking contrast to 'rock-and-roll' which 'just grew on people'), once established, there could be no doubt of the twist's enormous and compulsive appeal to millions. There is a compelling drive about twist music which makes people want to move their bodies to it, and once the novel sight of English people using their hips in a dance became acceptable, inhibitions quickly faded away. A great part of the appeal of this dance lay, of course, in its simplicity and its individuality. No one could say any longer: 'I don't dance', since no steps needed to be learnt. The movements could range from the wild exhibitionism of an athletic teenager to the controlled subtlety of the 'middle-aged' version, as demonstrated by Victor Silvester in his television series of dancing lessons.

It would, indeed, be a mistake to think of the twist as the personal property of the young. Normie Dwyer[7] has pointed out that the simplicity of the dance and its weight-reducing properties made the twist a dance-craze with the 'over-forties' and quotes an opinion from this age-group: 'The older folks like it because you move quite separately and therefore don't have to worry about your partner's feet. And the movements are so easy . . .'

Of course the twist could look grotesque when performed by a stout, elderly, untalented man or woman – but this surely would have been equally true, of say, the nineteenth-century polka. The alleged vulgarity or flaunted sexuality of the twist has also come under fire, but again the sexual aspects of any dance can be either subdued or exaggerated according to taste and temperament. In any event, those who enjoy (or used to enjoy) dancing the twist can count themselves in good company, artistically and socially. From the artistic point of view, Robert Helpman has demonstrated on television that he is an expert twist exponent. Socially, the twist can be said to have received the highest possible cachet when it was included in the programme at the Queen's dance given at Windsor Castle in April 1963, to celebrate Princess Alexandra's engagement.[8]

The twist reached the height of its popularity in the early months of 1962. By the spring of 1965 it had become completely out-dated, having been superseded first by the 'blue-beat' and then by the 'shake'. The latter was a curious, highly individualistic dance in which the feet hardly moved but the legs vibrated, the hands gesticulated, the shoulders swung and the head quivered and twitched. No particular partner was necessary – it could be danced in a mixed group, or by a group of boys only or girls only. Each dancer appeared to be utterly self-absorbed, wearing the rapt expression of one in a closed-in private world.

The shake was a 'mod' dance (linked with the 'mod' cult which reached its height in Britain in 1963–64) but its advent and some of its movements can be understood better if its less well-known predecessor, the blue-beat, is first examined. Towards the end of 1963, 'rhythm and blues' which had long been popular in America, enjoyed a vogue in Britain.[9] This type of music – noisy and hypnotic, epitomized by the Chuck Berry sound – might be described as 'blues' songs 'hotted-up' to swing music, sometimes slow, sometimes fast but always with a strong, rhythmic, hypnotic beat. The Mersey groups made considerable use of this musical form and soon the basic twist sound (and dance) became rather old-fashioned.

No particular dance seems to have been done to rhythm and blues, but this new sound paved the way for the coming of blue-beat. The real name of blue-beat is the 'ska' or 'ska-blues', a form of music and dance well-known in Jamaica. In Jamaica the ska derives from the dancing and music inside a religious revivalist cult known as 'Pocomania'.[10] When combined with American rhythm and blues (which swept over Jamaica in the 1940s) Pocomanian music and dance became the ska.[11] As far as is known, the dance and the music were first introduced into Britain by West Indian immigrants in 1959 or 1960. A number of blue-beat records were made and launched about that time but they were aimed largely at the West Indian market and, naturally, were not widely-known outside the coloured communities and certain clubs in Soho and Brixton.

In March of 1964, however, Millie Small, a Jamaican teenager, produced a ska version of 'Lollipop' – an old American pop song. It was an immediate success and, retitled the 'blue-beat sound', the new musical idiom and a new dance to match it, caught on with teenagers throughout the country. 'Now comes the blue beat'. Ezz Rico, a Jamaican band leader explains how to dance it: 'Imagine you have a terrible tummy-ache and a twitch at the same time. You've just got to move around to relieve the pain – well, man, that's blue beat. It may look like you're suffering but the truth is, you're having a whole heap of fun.'[12] A teenager, interviewed for *Generation X*, puts it this way: 'They all dance the blue beat – stiff at knees, throw arms everywhere. Hips to the side four beats at a time and the rhythm is like a locomotive thumping along a track, sound like a drum and the words are really mad.'[13]

Different versions of the dance there might have been,[14] but about the instantly recognizable 'ska' or blue-beat music there was no doubt – a fast, hypnotic, monotonous rhythm and a very heavily accented 'off-beat'. In its hey-day in 1964 all manner of contrived and commercialized blue beat was perpetrated and soon enough the distinctive music went the way of other teenage popular crazes. The accompanying movements, however, did not die out and became the basis of the very widely known 'shake',[15] both in Britain and in the U.S.A. This is yet another example of culture diffusion as an explanation of new dance-forms, and is particularly interesting in that here a small immigrant minority culture has influenced the dominant culture of the host community.*

The 'Mersey sound', 'rhythm and blues', 'blue beat' and so on are of course bound up with one of the most striking teenage phenomena of the sixties – the springing up all over the country of 'groups', from

* See Plate VII, page 114.

Plate VII West Indians demonstrate the Ska or Blue Beat: 1964

Plate VIII Mod Girls dance The Block at Soho's Scene Club: Summer 1964

the famous Beatles and Rolling Stones to hosts of semi-professional and amateur groups all over the country. There are now said to be at least 25,000 beat-groups in Britain: young people, making music for young people, but not, the cynic will add, without the aid of the middle-aged middlemen of the pop music industry – the managers, disc jockeys, recording supervisors and P.R.O.s. This is not the place to discuss the merits or demerits of pop music, nor to analyse its hold on the young, but the point must be made that contemporary pop music and contemporary dancing can never be separated, and that any change in the musical idiom will bring about a change in the dance-form.

Part of the appeal of the groups and the shake has been well put by an articulate (University) teenager (May 1964):

> It's been a good term socially, thanks to the marvellous Mersey beat, as Aberdeen like every other town in the British Isles has its local groups and we have a student group as well. The great thing now is for societies to hire a group for an evening to have a party in the Dive in the union. This is small, dark and cellar-like and when you get it crowded with fanatically yelling and shaking people and the group pounding away, the atmosphere is terrific. The electric guitar is absolutely made for such a small stuffy hole – you can really feel the music and I find that the insistent beat results in a feeling very like being drunk. Of course it gets terribly hot – even the walls are streaming and after an hour or so of frenzied activity one feels completely limp. But this is marvellous once in a way, letting oneself go and shaking away all troubles and worries.[16]

The reference here to a 'feeling very like being drunk' provides anecdotal support to certain hypotheses arising from recent experimental investigations of the effect of music on the central nervous system.[17] Electroencephalograph (E.E.G.) studies are showing that monotonous rhythmic stimulation, if fast, (beyond five pulses per second), can cause tension, anxiety and distress, and that, if slower, can have a hypnotic effect, inhibiting cortical control and allowing release of emotional response, exactly in the way that alcohol does. The 'intoxicating' element in a steady basic, monotonous beat is of course utilized to the full by the popular beat groups of today, who tend more and more to dispense with the supporting melody instruments and concentrate solely on the amplified guitars and drums of the rhythmic section.

In the 'wake of the shake' came a never-ending stream of gimmick

dances (Zizzle, Whack, Bang, Block,* Bird, Duck, Frug, Jerk . . .)
but in all of these there was an element of blue beat or shake. These
dances were all, to a certain extent, 'mod' dances in that they tended
to be initiated by mods in their own clubs, but in a mysterious fashion
they were rapidly picked up by dancing teenagers everywhere. The
mod movement began in London as early as 1960, starting as a tiny
minority cult, fanatical in standards, restricted to boys, cool, self-
involved, and centering round clothes and personal appearance.
Within three years, the movement (now including girls) had developed
into the biggest teenage cult (and industry) that Britain has ever
known, producing Carnaby Street, 'Ready Steady Go' on television,
the purple heart, and – the essential uniform of the new mod – the
motor-scooter. The movement was also closely linked with the rise
to fame of pop groups like the Rolling Stones (in those days neatly
dressed with velvet-collared jackets) and the Beatles (equally dapper
in mod fashion).

As a reaction against the mods – a movement which, especially in
its early days, had distinct introvert, narcissistic and homosexual
undertones – there arose the rockers, a carry-over from the 'rock
generation' of the mid-fifties, characterized by an aggressive masculinity, which was symbolized by the leather jacket and the roaring
motor-bike. Needless to say, the rockers did not dance the new mod
dances. Either they were not interested in dancing, or, if they were,
they danced rock and twist with 'rocker girls' – a type of female just
as distinct from the mod girl as were the two male varieties. An
illustration of this is the reaction of a mod boy when I asked him, on
one occasion, whether he would ever invite a rocker girl to dance
with him. First, a look of blank astonishment, then incredulous
amusement that such a question could even be asked. There were
countless reasons why he would not: first, he wouldn't want to,
second, she wouldn't be able to do the mod dances, thirdly, she
would simply ignore him, fourthly, if in fact she were to accept, the
rockers would be on to him with fists and flick-knives and a gang-
fight would break out in the dance hall.

It was of course the open conflict, particularly the riots and gang-
fights at Brighton and Hastings on bank holidays, which brought
nationwide publicity to the rival teenage movements, although by
this time (1964) neither mods nor rockers had more than the vaguest
notion of what they were fighting about. The bank-holiday riots
proved to be the culmination of the whole mod movement, since after
this the fanaticism died out, as did the word mod itself.

The successor to the teenage mod involvement might be said to be

* See Plate VIII, page 115.

the 'hippies', but this non-indigenous movement (a watered-down version of the San Francisco 'flower-children') seems to be centered almost entirely in London and is unlikely ever to have the influence that the mods had. The hippy cult, with its 'love-and-beauty' philosophy, is unfortunately ineradicably bound up with L.S.D. and other drugs of the hallucinogen variety (assuredly more dangerous than the pep pills of the mod days) but on the credit side there is a certain emphasis on gentleness. It would of course be ludicrous to suppose that the permitted level of aggression amongst teenagers in general (or even hippies) is limited to the throwing of a flower, but it is none-the-less true that the organized yet aimless violence of the mod and rocker days is a thing of the past. So far as music and dance are concerned, the hippy emphasis on enjoyment has contributed to the emergence of teenage dancing out of the cool, narcissistic phase into a much more energetic form of dancing, often to 'psychedelic' music, where it is permissible to look wildly happy.

In every period so far considered, some link-up has been found between the dances currently in fashion and the climate of society.* To what extent is this true of the sixties?

One of the most striking things about dancing in the sixties is that, for the first time in the history of the social dance in England, there exists a gulf between young people (defined as between about thirteen and twenty-five) and the older generation. The over-twenty-fives dance the traditional ballroom dances, Latin American and jive and sometimes even the twist, dances which are regarded with some scorn by the young who tend to concentrate on beat dances, danced 'solo' without even a 'hand-hold'. The 'modern' dances are felt to belong to the young, in the same way that pop music is often considered to be exclusive teenage property.

This of course reflects the gulf, always present to some extent, but now manifest as never before, between young people and the older generation in our society. The 'cult of the young', as it is sometimes called, derives firstly from the sheer weight of numbers (resulting from the high birth rate at the end of the war and in the immediate post-war years, as mentioned in the previous section); secondly from the relative affluence of working teenagers in an era of high wages and full employment; and thirdly from the combined efforts of all commercial interests to woo the teenager, make him feel important and extract from him as much money as possible. Bearing in mind these factors, together with the rapid scientific advance and techno-logical change of the sixties which has the effect of putting knowledge and power in the hands of the young and rendering out-of-date the

* This question is discussed again in Part III.

traditional wisdom of their elders, it is not surprising that we should find ourselves living in an era where 'to be young' if not 'very heaven' is the only way to be 'with it'. And no one need wonder that this 'special generation' should have its own language, its own music and its own dancing.[18]

It is, moreover, very interesting that this style of dancing is 'classless' (as is pop music). The change in class attitude to dancing has already been traced – to dance well and with style being the mark of a gentleman from the thirteenth century to the late nineteenth century, after which comes a decline in social 'cachet', culminating in the idea that a good ballroom dancer must be something of a 'gigolo' or 'outsider'. There is no 'good' or 'bad' in modern beat dancing and there is certainly no style distinctive of any particular social class. This factor, too, must be a reflection of a change in young people's attitudes, this time in the sphere of social class. No one would deny that class consciousness still exists, particularly at the two extremes of the 'social ladder' but, in an age when a Liverpool accent provokes more acclaim than an Oxford one, and when a 'career open to talents' is on the way to realization, it is clear that the sociological dimensions of class, status and power are more confused and fluid than ever before.

It is not easy to explain the typical teenage style of dancing – that is, either 'solo' in a group or with a partner, but with no contact, not even a hand-hold as in jive or rock and roll. The obvious argument would seem to be that, in a permissive society, today's teenagers have plenty of opportunity elsewhere for contact with the opposite sex, and therefore prefer to use the dance to express their individuality and response to the music, than as an excuse for close physical contact with their boy or girl friends. It must, of course, be remembered here that certain types of music – particularly slow blues, or any 'mood music', especially when played late at night at parties – does indeed find teenagers dancing (or 'smooching') in couples as close, if not closer, than any previous generation. This, however, is nothing new, amounting as it does to a greater awareness of the partner than of the dance, and is not typical of contemporary teenage dancing.

To sum up, the style and technique of the modern dance-form is both complicated and paradoxical. The dancers look 'sexy' yet no bodily contact exists between partners, if partners there be; the dancers show the minimum of grace but the maximum of rhythm with intense concentration on the beat; there is a strong element of exhibitionism yet frequently the dancers appear self-absorbed and oblivious to the outside world; there are no rules to the dance yet, somehow, at any one time, most dancers seem to be doing the same thing. Perhaps these dances and this style of dancing are not inappropriate to an independent teenage generation brought up in a graceless and ugly environment, but surrounded by the spell of magical, syncopated beat: a generation less conscious of class than their predecessors: rebellious and individualistic yet strongly conformist within their own conventions: sexually alert and relatively uninhibited yet not without the self-consciousness and need for reassurance typical of adolescence.

Although this style of dancing is new, so far as England is concerned, it is of course anything but new in the history of dance. All primitive dancing is of this nature, the 'partnered-up' style being a product of the ballroom of civilization, and, in comparison, artificial and inhibiting. It may be that today's young people want to dissociate themselves completely from the traditional ballroom style of dancing and much prefer a link with primitive man. Indeed, in view of the theory that dancing preceded speech, one might go further and claim that contemporary social dancing has returned to the very beginning of the cycle – to the jungle! Certainly, beat music played in the modern idiom is so loud that conversation is both unnecessary and impossible during the dance, and thus 'the language of words is replaced by the language of the body'.[19]

XVI
Summary

At this stage, a socio-historical summary of the general findings will be useful, bearing in mind the following points. The sociologist is of necessity concerned with trends and generalities and not with unique occurrences or special instances. It is, therefore, legitimate in summing up the complicated pattern of the developing social dance in England from the Middle Ages to the present day to concentrate upon the changes and innovations in any period, rather than to mention every single dance known at the time. From the point of view of the relationship to society, what is continuing to be danced in any particular period is not so significant as what is new (for which the time must be ripe) and what is dropped, as out of date.

(a) *Court and nobles – Thirteenth century to 1900*

In the thirteenth century aristocratic and court dancing consisted of estampies, rounds and caroles danced in the artificial and restrained manner typical of the medieval approach of the knight to his lady. In the fourteenth and fifteenth centuries came the addition of the processional form of dance then made possible by the invention of chimneys which allowed a greater expanse of floor-space. Of great significance, too, was the influence of France, and French customs learnt from the nobles captured during the early years of the Hundred Years' War.

In the early sixteenth century, dance history in England is on a surer footing since, with the publication in 1521 of Copeland's *Manner of Dancing Bace Dances After the Use of France*, contemporary records become available. We know that the dance of sixteenth-century England for court and nobles was the Basse Danse, much influenced by the dances of the French court, which were watched and admired by Henry VIII and his courtiers at the Field of the Cloth of Gold. A further dance of court and nobles at this time was the slow and solemn pavane, characterized, as was the basse danse, by dignified steps, befitting the heavy dresses and long robes of the period.

Summary

In the second half of the sixteenth century the slow and dignified style of court dancing gave way to the gay and swift galliards, courantoes and La Voltas, so beloved of Queen Elizabeth I, and so much in keeping with the adventurous and joyous spirit of the Elizabethans and with their robust attitude to women. This was a period of greater harmony and freer mixing of the social classes than ever before in England and it is, therefore, not surprising that in this period (in addition to the dances already mentioned) the English country-dances of the 'people' were taken up by court and nobles.

Seventeenth-century England saw a decline in enthusiasm for the social dance with the death of Elizabeth, the new enthusiasm for ballet and masque, the Civil War, the execution of Charles I, and the establishment of the Commonwealth. In this century, apart from the country-dances which continued to be popular, the formal and stately type of dance came back into favour, with the gavotte, a devitalized galliard, and a much slower courantoe.

In the first half of the eighteenth century the best-known dance at court and assembly was the graceful, stylized, mannered minuet, essentially a product of its age and entirely suitable to the early eighteenth century world of fashion. By the second half of the eighteenth century, however, it was gradually ousted by the warmer contredanse, cotillon and allemande, and in the early nineteenth century by the French quadrille, and unforgettably, the waltz.

Increasing freedom in the relations between the sexes was now being paralleled by increasing freedom in dance-forms. Thus, the waltz – 'that indecent foreign dance' to quote *The Times* of 16 July 1816 – was to usher in an era of the 'closed couple' dance, as opposed to the more impersonal 'open couple' of minuet, quadrille and country dance. The waltz, rhythmic, romantic and full-blooded – utterly different from the dainty, precise minuet – fitted in so well with the romantic revival, and the trend towards naturalness and spontaneity that, aided by the Strauss compositions, it succeeded in dominating all other dance-forms until the advent of the polka in the 1840s.

The polka, another closed-couple dance, was gay, vital and spirited: well-adapted to the quickening tempo of social change in mid-nineteenth-century England. It became a craze in the year 1844 but died out before the turn of the century. The closing years of the nineteenth century saw social dancing at a very low ebb in England. Evangelical religion was no friend of the social dance; the army of workers, men and women, playing their part in the Industrial Revolution, had neither facilities nor energy for dancing, and the late Victorian upper classes and upper-middle classes were too industrious, too respectable (at any rate outwardly) and perhaps too inhibited to enjoy dancing. At all events, now, for the first time in the history of dancing in England, it became 'bad form' for a man to dance well.

(*b*) Folk – Thirteenth century to 1900

In rural England in the Middle Ages the most characteristic form of dance was the vigorous 'Morris' – strictly speaking, more of a ritual than a true social dance. In general, the country-folk celebrated holidays, weddings and all joyous occasions by dancing their boisterous and simple chain, ring and round dances, with a greater emphasis on enjoyment than on technique. In Queen Elizabeth's day, the more complicated 'new' country-dances became popular, dances containing specific patterns and figures, later to be included by Playford in his collection, and to continue in popularity for hundreds of years. Other sixteenth- and seventeenth-century dances of the English countryside were the jig and the hornpipe, the former a rapid dance-with-song for groups of young men and girls, and the latter also a vigorous group dance.

No one can point to a specific date when 'communal' country-dancing ceased to exist in England (and, indeed, there are small pockets where some traditional dances are still alive). The erosion of 'village green' dancing was a gradual process, an inevitable accompaniment to late eighteenth- and nineteenth-century industrialization, urbanization and the break-up of rural communities. The nearest one can get to a specific date is the report of a dance historian in 1906 that he could not find, even in rural areas, any trace of national or traditional dances, and that the 'country-folk' danced the waltz, polka and lancers just as did the 'upper classes', although with greater apparent enjoyment. From this date on, the more individualistic and 'atomistic' type of 'couple dancing' takes over from group or communal dancing, and there is no point in straining to find specific 'rural' as opposed to 'urban' dances, or much differentiation (except in style) between the dancing of the 'common people' and any other social stratum.

(*c*) General – Twentieth century

After the turn of the century, dancing (but of a very different kind from anything that had gone before) became extremely popular again. Apart from the tango craze of 1911–12, the predominating influence on dancing in England in the early part of the twentieth

Summary

century was unquestionably American ragtime. This type of music arrived in England around 1911, and dictated the free-and-easy one-step and early foxtrot of the days before the First World War. The restless and feverish post-war decade continued to revel in the syncopated music of the early jazz bands, but they wanted new dances. They came, of course, from America: notably the Charleston and the Black Bottom.

The thirties and the forties saw ragtime developing into the new rhythms of 'swing' music with swing dancing as its counterpart in the U.S.A. Jitterbug and jive was the answer in England, greatly influenced by the arrival of G.I. Joe in the early war years. Jive, sometimes frenzied, was the dance of the young in the anxious days of wartime unheaval. The not-so-young tended to forget their worries in the group participation dances of the day: novelty dances to the accompaniment of a particular song, country, square and 'Old Time'.

In the decades after the war innovations in dancing can be summarized as, on the one hand, Latin American which makes a steady minority appeal to those who, in changing times, seek a change from the traditional ballroom dances: and, on the other hand, the new partnerless dances such as the twist and the shake and their successors which have such a strong appeal for the confident teenagers of today who, possibly, prefer to use the dance to express their individuality and even to 'show off' rather than as an excuse for an embrace. The strong emphasis on rhythm and beat to the exclusion of melody in this type of dancing is an indication that contemporary teenage social dancing has, in some respects, returned to the beginning of the cycle – to primitive dance, where (in extreme instances) the stamping of feet is the only accompaniment necessary.

Alternatively, this type of dancing can be thought of as 'progression' rather than 'regression'. Historically speaking, country-dancing of a communal or group nature gives way, with the break-up of communities, to partnered-up ballroom dancing with a concentration on couples rather than groups. This, in turn, is now replaced amongst young people by partner-less dancing, which, although individualistic, seems none-the-less, to be rooted in a striving for community feeling and group solidarity.

Testing of Hypothesis

At the outset of this study the hypothesis was put forward that variations in the social dance are never accidental, but are linked with all other aspects of society: in other words, that the social dance forms an integral part of the total culture pattern of any society. The sociological method used to examine this hypothesis was that of investigation, observation and analysis of 'repetitious uniformities of individuals and groups' in one country (England) over a given period of history (thirteenth century to the present day).

The hypothesis has been borne out in a general way by the socio-historical study. It may, however, be tested in a more specific way by enlarging on certain aspects of society and correlating changes in those aspects with changes in the social dance. For this purpose, the following will be considered:

    (1)   Relations between the sexes and the social dance.

    (2)   Social stratification and the social dance.

    (3)   Social prestige and the social dance.

    (4)   Movement, gesture and the social dance.

    (5)   Social and political history, culture diffusion and the social dance.

(1) Relations between the sexes and the social dance

The medieval attitude of chivalrous and distant love has already been linked with the constrained and artificial way of medieval court dancing, and has been contrasted with the more realistic and robust attitude to women of Elizabethan days, exemplified both in the Elizabethan dances (particularly La Volta) and in Shakespeare's plays. The eighteenth-century era of politeness and formality between the sexes, with the accent on manners, etiquette and convention, is mirrored in the stately gavotte and the precise minuet, while the nineteenth century sees an easing of constraint and the beginning of women's emancipation. It is no coincidence that the mid years of the nineteenth century fully accept waltz and polka (closed couple dances permitting a woman to dance with a number of different partners) and that the year 1869 sees the publication of J. S. Mill's *Subjection of Women*. The next stage is the casual, much more free-and-easy relationship between the sexes when, particularly after the First World War, newly-emancipated woman no longer has any claim to be regarded as mysterious and romantic. This new attitude to woman is typified in the casual, crazy and sometimes crude ragtime dances of the twenties, and continues, with modifications, into the era of jive, and particularly rock and roll, a dance where, sometimes, the girl can lead and the man has to follow.

The sixties are too close to permit of anything but speculation. Clearly, this is a period in which previously accepted norms of 'masculinity' and 'femininity' are changing, at any rate as regards outward appearance. Hair styles and clothes are becoming more and more interchangeable, culminating in 'unisex' fashions. As Harrod's 'Way In' have it: 'Male or female, you're all the same to us. One-sex clothes in two-sex sizes.' It can surely be no coincidence that an age which permits previously established masculine and feminine 'roles' to be mixed up in this way, also permits social dancing in an equally indiscriminate way – where girls may dance in a group of girls, boys in a group of boys, or boys and girls together, but without specific partners.

Following the lines of J. Langdon-Davies' argument in *The Dancing Catalans* this type of 'indicriminate' dancing may well reflect a more natural, or at any rate, less hypocritical attitude both to sex and to dancing than that of the older generation, with their partnered-up ballroom dances. His argument runs that ballroom dancing is an expression not of sex, but of suppressed sex, that it is a form of 'socially licensed sublimated promiscuity', pointing out that wives, for example, on the whole do not care to dance with their husbands, since 'dancing is precisely what they are permitted to do with other men'. He describes the 'innocence' of the highly-sexed Catalans in their dance, the 'Sardana', where men 'have not come to meet girls, nor are the girls' minds buzzing with thoughts about the men as such, all together are responding to another feeling, the feeling of being one of a group'. If a girl squeezes the hand of the man on her left three times she is only reminding him of the number of bars left in that section of the music. Anyone can break into any circle, and the Sardana circle may be composed of men and girls, or of men alone, or of girls alone – it is almost immaterial. The highly-sexed and virile Catalans, according to this argument, do not look on the Sardana as a substitute for sex, but as a form of sensuous delight and a social ritual, and (presumably) find direct rather than indirect sexual outlets.

This situation Langdon-Davies contrasts with the 'sex-obsessed' but at the same time 'repressed' men and women of northern climes, whose partner dances do not lead to direct sexual activity, but which are none-the-less, very much concerned with sex, in substitute form. Without going all the way with the argument, it is interesting and significant that modern beat dancing *does* mix up the sexes in the indiscriminate way that the Sardana does (although bearing no other resemblance to this dance) and that this type of dancing is typical of a generation which is direct and outspoken in its sexual attitudes.

(2) *Social stratification and the social dance*

In medieval times there was a marked difference between the dancing of the nobles and that of the peasants or common people. The couple dance known as the 'estampie' was, it is thought, a dance of the court alone, and although rounds and caroles were danced by both strata, the solemn stepping of the nobles so little resembled the cavorting of the 'folk' that they could scarcely be regarded as the same dance. Similarly, in the early sixteenth century there was a pronounced distinction between the dances of upper and lower strata, the dignified and stately Basse Danse and pavane being danced at court and by the upper classes but not by the common people. The dances of the countryside were 'democratic' in that they were ring and round dances without a 'head' or leading couple, whereas the court dances tended to be of the 'processional' type which eminently suited a hierarchical society, since the order of precedence in the dance could be exactly matched to social rank.

Thus, from medieval times up to mid-sixteenth century, the wide gulf between 'high' and 'low' in society was paralleled by marked differences in the social dance. In the second half of the sixteenth century, society was still rigidly stratified, and, correspondingly, there were many dances (for example galliard, couranto, La Volta) which belonged to court and nobles and not to the people. In this period, however, there was a tendency for a somewhat easier mixing of the different estates and in Elizabethan England it was by no means unusual for the lord of the manor and his family to join in 'country-dancing' with his tenants, on high days and holidays. It goes without saying that this mixing implied complete acceptance, on everyone's part, high and low, of his strictly defined 'station' within a rigid social structure. These attitudes continued into the seventeenth and eighteenth centuries, with the eighteenth century minuet typifying the gulf between the strata, but the country dance still affording frequent possibilities for mixing, on appropriate occasions.

As the 'estate' type of social stratification began gradually to dissolve into the 'class structure' system in the nineteenth century, there were considerable changes. In the course of the nineteenth century there came to be a strong similarity in the dances of all social classes, since the dances of the day (quadrilles, lancers, waltzes and polkas) were becoming widely known and enjoyed by all. The question then was whether the upper classes could preserve the exclusiveness not of *what* they danced, but of *where* they danced.

Almack's, in the early years of the century, set a standard of exclusiveness which became a byword, and the other early assembly rooms did their best to copy this impossible standard. The assembly rooms kept their exclusiveness during the first two-thirds of the century but they were fighting a losing battle in the face of a society steadily moving towards a more democratic way of life. The assemblies gradually grew less fashionable and in the last third of the century a number of 'popular assembly rooms' were built, to cater for public demand. It would of course be a mistake to see in this development any evidence of a diminishing 'class consciousness' in England in the latter part of the nineteenth century. When the original assembly rooms became less fashionable, 'society' ceased to patronize them and preferred to dance at balls given privately by society hostesses in large town residences. In the actual dance-forms, an interesting class aspect persisted into the twentieth century, in that the popular assemblies featured sequence dances, such as the veleta, never to be seen at a society function, and preferred the '*trois temps*' waltz to the more fashionable '*deux temps*'.

The advent of the modern Palais de Danse after the end of the First World War was the beginning of dancing for the 'masses', or the real democratization of the social dance. Partly this was a question of demand and supply. At the end of the war, the mass of the population, better off in the days of the post-war boom than ever before, had a great urge to dance, but not to string orchestras playing veletas and lancers. They wanted modern jazz bands and the new ragtime dances, but could not afford to patronize the fashionable hotels and restaurants which provided them. For this new dancing public, the Palais de Danse was to be the answer. The first was the Hammersmith Palais de Danse, opened in 1919, soon followed by the Palais de Danse in Birmingham. These and others which followed had perfectly sprung spacious floors and top-quality modern orchestras. In 1920, for example, Hammersmith Palais featured Dominic la Rocca and the famous 'Original Dixieland Jazz Band' from America, while in the 1960s, one of the bands which plays regularly at the Hammersmith Palais is the well-known Joe Loss and his orchestra. It is an interesting and by no means insignificant sidelight on the democratization of the social dance that this was the band chosen by the Queen to play at Windsor Castle for the ball given in April 1963 to celebrate the engagement of Princess Alexandra.

The success of the Palais de Danse encouraged the opening of popular dance halls and dance-hall chains everywhere in the British Isles. It can thus be said that ballroom dancing is now fully demo-cratized, in the sense that the best facilities are within the reach of all, and that the same dances are performed regardless of social class position. The 'ultimate' in democratic dance-forms has perhaps been reached with contemporary 'modern beat' dancing. Here the only barrier is that of age group. Since no special style has to be learnt and no particular steps have been handed down by tradition, young people of widely varying background, experience and education can join in freely if they so wish.

There is still, however, a great gulf between *where* the different social classes dance, and how much they pay. The 'deb.-type' young girls and their partners, for example, who do the modern dances at Annabel's or at the Saddle Room, or who dance more formally at Queen Charlotte's Ball are enjoying the same dances as the shop assistants and typists at the local discothèque or Palais, but they will never meet. This is inevitable, and taken completely for granted, in our society where class boundaries are fluid and fluctuating but where, for that very reason, consciousness of class goes very deep.

(3) *Social prestige and the social dance*

In medieval times it was a mark of courtly grace to dance well. In fourteenth-century England, Chaucer's squire could 'juste and eke dance and well pourtraie and write' and indeed from the Middle Ages to mid-nineteenth century there was no break in the attitude that skill in dancing was one of the accomplishments which carried great social prestige.

In the late Victorian era this ceased to be true. To dance with skill and grace was no longer the hallmark of a gentleman; at its mildest, it was distinctly bad form and at its worst was indicative of a rake or gigolo.

This reversal of social attitudes was originally due to the influence of evangelical religion on all classes of society, resulting in the outward preserving of the respectabilities of a sober, industrious and serious way of life. But the fact that dancing was at this time be-coming a pastime available to the masses contributed greatly to its loss of social prestige especially as the masses rapidly became much better dancers than their social betters. Now that dancing is available to all, any social cachet that may still remain applies only to *where* one dances and not *what* or *how*.

(4) *Movement, gesture and the social dance*

Since, at the outset of the study, dancing was defined in terms of rhythmical movements, a word has to be said about the way in which changes in movement and gesture of the social dance correlate with changes in society.

In many instances, the movement of the social dance can be seen to reflect the movements of contemporary everyday life, at any rate for those classes in society who dance. This can be seen very clearly in the '*révérences*' or bows and the stately slow tread of the Basse Danse and also in the bows, curtseys and tiny precise steps of the minuet. (The movements of the dance are of course dictated to a considerable extent by another aspect of the culture pattern – the clothes currently in fashion.) The mirroring of the movements of everyday life can equally well be seen in the 'natural walking movement' of the one-step of the 1920s, in the 'shaking hands' position of the partners in jive, and in many figures of the ballroom rumba which represent such everyday Cuban movements as stepping on cockroaches, or walking round the rims of discarded cart-wheels.

'Movement always tells the truth', says Martha Graham, a statement which must mean more than the mere reflection of everyday life. The dance-sociologist would take this to mean that the movements of the social dance are an expression not only of contemporary life, but also of the mood of the times: whether the movement is that of the dignified Basse Danse and pavane, the leaps and whirls of La Volta, the mincing intricate steps of the minuet, the casual walk of the one-step and early foxtrot, the contortions of the twist or the twitchings of the shake.

It would undoubtedly be too facile to see in the movements of twist and shake and their successors a reflection of a 'mixed-up', drug-taking younger generation, though the analysis is tempting, particularly in the case of the tense jerkiness of the shake. Observations along these lines can only be speculative, and any analysis of the sixties must wait until the decade can be seen in perspective.

(5) *Social and political history, culture diffusion and the social dance*

At all periods a close relationship can be seen between dance-history and social and political history, particularly when it involves the movement of peoples. This is illustrated by such examples as: the coming of the carole and estampie to England following the Albigensian massacre in Provence in 1208; the influence of the captured French nobles during the Hundred Years' War on the shaping of the Basse Danse in England; the setback to social dancing and the concentration on 'indoor' forms during the period of the Commonwealth; the upsurge of English interest in Scottish dances following the repeal in 1781 of the 1746 Act of Proscription, and the prowess of the Scots in the Peninsular Wars; the artificial prolongation of the life of the minuet in England by émigré French aristocrats; the success of the polka, polonaise, mazurka and redowa after the Polish Revolution of 1831; the innovations brought into the social dance by the arrival of American troops in both World Wars; and, finally, the institution of Negro slavery in North America, South America and the West Indies giving rise to such different developments as jazz and jazz dances in the North, Latin American music and dancing in the South, and the ska in Jamaica, subsequently to form the basis of the shake in Britain.

Functional Analysis

There now remains the task of analysing the functions of social dancing for the period in question in terms of the four major problems enumerated in the Introduction (Chapter I).

It is clear from the outset that dancing, in this context, will not be found to be a functional pre-requisite for survival, as was the case with tribal society. Nevertheless, as dancing is seen to form a regular and recurrent pattern of activity throughout the period, it is not unreasonable to look for the possible functions it fulfils, albeit of a less important order.

In so far as the social dance, in the period under review, reflects the structure of social stratification it clearly contributes to 'pattern maintenance' in society and also to the furthering of 'integration' in terms of patterns of authority and common values. This contribution to pattern maintenance and common values is further borne out by the fact that dance-forms change – for example from 'open' couple to 'closed' couple as the sex attitudes of society alter. In addition, social dancing has a distinct 'socializing' function in that it helps adjustment to normal social life, particularly between the sexes.*

* This aspect is brought out in many of the questionnaire replies, Part III.

The connection of dancing with the general social function of 'role differentiation' is shown by the fact that throughout the period men and women have performed different roles in the social dance (except for contemporary teenage 'modern' dancing). In particular, in so far as the 'couple dance' is concerned, the man has always 'led' and the woman has 'followed', in accordance with the norms of a masculine-dominated society. Now that male and female roles (amongst young people) are much less clearly differentiated it is of great interest that their social dancing no longer needs to discriminate between the sexes, i.e. both boys and girls dance in the same style and there is no need for partners, and hence no need for 'leading' and 'following'.

One of the functions which dancing most clearly fulfils is that of 'tension management'. In the period under review, this emerges clearly in the increased enthusiasm for dancing in times of war and of post-war social upheaval. The particular contribution that group dancing makes to the solution of this problem has already been remarked, in the revival of 'Old Time', square and country-dancing in the early days of the Second World War.

Of all societal goals, the most fundamental is surely that society should reproduce itself. Here, too, social dancing can be seen indirectly to have a functional aspect. In primitive societies, dancing is frequently openly erotic, sexually exciting and leads directly to 'mate selection'. In 'civilized' society, social dancing is more aptly termed 'sub-erotic', but the sexual ingredient is no less essential for being less obvious. From the point of view of 'mate selection', dancing has always been one of the recognized ways of bringing young people of different sexes together. Eric Morley, a director of Mecca, has estimated that sixty per cent of marriages originate on the dance floor, whether it be Saturday night at the Palais or a coming-out ball at the Savoy, pointing out that: 'The British are very free, but also very conventional. A boy can't approach a girl in the street but he can at a dance, and it is part of the code of the dance hall that she can say no if she wants to.'[1]

A survey carried out on marriages contracted in England in the fifties, while not bearing out this high estimated percentage, does in fact show that, in the age group sixteen to twenty-four, more brides first met their future husbands at a dance than in any other way.[2] In this connection, it is interesting that there are 3,000 to 4,000 regular dance halls in Britain and that approximately 6,000,000 (mostly young people under twenty-five) go dancing every week.[3]

Finally, people dance not only to make social contacts but also 'for fun' – for the pure pleasure in motor activity and expressive body movement. This 'function' may not be in any way comparable to the function that dancing has in primitive society, but it is nevertheless an important factor in explaining the universality and the persistence of dancing as a pastime, especially if allied with the view, expressed in Chapter II, that this method of expression is part of man's innate biological make-up.

PART III
SURVEY

XVII
Preface to Survey

Of the making of surveys there is no end, and of many it could be said that 'nothing has a drift or a relation; nothing has a history or a promise. Everything stands by itself, and comes and goes in its turn, like the shifting scenes of a show . . .'[1] The intention of the present survey is to avoid this charge of 'unrelatedness' by providing a specific integration of empirical research and social theory.

In preceding chapters, consideration has been given to many hypotheses with regard to the social dance and society, couched within the context of structural/functionalist sociological theory and studied historically. The relationship between the social dance and other aspects of society is, however, a matter which lends itself not only to socio-historical enquiry but also to contemporary research – a fact which makes a survey such as this necessary for the sake of completeness. Those hypotheses which relate to past ages can be studied only on the basis of documentation, but any hypothesis relating to the contemporary scene can undoubtedly be clarified by first-hand empirical enquiry. Two major hypotheses of the latter type have been put forward in Part II:

(1) The hypothesis that the present-day changed style of teenage dancing can be interrelated with certain concomitant changes in society.

(2) The hypothesis of a basic similarity between modern beat dancing and the dancing of primitive societies.

One purpose, therefore, of the present survey (a purpose which comes within the broader aim of collecting the fullest possible data on the dancing habits and attitudes of young people) is to discover whether empirical research confirms, refutes or alters any of these hypotheses.

As well as being 'theory-testing', surveys can of course be 'theory-generating'. With this in mind, a secondary purpose of the survey is to find out whether, in this instance, empirical research throws up fresh hypotheses, which in turn may suggest new theories and fresh lines of research.

Both of these purposes have, in some considerable measure, been served by the research data. The extent to which further light is thrown on the first two hypotheses is discussed in section 7.1. The measure of confirmation given to the second hypothesis would suggest further sociological research directed to discovering the forces and constraints in advanced industrial society which lead its young people to seek satisfactions and self-expression in ways more typical of primitive society. Finally, the findings with regard to individual differences between (a) keen dancers and non-dancers; and (b) 'ballroom' dancers and 'beat' dancers, suggest further inter-disciplinary research into the links between personality structure, environment, and the need (or lack of need) for these particular motility patterns.

XVIII
The Survey*

1. Previous Surveys

Over the past twenty years there have been a number of investigations[1] into the leisure activities and interests of young people, some of which have touched, *inter alia*, on dancing. These studies indicate that, over the past fifteen years or so, there has been a marked increase of interest in dancing. M. Stewart, for example, who investigated the leisure activities of school-children in the same part of Essex in 1946[2] and in 1958[3] has pointed out that, over the twelve years in question, dancing, like record-playing, had become a 'regular pastime' for large numbers of school-children.[4] Similarly, T. Veness, in an enquiry conducted in 1956[5] into young peoples' spare-time activities found that, in comparison with other social activities mentioned, interest in dancing was high for modern school and technical school girls, particularly the latter. She concludes that 'it is probable that interest in dancing has risen considerably over the past decade (of which our investigation comes in the middle).'

In 1950 L. T. Wilkins[6] found that 43% of male adolescents and 17% of female (age range 15–19), in Britain, were not at all interested in dancing. By way of comparison, the Crowther Survey[7] carried out in the summer of 1957, has the following evidence for participation in dancing:

TYPE OF ACTIVITY AND NUMBER OF EVENINGS
SPENT ON IT DURING WEEK PRIOR TO INTERVIEW

	Dancing		
	One evening %	Two evenings %	Three or more evenings %
Grammar and Technical School-leavers			
Girls	30	13	5
Boys	25	16	10
Modern School-leavers			
Girls	25	11	7
Boys	25	11	8

* A greatly abridged version of this Survey first appeared in 'Dance Teacher', February 1968.

It is perhaps difficult to make a direct comparison between Wilkins (1950) and Crowther (1957) but, bearing in mind that the interviewing for the Crowther Survey took place during the season least associated with dancing and that the figures relate to active participation in one specified week, it would appear that, compared with the Wilkins figures, the Crowther Survey shows that in the intervening years there was a considerable development among boys of interest in dancing, 51 % of grammar and technical school-leavers and 44 % of modern school-leavers having spent one or more evenings dancing in the week prior to the interview.

All previous surveys have included dancing, if at all, as one of many social activities and have of necessity been cursory and generalized in their treatment of this topic. The authors of the Crowther Report are aware of this, and point out,[8] with reference to the figures for 'Sports', 'Dancing' and 'Cinema': 'It is possible that a much more detailed investigation than was practicable within the scope of this survey would reveal differences of degree and quality, in the activities of the various groups, which do not emerge in the very generalized outline of leisure activities given here.'

To provide such a detailed investigation, albeit on a small scale, with reference to dancing was one of the tasks of the present survey.

2. The Present Survey

2.1. PURPOSE

The overall aim of this survey was to find out as much as possible about the part played by dancing in the lives of young people* in contemporary society. So far as is known, it is the first detailed investigation into teenage† dancing. The *specific* aims of the survey were to get information on the following points:

	QUESTIONNAIRE
(i) The frequency of teenage dancing	Question (1)
(ii) To what extent is 'ballroom dancing' excluded from their pattern of dancing?	Question (2)
(iii) Is this exclusion (where it occurs) voluntary or not?	Question (3)
(iv) To what extent do they find partners unnecessary?	Question (4)

---

* Defined as, roughly, within age-group 13–23. Twenty-four (5·7%) of the total were somewhat older, falling within age-range 24–30. (See footnote on page 140).
† 'Teenage' is used here sociologically rather than literally. (See note above).

(v) What is their general motivation for going dancing?	Question (5)
(vi) Where does the enjoyment come from?	Question (6)
(vii) To what extent do they regard the modern beat dances as belonging exclusively to their generation?	Question (7)
(viii) What needs and drives find satisfaction and outlet in this style of dancing?	Question (8) plus Interview
(ix) In what way do 'ballroom dances' fail to satisfy these?	Question (9) plus Interview
(x) Is there a link-up between these needs and drives and the nature of present-day society?	Interview
(xi) What is the break-down in terms of age, sex, educational background and socio-economic class for the answers to points (i) to (x) above?	Question (10)

2.2. METHOD

The method used was that of postal questionnaire,* followed up, in some cases by an informal interview, incorporating the Eysenck Personality Inventory.† Three pilot studies were made, two with polytechnic students, and one with working teenagers at a youth club before the final draft of the questionnaire was decided upon. With each study, the form was progressively simplified, some additions were made to question (2), and the instructions were made more explicit.

The sample was drawn from young people in every major type of educational establishment within the I.L.E.A., catering for the age-group 13 to 23, viz: secondary school; college of further education (day college); college of higher education (area college); polytechnic (regional college). The sample thus draws upon schoolgirls, working teenagers (boys and girls) in part-time further education, girls doing a full-time secretarial course, boys and girls doing a full-time business studies course, and polytechnic students (predominantly male) doing a full-time degree or equivalent course. Details are given in Table 1 overleaf.

Sampling was achieved in the following way. In the case of the college of further education (boys and girls) and the polytechnic, full access was allowed to the college records, which enabled me to take a random sample of every fifth student's name and address (excluding, for the polytechnic, part-time and post-graduate students).

* See Appendix K.
† See Appendix L.

139

The Survey

In this way, 400 questionnaires, accompanied by letter, were sent out: 200 to polytechnic students, 100 to 'day release girls' and 100 to 'day release boys'. One 'batch' of reminders was sent, respectively, to the polytechnic sample and to the 'day release boys'. The final number of replies received is shown in Table 1 below.

It proved impossible to follow this sampling method in the case of the other two educational establishments (the school and the college of higher education), and the writer had to have recourse to friends within, who agreed to distribute questionnaires to certain

TABLE 1

The Sample

Educational Category	Age-range	Sex	Number of replies received		Total
			F	M	(F plus M)
Secondary Technical School	13–15	F	29	—	29
College of Further Education. P.T. 'Day Release'	16–21	M		54	
		F	53		107
College of Higher Education. Post 'A' level: Secretarial F.T.	18–23	F	55		55
College of Higher Education. Post 'O' level. Business Studies F.T.	16–21	M		42	
		F	46		88
Polytechnic. Degree level F.T.	17–23+	M		134*	
		F	6		140
Totals			189	230	419

NOTES ON THE TABLE

  (i) Abbreviations: P.T. – Part time. F.T. – Full time.

 (ii) The secretarial course at the college of higher education requires one 'A' level pass for entry: in practice most students have more than one. The business studies course requires four 'O' level passes.

  * Twenty-four of these fell within the age-range 24–30.

classes, and to collect them (in class time). This method provided for 100% return of questionnaires, as no student proved unwilling to co-operate. The number of replies is shown in Table 1.

Subsequently, all the information (with the exception of the answers to the 'open-ended' questions) was coded, transferred to punched cards and sorted by machine. The answers to the 'open-ended' questions were then analysed and a summary made, according to the pattern which emerged.

It was decided to study the polytechnic group more intensively by means of a follow-up interview. The returned questionnaires fell roughly into four categories: (a) the non-dancers, (b) the keen dancers (defined as those who liked both 'beat' *and* 'ballroom' dancing and whose reply to question (1) was 4 or above), (c) those who liked modern 'beat' but disliked 'ballroom' dances, (d) those who liked 'ballroom' dances but disliked modern 'beat'. A random sample of five students in each category was taken and a letter was sent asking for their further co-operation. Unfortunately, by this time some students were involved in their final examinations and others had already gone down. In seven cases it proved impossible to get a personal interview, but these seven co-operated by letter, answering a short list of questions and returning a completed E.P.1. The remaining thirteen students were personally interviewed. The interviews were informal, but guided and, on average, lasted fifteen minutes, excluding the time taken to complete the E.P.I.

2.3. LIMITATIONS OF THE METHOD

The first and most obvious limitation is the problem inseparable from all postal questionnaire surveys – that of the 'non-responders', especially in so far as this may mean a bias in the forms returned. Commonsense would lead one to suppose that the non-responders would be less interested and involved in the subject of the questionnaire than the responders, and on this assumption the returns would be biased in the direction of those interested in dancing. Particular note was taken of the late responders, and of those who responded only after a reminder, on the assumption that they might have something in common with the non-responders. These were not found to differ in any particular way from those who responded normally, and it may therefore be assumed that any bias that exists can be only slight.

The second limitation is that the sample contains no working teenagers, other than those who are attending part-time further education. In fact, strenuous efforts were made to obtain access to a more representative list of working teenagers through two channels: (1) school records of school-leavers, and (2) records of young people registered for insurance purposes (held by the Youth Employment Service). Clearly, a random sample drawn from either of these sources would include working teenagers not participating in further education. To this end, letters were written to various authorities and interviews attended with representatives of the I.L.E.A. in May 1966. After an interval of two months a flat refusal was given on both fronts – no access was to be permitted either to school-leavers' records or to Youth Employment files.

It is, however, worth pointing out in this connection that the recent publication: *Adolescents and Morality* by E. M. and M. Eppel concerns itself only with young people attending 'day release' courses. Professor Sprott in the foreword[9] remarks: 'Anyone who protests about the unrepresentativeness of the sample must back up his argument by giving evidence that the "focal concerns" of young people who do *not* attend day-release courses is significantly different from the "focal concerns" of those that do' and continues: 'I do not feel that the sample is unrepresentative . . .'

Of much greater relevance to the point at issue in the present study are the findings contained in the Crowther Report on the leisure activities of school-leavers, where a comparison is made,[10] *inter alia*, between boys and girls who have had *no* full- or part-time further education, and those who are attending part-time classes. So far as frequency of dancing is concerned the following conclusion is drawn: 'It is interesting to note that dancing more than once a week did not on the whole occur less frequently amongst those participating in further education' (as compared with those not attending part-time classes). It thus seems reasonable to assume that, so far as dancing is concerned, a sample of teenagers drawn from those attending part-time further education is not markedly unrepresentative of working teenagers as a whole.

A further limitation is the absence of a sample of secondary technical boys for purposes of comparison with the girls. This omission is explained by the attitude, already outlined, of the I.L.E.A. Similarly, the inconsistency of sampling methods between, on the one hand the polytechnic and the college of further education and, on the other hand, the secondary technical school and the college of higher education is entirely explained by the difficulties of gaining access to records: difficulties so great that any offer of help had to be grasped even at the cost of sampling consistency.

It must, however, be added here that the attitude of the students concerned in the survey was in striking contrast to that of officialdom.

I would like to pay tribute to their interest and co-operation, as shown in the pilot studies, in the interviews and also in the answering of the questionnaires. The fact that out of 420 returned questionnaires only one was frivolous speaks for itself.

2.4. RESULTS

The results are set out in Tables 2 to 32, Appendix J.

2.5. Discussion of Results

(In the Tables percentages are shown to one decimal place: in the discussion the nearest whole number is sometimes taken.)

2.5.1. FREQUENCY (TABLES 2 AND 3)

(Question (1) on Questionnaire).

2.5.1.1. Frequency and Educational Category

The figures show that the great majority of young people represented by the sample have some interest in dancing. If one takes the category 'once a year or less' as evidence of lack of interest, only 9% (approx.) of the whole sample comes under this heading.* The highest percentage showing lack of interest is in the educational category 'Day Release Boys' (17%) and the lowest is to be found in their counterparts, 'Day Release Girls', the figure here being nil.

If one takes the category 'once a week or more' (Table 3) as evidence of considerable interest, the secondary technical schoolgirls lead the field (81%) followed by 'Day Release Girls' (64%). Polytechnic degree students come lowest (23%).

There are interesting differences in the *modes* for the categories (see Table 2), viz.:

Secondary technical schoolgirls	Several times a week
'Day Release' girls	Several times a week
'Secretarial Course' girls	Once a week
'Business Studies' boys	Once a week
'Business Studies' girls	Once a month
Polytechnic students	Once a month
'Day Release' boys	{ Once a month
	{ Once a year or less

---

* Not everybody coming under this heading is necessarily totally uninterested –
e.g. one respondent who ringed (8) in question (1) in the questionnaire added an explanatory note 'Have taken many lessons but just have no sense of rhythm'.

143

Broadly speaking, there is a pattern of agreement between the figures for 'once a year or less', 'once a week or more' and the modes, giving the following order of interest in dancing. The order goes from 1 – the most interested category – to 7 – the least interested.

1. Secondary technical schoolgirls
2. 'Day Release' girls
3. 'Business Studies' boys
4. 'Secretarial Course' boys
5. 'Business Studies' girls
6. 'Day Release' boys
7. Polytechnic degree students

The smallness of the sample of secondary technical schoolgirls precludes much discussion of the fact that they come out as the category most interested, but it is worth mentioning again that the survey carried out by T. Veness showed technical schoolgirls (as compared with modern and grammar) to have a particularly keen interest in dancing. It is also worth bearing in mind that 'frequency' of dancing does *not* (see the wording of the questionnaire) necessarily mean 'going out dancing' or to 'dances'. The fact that the polytechnic degree students come at the bottom of the Table is not surprising, in view of the more demanding nature of their studies.

2.5.1.2. Frequency and Sex

Taking the sample as a whole, and retaining the broad groups 'once a week or more: once a year or less', Table 3 gives the following comparison:

A *Once a week or more*   Males 30%   Females 51%
 Once a year or less   Males 13%   Females 5%
 Both these comparisons are significant at the ·01 level and indicate that girls have a greater interest than boys in dancing. This is confirmed by the figures for the homogeneous sample 'Day Release' boys and 'Day Release' girls, age-range 16–21, thus: (Table 3).

B *Once a week or more*   Males 32%   Females 64%
 Once a year or less   Males 17%   Females 0%
 These figures are also significant at the ·01 level. Interestingly enough, this appears to be contradicted by the figures from the equally homogeneous sample 'Full time: Business Studies Boys and Girls', age-range 16–21 (Table 3) thus:

C   *Once a week or more*   Males 50%   Females 32%
   Once a year or less   Males 4·8%   Females 8·7%
but statistical analysis shows that neither of these comparisons shows a significant difference.

An amalgamation of the 'Day Release' and the 'Business Studies' samples (giving a total of 195 boys and girls, ranging in age from 16 to 21) produces the following result:

D   *Once a week or more*   Males 39·5%   Females 49·4%
   Once a year or less   Males 11·4%   Females 4·0%
but here again the differences are not statistically significant.

There is thus a certain amount of support for the general hypothesis that girls have a greater interest than boys in dancing, taking frequency as a criterion, but in view of the figures for C and D above, caution should be shown in making any predictions based on this.

2.5.1.3. Frequency and Socio-economic Class
(Tables 4 and 5)

The polytechnic students were asked to state occupation of father in order that they could be classified broadly into socio-economic classes. The classification adopted was the simplified structure frequently used in market research, viz.:

   (i) Higher professional, senior civil servants, etc.
  (ii) Middle professional, grammar school teachers, etc.
 (iii) Lower professional, bank clerks, lower grade civil servants, etc.
 (iv) Skilled workers: supervisory grades
  (v) Unskilled workers
 (vi) Casual workers: those on National Assistance, etc.

It must be pointed out that the analysis in Table 4 should be taken more as a general indication of socio-economic status than as an accurate picture, since it depends on (1) a sometimes vague, and perhaps occasionally 'upgraded' description of occupation, and (2) my subjective assessment of that description in terms of the socio-economic classification (i) to (vi) above.

With this proviso in mind the figures were subjected to statistical analysis. In categories (ii), (iii) and (iv) the sample sizes were assumed to be large enough to justify normal confidence limits. For categories (i) and (v) which were very small, the significance was read from Poisson probabilities without calculating formal limits. These procedures indicated that the only result of any significance (with regard to link-up with socio-economic class) was that for category (v). In spite of the smallness of the sample here, the result was very unlikely to have been produced by chance. This can only be regarded, however, as a shred of evidence for the association of greater frequency of dancing with an unskilled working-class background, as compared with other socio-economic groups.

Table 5 – For reasons of policy, the secondary technical school-girls, the day release students and the full-time students in the college of higher education were not asked questions about their fathers' occupation. No precise data therefore is available, but, broadly speaking, it may be assumed that the day release students are predominantly from a working class background, and the full-time business studies students from a middle class or lower-middle class background. It is, therefore, interesting to compare results for the two age-groups 16–21 (see Table 5). This Table, of course, simply presents again, from a different aspect, some of the figures already discussed under 'Frequency and Sex'.

If the broad assumptions about social background are accepted, these results might appear to show a greater interest in dancing in middle class *boys* than working class *boys*, and, contrariwise, a greater interest on the part of working class *girls* compared with middle class *girls*. Statistical analysis however, shows that the differences obtained in Table 5 are *not* significant. These results (taken in conjunction with those for Table 4) would appear to indicate that, in general, the social class or socio-economic status of young people has little predictive value today with regard to frequency of dancing.

2.5.1.4. *Frequency: and Comparison with Crowther and Wilkins*

Table 3 affords a certain comparison with the Crowther Survey in 1957. The figures for girls who dance once a week or more (sec. tech. 81%, 'Day Release' 64%, secretarial 42% and 'Business Studies' 33%) do not differ appreciably (except for the secondary technical) from the figures in the Crowther Survey (see Table 1, page 140) viz.: grammar and technical school-leavers 48%, modern school-leavers 43%. (The 'Day Release' category in the present survey would undoubtedly contain girls both from secondary technical and modern schools). The figure for the secondary technical schoolgirls cannot usefully be compared with the Crowther figures since he does not have a separate heading for this category.

The same holds good for boys. Statistical analysis shows that the figures in the present survey – F.T. 'Business Studies' boys 50%, P.T. 'Day Release' boys 31%, do not differ significantly from the Crowther percentages of boys who spent one evening or more a week dancing, viz.: grammar and technical school-leavers 51%, modern school-leavers 43%. (No direct comparison can be made between the polytechnic students and the Crowther samples.)

There is, however, a striking difference between the figures in the present survey for those who dance 'once a year or less', viz.: Boys 13%, Girls 5% and L. T. Wilkins' findings in 1950 that 43% of adolescent males and 17% of adolescent females were not at all interested in dancing.

It seems reasonably clear that this comparison supports the hypothesis that in the fifties young people (particularly boys) came to have a much greater interest in dancing than had been the case before. This trend ties in with the coming of rock and roll music and dancing and has, of course, continued into the sixties, associated with the general upsurge of pop music, groups, and the popularity of the twist, shake and 'beat' dances.

2.5.2.1. Degree of Interest in Various Dances
(*Table 13, Questions (2) and (3)*)

Table 13, which has been compiled from the data in Tables 6 to 12 inclusive, shows, for each educational category, the three dances most commonly danced by members of that group, the dance most frequently shown as their first preference, and the dance most frequently shown as the one they would like to learn.

'Shake or Beat' falls for all groups in the category of the three dances most commonly danced. It is danced by nearly all the secondary technical schoolgirls, the secretarial course girls, the day release girls, the business studies girls and the business studies boys – the percentages being, respectively, 93, 91, 91, 89 and 89. But in the case of the day release boys and the polytechnic students it is danced by only 63%. Slightly more boys in the day release group dance rock (67%) and twist (65%) than dance shake or beat, and the same percentage (63) dance jive. In the case of the polytechnic students, considerably more dance both waltz (74%) and twist (72%).

In all categories except day release boys and girls and polytechnic students, shake or beat is most frequently shown as first preference. But there are considerable differences within the categories putting it first, thus:

Secondary technical schoolgirls	97%
Business studies girls	61%
Day release girls	51%
Business studies boys	45%
Secretarial course girls	38%

The dance most commonly shown as first preference by the day release boys is slow blues (26% putting this first), followed by shake or beat (22%) (see Table 18), and for polytechnic students rock (21%) followed by jive (19%) and then by shake or beat (17%) (see Table 12). The relative unpopularity of 'shake or beat' in the polytechnic group can be explained by the higher proportion of older students (see Table 18 for correlation with age) but this cannot be the reason in the case of the day release boys.

A remarkable fact, which no one could have predicted, is the emergence of the tango as the dance most frequently shown to be the one young people would like to add to their repertoire. Apart from the youngest age-group – the secondary technical schoolgirls – and the business studies boys (very few of whom wish to learn any new dances – see Table 21) the tango holds pride of place as the dance which people wish to learn. The reasons for this can only be speculative, but they are probably to be found in the arresting nature of tango music and the sense of drama and temperament associated with this dance. Four (14%) of the secondary technical schoolgirls indicate that they would like to learn the waltz, which shows, at any rate, that they have not unanimously rejected 'the past' in dancing. The same number would like to learn 'folk', but as they all specify 'Zorba's dance' here, this is 'folk' in a very modern sense of the word.

2.5.2.2. Degree of Interest in Ballroom Dancing (Table 14)

Table 14 shows at a glance the extent to which ballroom dancing has been 'rejected' by various categories of the young. Tango has been included since technically it is a 'standard ballroom dance' but, as it is rather rarely danced by the general public and does not have the same 'image' as the other ballroom dances (hence probably the interest in learning it, already mentioned) it might be better to exclude it for purposes of discussion.

The percentage who 'have no interest' was taken from the data in Tables 6 to 12. This comprises the people who indicate in answer to Question (2) that they do not dance the particular dance and in Question (3) do *not* mention it as one they would like to do/learn.

The following Table shows the 'rank order of rejection' for each of the ballroom dances excluding tango, ranging from (1) (the group showing the highest percentage of rejection) to (7) (the group showing the lowest percentage).

It is clear that the youngest age-group (13 to 15 secondary technical schoolgirls) are the least interested, as might have been predicted, and the older students (polytechnic and secretarial girls: 18 to 23 plus) the most interested. There is little doubt from the Table that the business studies boys and girls are less interested than the part-time day release boys and girls of the same age-group (16 to 21), but why this should be is not so clear. The explanation may be that the day-release boys and girls, being 'working teenagers' tend to identify more with the 'adult world' and to leave the 'teenage sub-culture' behind earlier than the full-time students.

WALTZ	%	FOXTROT	%	QUICKSTEP	%
(1) Sec. tech. girls	55	Sec. tech. girls	93	Sec. tech. girls	93
(2) Bus. st. boys	43	Bus. st. girls	81	Bus. st. girls	81
(3) Bus. st. girls	35	Bus. st. boys	79	Bus. st. boys	69
(4) Day rel. girls	34	Day rel. girls	76	Day rel. boys	56
(5) Day rel. boys	30	Secretarial girls	65	Day rel. girls	47
(6) Secretarial girls	29	Day rel. boys	63	Polytech. st.	39
(7) Polytechnic st.	20	Polytechnic st.	56	Secretarial girls	38

The Table also shows that the *waltz* is by no means rejected, more than half the young people in every group except the youngest (and almost half of them) either dancing it or wishing to learn.

The *foxtrot* is decidedly 'out', being firmly rejected by more than 60% in every category except the polytechnic, and even there by over 50%.

The *quickstep* comes midway, being rejected by more than 50% in four groups, but surprisingly popular ('accepted' by more than 60%) amongst the secretarial girls and the polytechnic students.

Table 15 indicates quite specifically the percentage of young people in each group who 'do not do' any or all of the 'standard four' ballroom dances, but who would like to learn/do them. Percentages for the waltz are generally low compared with the other dances, but this is because, relative to the other ballroom dances, it is already well-known. Once again, the fact that the business studies groups have a lower interest in ballroom dancing than the day release groups is confirmed.

2.5.2.3. *Degree of Interest in Latin American Social Dancing* (*Table 15*)

The information here was compiled in the same way and on the same basis as that for Table 14. 'Lack of interest' here, however, cannot be taken to mean 'rejection' as was assumed with the ballroom dances. It is just as likely to mean that the person has no idea what the dance is, since Latin American dancing is still very much a minority interest. Indeed, the appreciably higher figures for interest in the 'cha-cha' (shown by every one of the seven groups) can be explained by the simple fact that this type of dance music is more frequently played than the others.

However, a 'rank order of lack of interest' in terms of (1) percentage least interested, to (7) percentage most interested, is of value in comparing the relative penetration of this comparatively recent form of social dancing amongst the various groups.

	SAMBA	%	RUMBA	%	CHA-CHA	%
(1)	Bus. st. boys	92·9	Bus. st. boys	88·1	Bus. st. boys	54·7
(2)	Day rel. boys	79·6	Bus. st. girls	80·5	Day rel. boys	51·8
(3)	Bus st. girls	73·9	Day rel. girls	80·5	Polytechnic st.	39·3
(4)	Day rel. girls	73·9	Day rel. boys	79·6	Secretarial girls	34·5
(5)	Polytechnic st.	66·5	Polytechnic st.	76·4	Bus. st. girls	34·5
(6)	Secret. girls	65·4	Secretarial girls	72·7	Sec. tech. girls	34·5
(7)	Sec. tech. girls	65·4	Sec. tech. girls	72·7	Day rel. girls	32·6

The two points which emerge most clearly from this table are (i) the considerably greater popularity of the 'cha-cha' as compared with rumba and samba and (ii) the greater degree of interest, in general, in Latin American social dancing amongst the secondary technical schoolgirls and the secretarial course girls as compared with the other groups.

2.5.2.4.* *'Modern Beat' Dancing: Degree of Interest and Extent to which 'Partnerless' (Questions (2) and (4))*

1 Educational Categories (Table 16)

This Table (repeating some of the information in Table 13) shows for each educational category the percentage who dance the modern beat dances, and also the percentage who, on occasion, dance without a partner. All beat dancing is 'solo', to the extent that there is no contact with the partner, but many young people dance without any specific partner at all, and this is the point which it is desired to investigate here.

The two categories showing the highest percentages for 'partnerless dancing' are the secondary technical schoolgirls (72%) and the day release girls (64%). The two categories with the lowest are the secretarial course girls and the polytechnic students (with 13% and

* The questionnaire sent out early in 1966 specifies 'Shake or any Modern "Beat" Dance'. The discussion will use the generic term 'beat' or 'modern beat'.

14% respectively). There is undoubtedly a correlation here with age (see Table 19 for confirmation) and, in all probability, not only a correlation but also a causal relation, at any rate so far as the secondary technical schoolgirls are concerned. It seems reasonable to suppose that secretarial girls (age-range 18 to 23) and polytechnic students (age-range 18 to 23 plus) are more likely to have partners when they go dancing than are the schoolgirls, age-range 13 to 15. This would not entirely explain the high percentage of day release girls who on occasion dance without partners, since they fall within the age range of 16 to 21, but the explanation here is probably the fact (demonstrated many times already) that this group is particularly keen on dancing. An additional factor which might well enter into the low percentages shown here for secretarial girls and polytechnic students is the possible association of solo gyrations with 'young mods' (see Comment 13, Table 32) and as such hardly in keeping with the dignity of would-be secretaries or the maturity of degree students.

2 Sex *(Table 17)*

The figures in Table 16 suggest that there is a sex difference with regard both to the popularity of beat dancing and the acceptability of dancing it without a partner. To test this, Table 17 analyses the figures in terms of the entire age-group, 16 to 21, ignoring the other groups, in order to keep the age-factor constant.

The figures in Table 17 are significant at the ·01 level, which ties in with the fact that, even in 1966, more females than males go dancing and also with the fact that, even when they do go to dances, the males do not always dance. (See the censorious Comment 8 under 'Reasons for liking Ballroom', Table 27). This is not intended to imply necessarily that all the girls dancing 'solo' would prefer to have partners. (See Comments 1 to 5 under 'Reasons for liking Beat', Table 27).

3 Class *(Table 18)*

This table shows the breakdown of beat dancing and 'partnerless' dancing in terms of class, again making the assumption that the day release sample is working-class and the business studies sample middle or lower-middle class.

The comparisons, 90·6% working class (female) with 89·1% middle class (female), and 63% working class (male) with 78·6% middle class (male) for those who dance beat dances are not statistically significant. Both comparisons (i.e. male and female working class/ middle class) for those who dance 'partnerless' are however, statistically significant, at the ·01 level.

4 *Age* (*Table 19*)

This table analyses those who dance the beat dances, and also those who dance them sometimes without a partner, in terms of age. There is a very clear connection between age and the likelihood of dancing without a specific partner, as can be seen from the positive correlation of +0·98 obtained by comparing the rank order for age with the rank order for percentages (for each age) who dance without partners. A positive correlation of +0·92 is obtained if a similar comparison is made for age and the total percentages dancing beat dances for every age, and if the age-gradation is made somewhat less fine, as indicated below, an exact positive correlation is obtained, viz.:

Age-group	No. in group	No. dancing beat dances	Percentage
13–15	29	27	93·1
16–18	179	157	87·7
19–21	120	147	81·6
Over 21	64	45	70·3

2.5.3. 'AGE-BAR' OR NOT, FOR MODERN BEAT DANCES (QUESTION 7, TABLE 20)

The most 'tolerant' group is the youngest – the secondary technical schoolgirls – of whom 48% are of the opinion that 'age does not matter'. They are followed by the oldest – the polytechnic students – of whom 44% are of this opinion: put nicely by one student . . . 'If it's not immoral, or illegal – then do it!' The secondary technical schoolgirls may come into the 'tolerant' category simply because they like the beat dances so much that they would not like to deprive any one of such joy, and the polytechnic students because maturity brings a tolerant attitude. Neither of these explanations, however, fits the day release boys whose 'tolerant percentage' (42·5%) is almost the same as that for the polytechnic students. The day release boys do not share the enthusiasm of the secondary technical schoolgirls for these dances, nor are they older than the others in the sample. It may be that many of them are not particularly interested and 'just couldn't care less' whether older people do these dances or not.

The most 'intolerant', or to put it better, perhaps, the most 'age-conscious' group is the business studies girls, of whom only 26% take the view that age does not matter. Taking those who do think age matters, there is a striking consensus of opinion, which is found in every group and most notably in the secretarial girls, the business studies boys and the business studies girls, that these dances are not suitable for those over the age of thirty. The three groups named above, interestingly enough, are all in the same college, but it is rather difficult to see that this could be a relevant factor.

2.5.4. WISH TO LEARN NEW DANCES (QUESTION 4)

This is a suitable point at which to discuss the differences that emerge amongst the groups on the question of whether they wish to learn any dance they do not already do. The questionnaire does not specify 'learn' but it is legitimate to assume that any positive answers here Question (3), imply a willingness to 'learn', even if perhaps only on a 'picking-up' basis by watching others.*

Table 21 – It is interesting that more than half the young people in all but two groups (business studies boys and business studies girls), and more than half of the whole sample, would like to add a new dance to their repertoire from the list given in Question (2). Almost by definition this means a dance other than shake or beat (which requires no learning), although it must be pointed out here that two of the day release girls (see Table 7) and four of the day release boys (see Table 8) did in fact specify 'shake or beat' here. The day release girls prove to have the highest percentage (64) interested in learning something new, closely followed by the secondary technical school-girls (59). These two groups have already been placed second and first respectively in rank order for interest in dancing (see page 144). The remaining five groups can be placed in rank order for wishing to learn something new as follows:

1st Polytechnic
2nd Day release boys
3rd Secretarial girls
4th Business studies girls
5th Business studies boys

* A positive answer here *might* mean that the person knows the dance (e.g. having learnt it, say, at school) and lacks any opportunity for dancing it, but this is unlikely and any such case would probably have been indicated on the form.

This does not in any way follow the rank order for interest in dancing as did the first two categories discussed, but there is an inverse correlation of -0.9 with 'first preference for beat and shake' – thus:

	Wish to learn		First preference Shake or Beat	
%	Rank order	Category	%	Rank order
59	1	Polytechnic	17	5
54	2	Day release boys	22	4
50	3	Secretarial girls	38	3
39	4	Business studies girls	61	1
24	5	Business studies boys	45	2

This inverse correlation, however, does not hold if the secondary technical schoolgirls and the day release girls are included. The explanation of all this may well be that the real enthusiasts can express a marked preference for 'shake and beat' as indeed they do, but are sufficiently interested in dancing to welcome anything new. For the less keen, however, a preference for shake and beat (the easy all-purpose and all-occasion dance) tends to preclude the necessity for, and hence interest in, learning and doing other dances.

2.5.5. REASONS FOR GOING DANCING AND REASONS FOR ENJOYMENT
(QUESTIONS (5) AND (6), TABLES 22 AND 23)

Table 23 makes it clear that 'To meet or be with the opposite sex' is the reason most frequently given first preference by *all* the male groups. It is also quite unmistakably the reason most frequently given first preference by the secondary technical schoolgirls. In *all* the female groups, with the exception of the secondary technical schoolgirls the reason most frequently given first preference is that they enjoy dancing. Perhaps the only comment to make here is that if the girls go dancing because they enjoy it, and the boys go in order to meet the girls, it probably all works out. The schoolgirls are presumably at that stage of adolescence when they are more interested in boys than in anything else. It is interesting that the two reasons which the day release girls most frequently put first do not include 'to meet or be with the opposite sex', the second being 'because a particular group is playing'. This probably ties in with the fact that they come second highest in the list for 'partnerless dancing' (64%), and links up interestingly with some of the answers to the open-ended questions (see particularly (1) to (5) under 'Reasons for liking Beat', Table 27).

It is noteworthy that the reason 'because the dance is run by an organization you belong to' is most frequently put last by every group except the polytechnic students. This seems to bear out one's impression that young people today dislike being organized and value their freedom of movement. The polytechnic students, being older, are likely to have more organizational affiliations and responsibilities. The fact that they most frequently put last 'because a particular group is playing' shows, presumably, that a great many of them have outgrown the phase of enthusiasm for the 'groups'.

Tables 24 and 25 – Question (6) was asked in addition to Question (5) because, in my view, the motivation for going dancing does not necessarily coincide with the reason for enjoyment of the activity. Table 25 looked at in conjunction with Table 23 bears this out for the secondary technical schoolgirls and the day release boys. Both these groups most frequently put first as their motivation for going dancing 'to meet or be with the opposite sex' but when it comes to reasons for enjoying dancing they both most frequently give first preference to 'the music and rhythm'. Apart from these two groups there is a close correspondence between the answers to Question (5) and (6). Thus, the business studies boys and the polytechnic students who in Question (5) most frequently put first: 'to meet or be with the opposite sex' reinforce this in Question (6) by most frequently giving first preference to the 'presence of the opposite sex'. Similarly, the day release girls, the secretarial course girls, and the business studies girls, who in Question (5) most frequently gave first preference to 'enjoyment of dancing' as a motivation, reinforce this in Question (6) by most frequently putting first 'the music and rhythm' as the reason for enjoyment.

Unanimously, all groups most frequently put last the reason 'the steps and movement'. Here – in conjunction with the fact that five out of seven groups most frequently put first 'the music and rhythm' – is empirical evidence in the sixties of the continuing validity of the point made in Chapter X, 'Up to 1910, no matter what the dance, the main attraction lay in the actual steps, and in some cases, the exhilarating movement. After 1910, the main attraction was unquestionably the rhythm . . .'

155

2.5.6. ANSWERS TO OPEN-ENDED QUESTIONS (QUESTIONS (8) AND (9), TABLES 26 TO 32)

Tables 26 to 32 contain the answers given to the open-ended Questions (8) and (9) in the questionnaire. The instruction (b) 'Leave blank if you do not care one way or the other' was inserted to avoid the possibility of producing attitudes where none really exist. It may be assumed, therefore, that all the attitudes expressed in these Tables are genuinely held, and further that the number of reasons produced, under each heading, is a measure of the extent of the general attitude of like/dislike in the sample. It should be pointed out here, however, that the 'number of reasons' is not invariably the same as the number of respondents giving reasons. If a respondent gave two or three quite different reasons in one response, these were enumerated separately, in order that they could be counted for purposes of the summary.

These summaries have been made, wherever appropriate, in the Tables in order to show the general pattern of responses.

The Tables might be regarded as 'speaking for themselves' but a brief discussion of each may serve to highlight certain points.

Secondary Technical Schoolgirls (*Table 26*)

The striking thing here is the unanimity of the group. Even the two non-dancers of beat dances (see Table 3) do not express dislike, since the responses under 'dislike beat' are nil. Twenty-seven reasons are produced (often inarticulate) for liking beat, usually in terms of energetic movement and modern qualities. Nineteen (much more specific) reasons are given for disliking ballroom dancing, generally because of its old-fashioned, square and boring image. The degree of repetition in the answers makes one suspect that there was a certain amount of 'looking to see what someone else has written' (this was a questionnaire done in class), but, even so, it is more likely to be the wording than the attitude that was copied.

Day Release Girls (*Table 27*)

Forty-seven reasons were produced for liking beat dancing, with a certain emphasis on freedom *from* having to have a partner, and a freedom *to* express oneself in a creative way (perhaps summed up by (8): 'You can express how you feel when you dance modern'). Fun and excitement are also stressed but much less emphasis is given to being 'modern' than was the case with the secondary technical schoolgirls.

The Survey

Only one girl in the sample expresses an attitude of dislike for beat dances but she does so in a very uncompromising way: 'They are a waste of energy and look silly'.

Thirty-two reasons were given for liking ballroom dancing – a strong indication that the enthusiasm for beat in this group by no means precludes the enjoyment of the more conventional form of dancing. (This is confirmed by the fact that only eight reasons are found for disliking ballroom dancing, and by Table 14 which shows that waltz and quickstep are reasonably popular). Stress is given in the answers to the more 'interesting steps', to the fact that these dances are graceful and 'look nice', and that one can get to know one's partner. An interesting reply which will be discussed further is (24): 'It closes the gap between old and young if you can dance "their" dances with them'.

Day Release Boys (Table 28)

In comparison with the day release girls, fewer reasons are given for liking beat dancing and ballroom dancing – (27) and (28) respectively, compared with (47) and (32).* This is another indication of the much lower general level of interest in dancing in this group as compared with the girls. It is rather remarkable that more reasons were produced for liking ballroom than beat in this group, but it may be remembered from the discussion of Table 14 that these boys by no means rejected ballroom dancing.

Those who like beat dancing do so because these dances are easy to do, informal, energetic, good fun, and have a strong beat and rhythm. Amongst those who give reasons for liking ballroom dancing there is an interesting stress on its utilitarian aspect, in terms of 'usefulness on social occasions' – e.g. (2): 'It is always handy to know how to do them later on in life'. This seems to be a form of 'anticipatory socialization' with the respondent clearly thinking beyond his present teenage group.

The final point to be made here is that although this group expresses far fewer opinions than the day release girls for 'liking beat' and 'liking ballroom', they have six reasons for 'disliking beat' compared with only one for the day release girls. Once again, this is evidence for the greater popularity of beat dancing with girls than with boys.

* This section is largely impressionistic and detailed statistical analysis is not considered appropriate.

Business Studies Girls (*Table 29*)

Thirty-five reasons are given for 'liking beat' mostly in terms of being easy to do, the music and rhythm and the fun and excitement. It is interesting that, unlike the day release girls, not one mentions the 'creative self-expression' aspect.

Only thirteen reasons are given for liking ballroom dances, mostly in terms of their grace and elegance. As with the day release girls, only one reason is given for disliking beat dances (the self-conscious one of looking and feeling stupid), but many more reasons (eighteen compared with seven) are given for disliking ballroom dancing (in the usual terms of its being out-of-date and requiring lessons).

Business Studies Boys (*Table 30*)

They give thirty reasons for liking beat dancing mostly for the usual reasons of 'letting off steam', the beat and rhythm and excitement, but it is interesting that, for the first time, a quite specific sexual reason appears in several responses: e.g. (18): 'It makes me feel very sexy towards the opposite sex'. This ties in with the fact that this group most frequently gave first preference to the motivation for going dancing: 'to meet or to be with the opposite sex' and also most frequently put first 'the presence of the opposite sex' as a reason for enjoyment, but why this group should be more sexually aware, or possibly just more honest and uninhibited, remains a mystery.

Fourteen reasons are given for liking ballroom dancing, again an indication that the young have by no means entirely rejected these dances 'of the past' (as they are frequently described). The 'usefulness on social occasions' is again brought out here as it was with the other group of boys, aged 16–21.

Compared with the business studies girls, more reasons are given for disliking beat dances (four compared with one) and one boy *dislikes* these dances for their 'sexual manifestations' – thus showing, that with dancing as with everything else, one man's meat is another man's poison.

Fifteen reasons are given for disliking ballroom dancing, stress being laid on its slow, uninteresting and boring characteristics.

Secretarial Course Girls (*Table 30*)

The greater maturity of this group (age-range 18 to 23, compared with 13 to 15, and 16 to 21) and their superior intellectual background ('A' level, compared with 'O' level or less) is reflected in their more articulate and thoughtful answers.

Thirty-two reasons are given for liking beat in the usual terms, but here the element of 'creative self-expression' appears again, e.g. 'You can express yourself without restriction: can dance how you like'. A thoughtful answer which is discussed further is: '*All young people* – therefore not open to criticism from other age-groups.' A very interesting answer which brings out with great clarity an essential difference between this type of dancing and conventional 'ballroom' is (26): 'I can be in the company of my friends and yet they cannot impose themselves on me when dancing'.

Fourteen reasons are given for liking ballroom dancing, mostly in terms of gracefulness and the pleasure of moving with a partner. One answer (19) is unusual, however, and seems to show considerable psychological insight: 'For those who cannot let themselves go – it gives them an opportunity to dance without feeling self-conscious or ridiculous: there is safety in learned steps.'

Ten reasons are given for disliking beat dancing, but none, except possibly (1) is for self-conscious reasons. Seventeen reasons are given for disliking ballroom dancing – mostly in the usual terms, but quite specific mention is made here of dislike of the bands, the music and the rhythm associated with ballroom dancing.

Polytechnic Students (*Table 32*)

Seventy-five reasons are given for liking beat dancing, but it must of course be remembered that this is a sample of 140. The reasons here tend to follow the general pattern but there is rather an emphasis on relief of tension and emotional outlet. As always, the factor of rhythm and beat is stressed – put rather well as (50): 'They allow oneself to wallow in rhythm and to be soaked up to the eyeballs in "music".' Seven 'social and sexual' reasons (rather difficult to disentangle) are given here, but it is perhaps surprising that there should be so few, in view of the fact that this group, like the business studies boys, most frequently gave first preference to 'To meet or be with the opposite sex' as motivation and to 'the presence of the opposite sex' as a reason for enjoying dancing.

Fifty-seven reasons are given for liking ballroom dancing, largely in terms of having contact with a partner (e.g. (12): 'I enjoy dancing *with* a partner rather than *at* one'), the enjoyment of the steps and movement ('real dancing') and social usefulness (e.g. (38): 'One can pile on the charm and impress the boss's wife'). The latter (coming from a full-time student) is a clear case of anticipatory socialization. One factor in the liking for ballroom dancing which might not have been predicted here is a certain emphasis on romantic and sophisticated atmosphere (see (44) to (50)).

159

Thirty-one reasons are given for disliking beat dancing, the self-conscious factor clearly emerging on several occasions. Fewer reasons are given for disliking ballroom dancing and these are mostly along the lines of difficulty, dullness and formality.

OVERALL IMPRESSION OF ATTITUDES

Taking a synoptic view of the seven groups, there is a striking measure of agreement that:

(i) Those who like beat dancing do so because it is easy, great fun, energetic, rhythmic and without rules.

(ii) Those who dislike it do so because they consider it looks foolish and ridiculous, and is not 'real dancing'.

(iii) Those who like ballroom dancing do so because they like to have contact with a partner, they enjoy the skill required, and (boys only) they think it will be useful in later life.

(iv) Those who dislike it do so because it is 'out-of-date', stiff, formal, disciplined and difficult.

2.6. *The Interviews and Personality Inventories*

A follow-up study was made of a small group of polytechnic students. Their replies to the questionnaires tended to fall into the following pattern: (i) Those who liked both beat and ballroom forms of dancing (with reasons); (ii) Those who expressed a liking for ballroom dancing (with reasons) and a dislike for beat (with reasons); (iii) Those who expressed a liking for beat (with reasons) and a dislike for ballroom dancing (with reasons); (iv) Those who never or hardly ever danced (indicating 8 in Question (1), or writing 'Do Not Dance' across the form).

It was decided therefore to analyse the replies in terms of four categories:

(I) The 'keen dancers' (those who fell into category (i) above, and in addition danced once a fortnight or more);

(II) The 'non-dancers' (category (iv) above);

(III) The 'ballroom' dancers (category (ii) above);

(IV) The 'beat' dancers (category (iii) above).

A random sample of five students in each of the categories (I) to (IV) above was then selected, for interview. Seven out of the twenty were not available but answered questions by letter and returned a completed Eysenck Personality Inventory. The other thirteen students were interviewed informally for about fifteen minutes and then asked to fill in an Eyesenck Personality Inventory.

The following Table shows the individual and the mean figures for E (Extraversion) and N (Neuroticism) of the four groups. The twenty students concerned are designated by letters of the alphabet from A to T.

TABLE 33

	Group No. I			Group No. II			Group No. III			Group No. IV	
	E	N		E	N		E	N		E	N
A	15	7	F	16	13	K	19	11	P	15	15
B	17	9	G	7	10	L	17	14	Q	19	11
C	17	4	H	4	5	M	14	11	R	16	13
D	22	5	I	12	13	N	15	6	S	19	10
E	17	18	J	5	14	O	18	7	T	20	6
Total	88	53		44	55		83	49		89	55
Mean	17·6	10·6		8·8	11		16·6	9·8		17·25	12·25

It will be seen that the mean for Extraversion in category II, the non-dancers, is 8·8 compared with 17·6, 16·6 and 17·25 for categories I, III and IV respectively. Analysis of variance confirms beyond possible doubt that category II has a significantly lower mean than the other categories. (Any difference of means between any pair greater than 1·45 is significant at the ·05 level: it can be seen therefore that group II mean differs very significantly from all the others.)

Clearly this means that the 'non-dancers' are less extraverted than any of the 'dancing' categories, but does this mean that (compared with the general student population) the 'non-dancers' are 'abnormally' introverted or that the 'dancers' are 'abnormally' extraverted?

The published mean for E for the student population is 11·095 – so that in fact only group II (the non-dancers) yields a mean which is in any way consistent. It is somewhat below the published national mean, which is what one would expect, as it is a specially selected sample of 'non-dancer' students. It is clear, therefore, that groups I, III and IV (the dancers) are not only significantly more extraverted than the non-dancers, but also significantly more extraverted than the general student population. One further difference between group II, on the one hand, and groups I, III and IV on the other, is the range of difference for the E score, group II having much greater variability. Calculations on the variances and standard deviations make groups I, III and IV look too homogeneous, compared with the published figures, and only group II has the degree of variability which conforms to the published national standards. In other words, the E scores for the 'dancers' (groups I, III and IV) not only have an 'abnormally' high mean but this high mean is produced because the individual scores are all high and are closely grouped together.

There is no simple explanation here, since, on the face of it, there seems no reason why a keen dancer answering the fifty-seven questions on the E.P.I. should 'invariably' (as happened here) have a significantly high E score. This 'over-homogeneity' is apparent in all the 'dancing groups', so whatever the factor is, it is one which underlies dancing in general and not 'beat' or 'ballroom' in particular.

The situation with regard to the N score (neuroticism or emotional instability) is completely different.* Analyses of variance yields no significant results. The mean for group III (ballroom dancers) is lower than the others but not in a statistically significant way. The mean scores here are also consistent with published standards.

It appears, therefore, that a pronounced liking for social dancing (of any kind) is positively correlated in a significant way with extraversion, as a personality trait, but that no significant correlation exists between liking or disliking social dancing and tendencies towards emotional instability.

It was thought that the interviews might yield some data on the underlying reasons why some people became keen dancers, others remained aloof, and yet others manifested strong likes and dislikes of particular forms of social dancing. No very conclusive evidence was forthcoming, but the following information gives some leads.

GROUP I: THE DANCERS

A *Pen picture.* Average height, slim, lithe. Good-looking. Fair longish wavy hair, coming down over ears. Strikingly dressed in clean and very bright blue jeans. Middle class. Had some dancing lessons at the age of 14. His father was a keen dancer. He is a member of quite a number of clubs but prefers classical to pop music. Beat music and dancing is his way of expressing himself – and he finds it completely natural to express himself in this way. He quite often

* These findings validate in an interesting way Professor Eysenck's claim that extraversion and neuroticism as measured in the E.P.I. are two dimensions of personality. which are quite independent of each other.

dances without music – e.g. in a classroom while waiting for the lecturer to appear.

Very willing to talk but inclined to be tense. (International Marketing student. Age 21.)

B *Pen picture.* Slim, neat, smallish. Gay. Casually but nicely dressed in jeans. Untidy hair. Started dancing at the age of 15 (youth club). He was fascinated and took 'outside' lessons while still at school. He could not persuade any of his schoolmates to join him in lessons, and walked up and down outside the dancing-school for hours before going in for the first time. Found it difficult to say why he was so keen – he 'just wanted to dance'. Middle class. Family background of non-dancing kind. He is musical: plays piano, viola, violin and organ.

Was a member of as many clubs and organizations as presented themselves (in Bridgewater).

Finds satisfaction in ballroom and beat dancing, but finds a different kind of satisfaction in beat. Tried to explain it along the lines of 'fear of freedom' and identification with a group. (Economics student. Age 22.)

C *Pen picture.* Tall, slim – general impression of lightness. Tight jeans, Longish hair. Attractive appearance. Relaxed and ready to talk.

Working class. Family not interested in dancing, He became interested about the age of 16. Had no formal lessons but watches television – especially 'Come Dancing' which is 'just great'. He is very interested in disciplined dancing to this kind of music, but likes the beat variety too. Says this kind of dancing can be 'sexy' but only sometimes. He doesn't mind not dancing *with* a girl, his interest is held by watching her dance opposite him. (Mechanical Engineering student. Age 20.)

D No interview. E.P.I. and letter. Became interested in dancing at age of 12, has never had any lessons: parents not dancers: is not 'musical'. (Civil Engineering student. Age 18.)

E No interview. E.P.I. and letter. Became interested in dancing about the age of 17, because it was 'good fun'. His parents are both keen dancers. He has never had any lessons and is not 'musical'. (Mechanical Engineering student. Age 20.)

GROUP II: THE NON-DANCERS

F *Pen picture.* Small and wiry. Unremarkable in general dress and appearance. Quite friendly and interested. Middle class. Has had some experience of social dancing because his mother insisted on his taking it up for a time but has dropped it completely.

He is very musical and plays the guitar – folk music. He plays for others to dance but has no wish to dance himself. Has a very intellectual attitude – e.g. goes to Cecil Sharp House for folk music sessions and despises anything 'commercial'. He sees the beat scene as commercialized and therefore despises it.

In unconventional, not a 'joiner', and does not like to be 'organized'. (Mathematics student. Age 22.)

G *Pen picture.* Very handsome, blond, and boyish-looking. Middle class. Well-dressed in neat and conventional suit. Well-brushed hair – short back and sides. He was introduced to dancing through lessons at school but dancing has never appealed to him – he finds plenty of other things to do. When he goes to parties he does not find it inconvenient that he does not dance: he finds people to talk to.

He likes classical music but does *not* like pop. It strikes no chord within him: and pop dancing even less. It would seem to him a very artificial way of expressing himself.

Wears badge in buttonhole: Scripture Union. (Economics student. Age 19.)

H No interview. Letter and E.P.I. The reason that he has never danced is the environment he was brought up in. Having been brought up to devote all his spare time to Christian activities (about which he has no regrets) there are many social activities, of which dancing is one, 'in which I have never participated, and have no desire to do so either'. (Mechanical Engineering student. Age 19.)

I No interview. E.P.I. only. (Electrical Engineering student. Age 23.)

J No interview. E.P.I. only. (Mechanical Engineering student. Age 21.)

GROUP III: THE 'BALLROOM DANCERS'

K *Pen picture.* Casually but conventionally dressed – e.g. cravat tucked into open-necked shirt. Nice-looking. Neat hair – short back and sides. A keen dancer and a good dancer: danced even more before he came to college.

Middle class. His parents are quite keen dancers. He is interested in ballroom, country and folk dancing, but definitely not beat. Is musical: plays piano, violin and guitar.

Likes classical music. Does not *dislike* pop music but would never buy a pop record. (Economics student. Age 20.)

L Quite conventionally dressed: suit. Unremarkable appearance. Short hair. Had dancing lessons of the ballroom type when about 15/16. Liked them and became a 'bronze medallist'. Likes classical music: does not like pop music. Stresses fact that he was not brought up in pop music atmosphere. Middle class. (Economics student. Age 21.)

M *Pen picture.* Average height, fair, good-looking in a non-flamboyant way. Well-brushed hair: short back and sides. Dressed in highly traditional 'square' sports clothes – i.e. blazer and flannels: but 'good' and well looked after.
Middle class.

At age of 16 to 17 first came into contact with dancing through the 'twist' but this did not make any great appeal to him and he only really wanted to dance after going to a formal ballroom type of dance at a girls' school. He then took up ballroom dancing seriously and became a competition dancer: eventually took his silver medal and became Junior Champion of West Kent. Is musical: plays recorder and trumpet.

Can see no rhyme or reason in beat dancing. Says that many who do these dances are in no way in time with the music. Rather intense. (Mathematics student. Aged 20.)

N *Pen picture.* Relaxed and friendly. Unremarkable in appearance, not particularly well 'turned out' – hair medium to short.

Lower middle/upper working class. His family is not musical but he is: plays piano, organ and clarinet.

He specially likes 'Old Time' dancing: realizes this is highly unusual but says it is 'great'. Took up dancing at age of 11 to 12, influenced by his family.

Does not like 'partnerless' dances. (Chemistry student. Age 21.)

O No interview. E.P.I. and letter. First became interested in dancing at age of 13. His family is keen on dancing and he has had lessons. He likes pop music and is himself musical.

GROUP IV: THE BEAT DANCERS

P *Pen picture.* Casually dressed in very modern style. Tight jeans. Hair very long: wavy and 'feminine' style coming down over ears.
Working class.

He dislikes not only ballroom dancing, but also those of his contemporaries who 'go in for it' – he says they are 'straight-laced, they wear "suits", sports coats, ties and cravats'. In a working class area such as Woolwich he says beat is identified with working class: hence those who like ballroom dancing see themselves as middle class and do not wish to be thought otherwise.

He says it is a question of identification – the beat dancers conform to their own group. He identifies with youth, hence he likes beat groups and beat dancing. Is also a member of a jazz club.

He sees ballroom dancing as identified with 'adult society': says he might gravitate towards it when 'too old' for beat. (Economics student. Age 20.)

Q *Pen picture.* Tall, slim, intense. Jeans. Longish hair. At age of 16 to 17 had ballroom dancing lessons under pressure from'Mummy and Daddy' but did *not* enjoy them. Says he is not very musical and found difficulty with the 'time' in ballroom dancing and in identifying which dance fitted which music.

Upper middle class. Was very much 'under the thumb' of his family at 16/17 but has now broken loose. Likes beat dancing which he identifies with rebellion: he can work off energy: he likes the loud music and has no difficulty in following the beat here. He says that beat dancing to pop music is so different from 'conventional' dancing that it might just as well be called something else: wishes that pop music were not called 'music'. Belongs to some clubs and sometimes practises on his own because he says how well you dance (in certain clubs) is very important. Thinks dancing is very much associated with going out with girls, since most girls like to dance. (International Marketing student. Age 19.)

R *Pen picture.* Tall, slim and graceful. Well-dressed in casual jeans. Very handsome appearance – longish fair hair.

Middle class.

Became interested in dancing at the age of 16/17 and had six lessons. Dislikes ballroom dancing because of the 'corny' sound.

Is particularly interested in rhythm, hence likes the beat dances. He also likes 'folk' and can do Zorba's dance, which he picked up by watching. Plays guitar. His family are not dancers.

In beat dancing he considers that the partner is important even though there is no contact: he much prefers to have a good partner. Described how 'mod girls' dance in groups of girls and are not interested in having male partners.

Friendly and ready to talk: slightly anxious. (Electrical Engineering student. Age 22.)

S *Pen picture.* Sports jacket. Unremarkable appearance. Small. He had ballroom dancing lessons at age of 16.

Middle class.

He thinks of ballroom dancing as conformist and he does not want to conform. Is musical and plays guitar.

Likes beat dancing because no matter what the music is you can always dance something to it. He goes with a partner always: he 'leads' and she tries to follow his style.

Not at all talkative – difficult to get more than just answers to questions. Rather defensive. (Mechanical Engineering student. Age 19.)

T No interview. Letter and E.P.I. Became interested in dancing at age of 12 and had about six lessons. He is musical and plays both 'folk' and 'classical' guitar. He likes both 'pop' and classical music. (Science student. Age 21.)

The smallest amount of information was obtained from group II, the 'non-dancers' which is probably in itself significant. The fact that two out of five in this group had unmistakable religious affiliations and involvements would appear to be significant, especially as this factor did not emerge in any of the other groups.

There was an unmistakable contrast between groups III and IV (the 'ballroom' and 'beat' groups). With few exceptions the students in group III wore clothes which would not have been out of place for young people before the war: sports jacket, blazer, open-necked shirt with cravat etc. and did *not* have long hair. Unquestionably, they do not identify with the 'beat generation' in any sense of the word.

Group IV, with one exception, had the long hair, the tight jeans and the off-beat appearance associated with 'modern youth' and the majority expressed some degree of rebellion or at any rate protest.

There seems little doubt that the predilection for beat dancing *or* for ballroom dancing (when these are regarded as mutually exclusive) is closely linked with processes of identification, reference group membership, and attitude to authority.

Group I (the dancers) seemed much more closely allied with group IV than with group III as regards appearance and general attitude. This seems quite understandable, since a liking for *all kinds* of dancing (including 'ballroom') is a very different attitude from that of group III. Indeed, it might be said that, from the point of view of their contemporaries, the attitude of group III is distinctly deviant, more so, probably, than that of group II.

The forces that produce the really keen (and almost certainly *good*) dancer of group I are probably a combination of nature and nurture (see the comment of 'B' group I, to support the idea of an innate element – he felt that he 'just wanted to dance') and the same might possibly be true to some extent of group II. With regard to groups III and IV, however, in the writer's view the important forces are likely to be almost entirely environmental.

Much of the foregoing is highly impressionistic and more research with much larger samples would be necessary before any firm conclusions could be drawn.

2.7.   *Discussion*

7.1. DISCUSSION IN RELATION TO PART II HYPOTHESES

Two major hypotheses with regard to contemporary dancing were put forward in Part II, viz.:

(a)   That the present-day changed style of teenage dancing (which started in 1960) can be interrelated with certain concomitant changes in society: for example, the greater gulf between the generations, a possible decrease in consciousness of class amongst young people, and a greater flexibility as between masculine and feminine 'roles' and 'norms'.

(b)   That there is a basic similarity between modern beat dancing and the dancing of primitive societies.

The first hypothesis is confirmed to the extent that, particularly in the interviews and in the answers to the 'open-ended' questions, beat dancing is:

(i)   regarded as part of the 'modern' way of life: ('They are the "in things" of the sixties'. Day release girl);

(ii)   identified with 'youth' as a separate stratum of society. ('All young people – therefore not open to criticism from other age groups'. Secretarial girl);

(iii)   'classless in that beat dancing was not found to be identified with any particular social class (Table 18 and relevant discussion);

(iv)   linked with greater independence and freedom of girls, and with a less clear differentiation between the sexes: ('You can dance on your own ... and not have to wait to be asked', day release girl.) ('One does not need a partner: a group of girls can do it together', day release girl.) ('If without a girlfriend you can still dance by yourself or with a crowd of boys', day release boy.)

The second hypothesis is substantiated to some extent by the emphasis in the replies on the uninhibited direct transmission of emotional experience through body movements – e.g. 'You can express how you feel when you dance modern' (day release girl). 'You can express yourself without restriction' (secretarial girl). These answers clearly show some link with primitive dance.

The stress given to beat and rhythm in the replies – e.g. 'The good beat and rhythm' (day release boy) and 'You can dance to the beat' (business studies boy) further strengthens the notion of a relationship with primitive dance where 'the most essential method of achieving the ecstatic is the rhythmic beat of every dance movement.'[11]

A third similarity is to be found in the frequent mention of release of tension – e.g. 'It gets your feelings out of your system' (business studies boy). 'Escape valves to get rid of pent-up emotions' (polytechnic student).

In primitive societies, the dance, often allied to ritual, plays a very special role in this kind of release.

2.7.2. GENERAL DISCUSSION

In summarizing the general conclusions to be drawn from the survey, it will be useful to bear in mind the particular points on which information was sought.

Of the young people represented in the survey, 40% danced once a week or more and 9% never danced, or danced very rarely. The remainder fell within the categories of dancing once a fortnight, once a month, once every three months or once every six months. It seems clear, from the low percentage never or hardly ever dancing, that dancing *does* play a considerable part in the lives of these young people, but the figures *by no means* bear out a picture of 'pop and beat-crazed' youth.

The figures bear out the hypothesis of other investigators that over the past two decades or so, there has been a considerable rise in interest in dancing, on the part of boys and young men. Taking the present sample as a whole, there is evidence, even so, that girls dance more frequently than boys, but this was not true of every group within the sample and should be regarded with caution.

With regard to frequency of dancing little weight can be attached to socio-economic class or to educational *background* (e.g. as between day release and full-time students of the same age-range). As might be expected, however, there were significant differences in actual educational *category* – i.e. girls at school (also the youngest group) ranking as the most frequent dancers, and degree (or equivalent) students at college (also the oldest group) ranking as the least frequent.

The general motivation for going dancing differed in an interesting way in the different groups. Out of five reasons the fact that they enjoyed dancing was the one most frequently put first by the members of all the female groups (except the secondary technical schoolgirls) whereas 'to meet or to be with the opposite sex' was the reason most frequently put first by the members of all the male groups, and also by the secondary technical schoolgirls – who, in this study, emerge as a distinctly uninhibited group. There were similar differences for the reasons given for actual enjoyment of dancing. Out of three reasons, 'the music and rhythm' was most frequently put first by the members of all the groups except the business studies boys and the polytechnic (predominantly male) students. The two latter groups most frequently gave first preference to 'the presence of the opposite sex' – thus, at any rate showing a logical and consistent pattern of behaviour, in that they went dancing to meet or be with the opposite sex, and once there, enjoyed dancing because the opposite sex was around.

The survey indicated that there is not the slightest doubt that, so far as dancing is concerned, the main attraction for young people lies in 'modern beat dancing' to pop music. This does not mean, however, that the teenage dances of past generations (jive, rock and twist) have been entirely ousted, nor does it mean that the 'quick, quick slow' conventional type of ballroom dancing is completely excluded. In this latter sphere, quickstep and waltz are holding their own, but the day of the foxtrot is dwindling. In every group there are some young people who 'do not do' the ballroom dances, but would like to have the opportunity to learn and do them. This applies to each of the 'standard four' ballroom dances: waltz, foxtrot, quickstep and tango but more to the latter than to the first three. The percentages concerned, however, are very small and certainly do not add up to an impression that 'beat' is being forced on youthful dancers who would prefer 'Silvester'.

The popularity of beat dancing and the acceptibility of dancing it completely without a partner decreased as one went up the age-scale (within the age-range 13 to 23) and, overall, girls showed a greater preference both for beat and partnerless beat than did boys. Partnerless beat dancing was more acceptable in working-class than in middle-class circles but socio-economic class had no part to play when considering beat dancing as a whole.

More than half of every group in the sample of young people considered age to be a factor entering into beat dancing and the greatest consensus of opinion in every group was that these dances are not suitable for those over 30. There is little doubt that young people *do*, on the whole, consider that these dances are for their generation alone, and therein, no doubt, lies much of the secret of their appeal (see, for example, the remark (24), Table 31 '*All young people* – hence not open to criticism from other age-groups'). This reflection of inter-generational hostility, however, was by no means common in the replies received, many of which showed a 'tolerant' attitude and even a willingness to 'close the gap' – for example, the remark of a day release girl ((24), Table 27): 'It closes the gap between young and old if you can dance "their" dances with them'.

An interesting side-issue which emerged from the answers to the open-ended questions was the element of aggressive hostility to ballroom dancing which entered into some of the replies from the girls: e.g. 'I HATE waltz' (secondary technical schoolgirl), 'That's easy to answer: RUBBISH' (day release girl), 'They're "out" and they make me mad and sick as well' (secretarial course girl). This aggressive attitude did not appear in any of the boys' answers. This clue that deeper levels of the personality may be touched on by an innocent-sounding question about dancing preferences is borne out by the interview studies, which indicate a distinct personality difference between group III (whose who liked 'ballroom' and disliked 'beat' dancing) and group IV (those who liked 'beat' and disliked 'ballroom' dancing).

The general tenor of replies indicated that beat dancing gave satisfaction because it provided an outlet for exuberant youthful energy – an opportunity to 'go mad', to 'let off steam' and jump around to a pounding beat without criticism from carping elders. It is clear that ballroom dancing, with its emphasis on discipline and skill, and its strong association with the adult world could not possibly satisfy such needs. The sexual element, often stressed by critics of beat dancing and the beat atmosphere, was certainly present in some responses, but judging from the majority of replies, it is only a part of the general atmosphere of 'fun and excitement'.[12]

Other needs and drives which emerged in the replies were those for freedom and self-expression, both of which were frequently said to be satisfied in beat dancing. The interviews with groups IV and I showed that a liking for beat dancing was often associated with a feeling of 'group solidarity' and an identification with beat as a way of life.

XIX

An Integration of Social Theory and Research

In the interests of integrating social theory and empirical research, consideration must now be given to the link between contemporary society and the drives, needs, and attitudes expressed in the survey. A preliminary discussion of the function of youth cults in general is helpful here.

In the first place, it is significant to recall Eisenstadt's hypothesis and findings that a specific 'youth culture' is most likely to develop in areas going through a rapid process of culture contact and change, and least likely amongst societies and groups in societies which maintain a traditional setting.[1] Thus, if there is no discontinuity between childhood, adolescence and adulthood there is no need or drive to develop a youth culture, but if there is discontinuity, if there is no easy transition, with clearly defined roles, from the world of childhood into the world of adulthood, the stage that is not provided for will form a world or 'culture' of its own.[2] Through participation in the youth culture the adolescent gets some compensation for some of the social experience denied to him in the adult world. If he feels 'out of things' he collects together with his peers so that they can have something to be 'in': on the principle of 'You exclude me, and I'll exclude you'.[3]

A second, but closely-linked approach, is to consider active participation in the contemporary teenage youth cult in terms of alienation from adult society.[4] Alienation can come about through feelings of insecurity (caused by disappointment with persons) coupled with feelings of inadequacy (caused by disappointment with rules). There is little doubt that modern industrial 'mass' society tends to foster both. On the one hand, the absence of strong, closely-knit primary groups and the emphasis on impersonality and impermanence of contact tends to produce feelings of insecurity, instability and rootlessness, while on the other hand the great gulf between what is held up as desirable and what is in fact attainable cannot fail to produce dissatisfaction and disappointment with the rules, and hence feelings of personal inadequacy. In an affluent society everyone aspires to wealth, which is in fact impossible: in an education-orientated society everyone aspires to a grammar school education which is equally out of the question. Those who patently cannot reach what appear to be the goals of society will tend to become alienated from it, rejecting its rules and norms in the process.

Any individual, however, even if alienated still has a need to conform, since he has learnt, consciously and unconsciously in his socialization period, that conformity pays. The conflict between the need to conform and the need to express alienation frequently results in some form of compulsive aggression. Sociologists have pointed to this process and have isolated three separate forms of deviance it can bring about: firstly, illness (in which case aggression is turned inwards), secondly, crime and delinquency (where aggression is turned outwards) and thirdly, rebellion, which usually takes some form of embittered and compulsive hostility.

The really significant point in the present analysis is, however, the fact that a fourth solution[5] to the conflict is now presented by the possibility of active participation in a youth cult, centering around beat music and dance, since in a beat club or atmosphere strong aggression to adult society can be expressed, but in a highly con- formist manner. The element of hostility to the adult world is unmistakable, since, if a pop group becomes acceptable to adults (as did the Beatles) young people will quickly transfer their allegiance to a more violent group which is still disapproved of by their elders (in this case, the Rolling Stones).

The emotional satisfaction from conformity in the youth cult situation is probably as great as the satisfaction derived from membership of a delinquent gang, but in this case the solution is not a delinquent or deviant one.[6] It is a solution which restores to the teenager a sense of status, compensating in some measure for the absence of any clear-cut role in a society which looks on him as half child, half adult. It gives him a sense of identity through identifying with his peers, and provides some measure of emotional satisfaction, security and integration.

The link between the needs, drives and satisfactions expressed in the survey and the nature of present-day society can now be made more explicit. Firstly, it is obvious that industrial routine and monotony (where these occur) can be made more bearable if at the end of the day's work there is some outlet for energetic, active self- expression in beat dancing. Secondly, and less obvious, is the fact that this activity not only releases pent-up energy but may well help to resolve a conflict (in a non-delinquent and non-neurotic way) that arises from feelings of alienation towards adult society. Viewed in this light, the present-day teenage cult, centering around beat music and dancing is not only a product of the time (in all the ways indicated earlier) but is functionally related to modern society in that it makes a contribution, in Parsonian terms, to the 'management' of emotional disturbances and tensions which otherwise might disrupt some part of the system.

Ballroom dancing, on the other hand, however delightful and even therapeutic it may be, for those who enjoy it, can make no contribution to the solution of this particular problem. It is strongly identified with adult society and involves isolated 'units' (couples) whose needs are for music and floor-space, not for other 'units'. Each couple dances its own steps and patterns, with no relationship to any other couples on the floor. 'Smooth dancing' (to use the professional term) in the ballroom is in complete contrast to the crowded cellar or tavern filled with teenage dancers 'rebelling' yet 'conforming', seemingly 'solo' but psychologically merged: bound together, as in primitive tribal rites, by the magic spell of the drum-beat.

Overall Conclusions

The picture that emerges consistently from the entire study is one of close relationship (at times functional) between the nature of society and the nature of social dance, be it 'normal' dance in primitive society, pathogenic dance in primitive or medieval society, social dance in England from the thirteenth century onwards, or contemporary teenage beat dancing. The hypothesis that the social dance and society are so closely related that the dance must be seen as a significant part of the total culture pattern has, it is hoped, been adequately demonstrated.

The findings seem, therefore, to warrant a closer rapprochement between dance historians and sociologists. The dance historian has always acknowledged that the social dance can never be properly understood or appreciated in isolation from the rest of society: the social anthropologist has always included the dance in his study of primitive cultures: now, surely, it is the turn of the sociologist to acknowledge that any society can be understood better if its attitude to dancing and its social dance forms are included in his investigations.

APPENDICES

Appendix A

Dance History

c. 1228–1240 Ms Harley 978 (containing three instrumental estampies). [In B.M.]

1394 Gower in 'Confessio Amantis' mentions a carole with a 'softe Pas'.
1377 The 'Kennington Mumming' – with Mummers and Royal party dancing on separate sides of the hall.

Fifteenth century, first half: *'Le Manuscrit des Basses Danses de la Bibliotheque de Bourgogne'*.

Fifteenth century, late: Ms found in Library at Salisbury Cathedral: Basse Dances noted on the fly-leaf of a Catholicon.
c. 1490–1500 Thoulouze: *L'art et Instruction de bien Danser* (forty-nine Basses Danses). The first printed book on dancing.
1501 The 'Westminster Disguisings'.
1512 Disguised actors take dancing partners from audience: 'disguisings gradually superseded by 'masks'.

1521 Copelande. 'Manner of dancynge of bace dances after the use of France'.
1531 Elyot: 'Gouvernour' gives the modern dances as 'Base Daunces, Bargenettes, Pavions, Turgions and Roundes'.

Social and Political History

1208 Albigensian Crusade.
1216 Henry III.
1236 Henry III marries Eleanor of Provence.
1272 Edward I.
1307 Edward II.
1327 Edward III.
1337–1453 Hundred Years' War.
1337–1360 Period of Success.
1396–1413 Period of Peace.
1377 Richard II.
1396 Richard II marries Isabella, French Princess.
1399 Henry IV.
1413 Henry V.
1422 Henry VI.
1445 Henry VI marries Margaret of Anjou.
1461 Edward IV.
1483 Edward V.
1483 Richard III.
1485 Henry VII.
1501 Henry VII's son Prince Arthur marries Katherine of Aragon.
1509 Henry VIII.
1514 Treaty of Peace with France.
1519 Emperor Charles V visits England.
1520 Field of the Cloth of Gold.
1547 Edward VI.
1553 Mary I.

Appendix A

Dance History

c. 1560 'Misogonus' – first literary reference to Country Dances.

1588 Arbeau: *Orchésographie*

1591 'The Queene's Entertainment at Cowdrey'.

1594 Sir John Davies *Orchestra* ('Brawls Rounds & Hays, Measures, Corantos and La Volta')

1596 *Thomas Nashe* 'Haue with you to Saffron Walden' mentions Rogero, Basileno, Turkeyloney, All Flowers of the Broom, Green Sleeves, Pepper is Black, Peggy Ramsey.

1651 *Playford: The English Dancing Master*. (The first printed collection of English country-dances).

1661 Académie Royale de Danse founded by Louis XIV, Paris.

1662 Samuel Pepys at Court Ball mentions branles, courantes and country dances.

1711 *E. Pemberton:* Published collection of Minuets for Schoolgirls (Dancing Master).

1729 *Soame Jenyns:* 'The Art of Dancing' gives the following French dances – rigadoon, loure, bourree, minuet, bretagne, courante.

1705–1761 Beau Nash: Master of Ceremonies at Bath.

1765 Almack's Opening Night.

1812 Waltz first danced in England.

1813 Ball to celebrate battle of Vittorio: 'Scotch dances' requested.

1815 Quadrille introduced to England.

1816 Waltz included in Court Ball.

1829 Galop introduced to England.

1844 Polka craze comes to England.

Social and Political History

1558 Elizabeth I.

1589 Hakluyt: Publication of '*The Principall Navigations, Voiages and Discoveries of the English Nation'*.

1603 James I.

1625 Charles I married Henrietta of France.

1642 Outbreak of Civil War.

1649–1660 Commonwealth and Protectorate.

1660 Charles II. The Restoration.

1685 James II.

1689 William III and Mary II.

1702 Anne.

1714 George I.

1727 George II.

1760 George III.

1793–1815 Wars with France.

1813 Battle of Vittorio.

1815 Congress of Vienna.

1820 George IV.

1830 William IV.

1831 Polish Revolution.

1837 Victoria.

1840 Marriage of Victoria.

Dance History	*Social and Political History*
1846 Costume Ball given by Victoria opened with polonaise.	
1847 Cellarius: *Fashionable Dancing* mentions quadrilles, valse, redowa, mazurka, cotillon.	
1850s Casino de Venise and other less 'exclusive' assembly rooms.	
1850 Lancers introduced to England.	
1852 Thomas Wilson: *The Art of Dancing*. Instructions for the Country Dance, Quadrilles, Valse a deux temps, Redowa, Polka, Schottische, Circassian Circle, Gavotte Quadrille.	1861 Death of Prince Consort. 1865 Slavery abolished in U.S.A.
1880 Cake-walk briefly popular in England.	
1888 Barn-dance (Military Schottische) came to England.	
1891 Sousa composed Washington Post March.	
1906 R. St Johnston records: No trace among rural population of any 'national dance'.	1901 Edward VII. 1910 George V.
1911 Irving Berlin: 'Alexandra's Ragtime Band'.	
1910–11 Boston comes to England.	
1911–12 Ragtime music comes to England.	
1911–14 Tango comes to England.	
1914 Irene and Vernon Castle: *Modern Dancing*. Description of 'one-step'.	1914–18 First World War.
1914 Early foxtrot introduced to England.	
1915 Savoy Hotel instals Ragtime Band (Murray's Savoy Quartette).	
1919 Hammersmith 'Palais de Danse' opened.	1918 Votes for women at 30.
1920 Dominic la Rocca and Original Dixieland Jazz Band play at Hammersmith Palais.	
1921 'Shimmy' and other 'jazz dances' come to England.	
1921 'Charleston' comes to England.	1926 General Strike.
1926 Conference of dance teachers on standardization of ballroom dancing.	1928 Votes for women at 21.

Appendix A

Dance History

1930s (late) Swing music and 'jitterbug' dancing in England.
1930s (late) Novelty social dances in England.
1940s Revival of 'Old Time'.
1946 Rumba taught in England.
1945 Decline of big dance bands.
1955 'Rock around the Clock' (Bill Haley & the Comets). 'Rock and Roll' dancing.
1960 Chubby Checker 'twist' records.
1961–62 'Twist' dancing.
1963 Twist included in dance given by Queen for Princess Alexandra's engagement.
1963 'Rhythm and Blues' in Britain.
1963 Beatles' first hit record: 'Love me do'.
1964 'Millie' – My Boy Lollipop Blue beat or Ska.
1964 to present:
(1) Shake.
(2) Modern 'beat' dancing.

Social and Political History

1929 Wall Street collapse.

1936 George VI.

1939–45 Second World War.

1952 Elizabeth II.

180

Appendix B

Some EXTRACTS from *Manner of dancynge of bace dances after the use of France:* Robert Copeland.

Published in 1521. The original is appended to a French Grammar in the Bodleian Library, Oxford.

'Here followeth the manner of dancing bace dances after the use of France and other places, translated out of French in English by ROBERT COPELAND.

'Ye ought to make reverence toward the lady, and then make two singles, one double, a reprise and a branle.

All begin with Reverence and end with Branle (called in French Congé) but the branle step can occur anywhere in the dance.

Doubles: The first double pace is made with the left foot in raising the body stepping three paces forward lightly, the first with the left foot, the second with the right foot, and the third with the left foot. . . .

Reprises: A reprise alone ought to be made with the right foot in drawing the right foot backward a little to the other foot. The second reprise ought to be made (when ye make three at once) with the left foot in raising the body in like wise. The third reprise is made in place and as the first also.

. . . every one of these paces occupieth as much time as the other. That is, ye wit, a reverence one note: a reprise, one note: a branle, one note.' [The book finished with a description of the following Bace Dances, some with two, some three, some four measures:

> Filles a marier
> Le petit rouen
> Amours
> La Gerrière
> La Allemande
> La Brette
> La Reyne]

'These dancers have I set at the end of this book to the intent that every learner of the said book after their diligent study may rejoice somewhat their spirits honestly in eschewing of idleness, the portress of vices.'

Appendix C

EXTRACTS from *Orchésographie:* Thoinot Arbeau.

Published at Langres in 1588. Translated by Cyril Beaumont.

The following extracts refer to the Basse Danse, pavane, galliarde, volte and courante. The complete work gives detailed instructions for all the figures and steps required in these, and several other dances.

> Dancing . . . is to jump, to hop, to prance, to sway, to tread, to tip-toe, and to move the feet, hands and body in certain rhythms, measures and movements consisting of jumps, bendings of the body, sidlings, limpings, bendings of the knees, risings on tip-toe, throwings-forward of the feet, changes and other movements . . .
>
> Dancing or saltation is an art both pleasing and profitable which confers and preserves health, is adapted for the youthful, agreable to the aged and very suitable for all, so far as it is employed in fit place and season without vicious abuse.

Arbeau in answer to Capriol gives instructions for the performance of certain dances:

Basse Danse
First when you have entered the place where the company is gathered together for the dance, you will choose some modest damsel who pleases your fancy and, doffing your hat or bonnet with your left hand, offer her your right to lead her out to dance. She having been well brought up will offer you her left hand, rise and follow you . . .

A well-bred damsel will never refuse the man who does her the honour of asking her to dance.

The airs of the Basses Danses are played in triple time and to each bar the dancer makes the movements of the feet and body according to the rules of the dance.

The first movement is the reverence, the second is the branle, the third two 'simples', the fourth is the 'double', the fifth is the reprise.

[There follow detailed instructions for performing some of these, for example]

Simple:
1st bar: one step forward with left foot
2nd bar: bring the right foot to the left

3rd bar: one step forward with right foot
4th bar: bring left foot up to right foot
(This completes two 'simples').

Branle:
1st bar: feet together: turning body to left
2nd bar: feet together: turning body to right
3rd bar: feet together: turning body to left
4th bar: feet together: turning body to right
gazing softly and discreetly at the damsel the while, with a side-long glance.

The following drum rhythm is continued throughout the Basse Danse:

Pavane
The pavane is easy to dance because it is only two simples and a double advancing, and two simples and a double retiring: and it is played in duple time.
The two simples and the double advancing are begun with the left foot: retiring they are begun with the right foot.

The following drum rhythm is continued throughout:

Galliarde
The Galliarde is so called because one must be blithe and lively to dance it. . . . It ought to consist of six steps as it contains six crotchets played in two bars of triple time but there are only five steps because the sixth note is replaced by a rest.

Air: Antoinette

1st step: pied en l'air gauche
2nd step: pied en l'air droit and so on for 3rd and 4th etc.
On the rest that takes the place of a note, execute a 'saut':
Then change and execute to the right everything that you did to the left and so till the congé.

La Volte
The Volte is a kind of gaillarde familiar to the people of Provence: it is danced in triple time.

When you wish to turn, let go of the damsel's left hand and throw your left arm round her back, seizing and clasping her about the waist. At the same time throw your right hand below her busk to help her to spring when you push her with your left thigh. She, on her part, will place her right hand on your back or collar, and her left on her thigh, to hold her petticoat or kirtle in place, lest the breeze caused by the movement should reveal her chemise or her naked thigh. This accomplished, you execute together the turns of the Volte described above. After having turned for as many cadences as it pleases you, restore the damsel to her place, when she will feel, whatever good face she puts on it, her brain confused, her head full of giddy whirlings, and you cannot feel in much better case. I leave you to consider if it be a proper thing for a young girl to make such large steps and separations of the legs: and whether in the Volte both honour and health are not concerned and threatened.

Air for La Volte:

La Courante

The courante differs considerably from the Volte: it is danced to light duple time, consisting of two simples and a double to the left: and the same to the right going forwards or sideways and sometimes backwards ... Note that the steps of the Courante must be sauté (jumped) which is not done in the Pavane or the Basse Danse.

For example, to make a '*simple à gauche*' in the Courante, you will spring off the right foot and come to the ground on the left foot for your first step, then spring off the right, at the same time falling into '*pieds joints*' (feet together).

And similarly for '*simple à droite*'.

Double à gauche:

Spring off the right foot, coming to ground on left foot for first step, making second step with the right foot, then spring off the right foot making the third step with the left foot: then spring off the right foot making the fourth step with the left foot and fall into the position '*pieds joints*'.

Similarly for '*double à droite*'.

Air for the Courante:

Appendix D

Fashionable Dancing: Cellarius, London 1847. Translated from the original French book *La Danse des Salons,* published in Paris in the same year.

The Valse à Trois Temps:

The gentleman should place himself directly opposite his lady, upright but without stiffness; joining hands, the left arm of the gentleman should be rounded with the right arm of the lady, so as to form an arc of a circle, supple and elastic.

The gentleman sets off with the left foot, the lady with the right.

The step of the gentleman is made by passing the left foot before his lady. So much for the first time.

He slides back the right foot, slightly crossed, behind the left, the heel raised, the toe to the ground. So much for the second time.

Afterwards he turns upon his two feet on the toes, so as to bring the right foot forward, in the common third position: he then puts the right foot out, on the side, slides the left foot on the side, in turning on the right foot, and then brings the right foot forward, in the third position. So much for the fourth, fifth and sixth times.

The lady commences, at the same moment as the gentleman, with the fourth time, executes the fifth and sixth, and continues with the first, second and third; and so on.

The preparation for this waltz is made by the gentleman; he places the right foot a little in advance, on the first time of the measure, lets the second time pass by, and springs on the right foot, in readiness for the third time, and to set off with the first step of the waltz. This prelude serves as a signal for the lady.

Before the first six steps are completed, they should accomplish an entire turn, and employ two measures of the time.

. . . The first three steps should contribute equally to the first half-turn; not so with the three last. At the fourth step, the gentleman should, without turning, place his foot between those of his lady, accomplish the half-turn, passing before the lady with the fifth step, and bring the right foot to its place with the sixth time.

The Valse à Deux Temps:

The music of the Valse à Deux Temps is rhythmed on the same measure as that of the à Trois Temps, except that the orchestra should slightly quicken the movement, and accentuate it with special care.

A step must be made to each measure: that is, to glide with one foot, and chasser with the other. The valse à deux temps differing from the valse à trois, which describes a circle, is made on the square, and only turns upon the glissade. It is essential to note this difference of motion, in order to appreciate the character of the two waltzes.

The position of the gentleman is not the same in the valse à deux temps as in that à trois. He should not place himself opposite his lady, but a little to her right, and incline himself slightly with the right shoulder, so as to enable him to move easily in accordance with his partner.

I have already expressed my regret at the title of à deux temps being given to this waltz instead of à deux pas. The term à deux pas would have avoided much confusion, by indicating that two steps were executed to three beats of the music; the first step to the first beat, letting pass by the second beat, and executing the second step to the third beat. By this means we are sure to keep time with the measure.

In the valse à deux temps, the gentleman begins with the left foot, the lady with the right . . .

Appendix E*

Popular Assembly Rooms of the Nineteenth Century

Laurent's Casino: This opened at seven o'clock, closed at half-past eleven, and the admission charge was one shilling. The following is a typical programme of 1848:

1.	Quadrille (First Set)	'Robert Bruce'	Musard
2.	Polka	'Souvenir de l'Hippodrome'	Fessy
3.	Valse	'Pas des Fleurs'	Maratzek
4.	Parisian Quadrille	'Le Comte de Carmagnola'	Bosisio
5.	Cellarius Valse	'New National Mazurkas'	Sapinsky
6.	Parisian Quadrille	'Don Pasquale'	Tolbecque
7.	Polka	'Eclipse'	Koenig
8.	Valse	'Le Romantique'	Lanner
9.	Parisian Quadrille	'Nino'	Coote
10.	Polka	'Polka d'Amour'	Wallenstein
11.	Parisian Quadrille	'Les Fêtes du Château d'Eu'	Musard
12.	Polka	'Les Amazones'	Val Morris

Mr Mott in Foley Street (Portland Rooms)
The Times, 17 April 1849:
Messrs Mott and Freres Soirees Dansantes, at the Portland Rooms, Foley St, Portland Place. Tomorrow, Wednesday and every Wednesday during the season. Subscribers' tickets to admit a lady and gentleman to eight balls. £1 10. Single tickets 2/6 each.
N.B. Messrs Mott and Frere continue to give lessons in all the fashionable dances, including the Redowa Valse, the Valse à deux temps, Polka, Mazurka, Schottische etc.

Programme: Portland Ball Rooms (Motts) (1847)
Mr. Henry's Ball
LA DANSE

1.	Quadrille Pastorale	Mysteries of Paris
2.	Lancers	Original
3.	Spanish Dance	
4.	Quadrille (Trenise)	Enchantress
5.	Polka	
6.	Caledonians	
7.	Cellarius Waltz	
8.	Quadrille Pastorale	Esmeralda
9.	Redowa Waltz	
10.	Polka	

11.	Sir Roger de Coverley	
12.	Quadrille (Trenise)	
13.	Polka	Don Pasquale
14.	Waltz	The Elfin
15.	Quadrille Pastorale	Maritana
16.	Polka	Bohemian
17.	Quadrille (Trenise)	Alma
18.	Circular Waltz and Post Horn Galop	
19.	Quadrille Pastorale	Irish
20.	Polka	
21.	Quadrille Pastorale	Royal Irish

Casino de Venise, High Holborn

The Times, 4 January 1858:

Casino de Venise, High Holborn. This world-renowned and elegant establishment is universally pronounced to be the leading feature of the Metropolis. Mr. W. M. Packer has prepared a grand and varied Christmas programme, which is nightly performed by the celebrated band under his direction, including the Rustique, Linda, Pantomime and New Lancers Quadrilles, the Delhi, Isabella and Whisper of Love Waltzes, the Captive, Havelock and Happy Thought Polkas, the Princess Royal Varsoviana, Belle Vue Schottische, Midnight Galop etc. commencing with a grand overture.

Doors open at half past eight and close at twelve.

Admission 1/–.

In the closing years of the nineteenth century the leading popular assemblies were those conducted by H. R. Johnson at Holborn Town Hall: Mr Arnold at Albert Rooms at the back of the present Scala Theatre: Mr Piaggio at his rooms in Winsley St near Oxford Circus. Favourite dances were waltz, barn dance, quadrilles, lancers, schottische, waltz-cotillon.

---

* See *P. J. S. Richardson:* The Social Dances of the Nineteenth Century.

Appendix F

Standardization of Ballroom Dancing in the 1920s

A 'figure' may be defined as: 'One of the regular movements of a dance, in which a certain set of steps is completed.' A 'standardized figure' is one which has been agreed by the leading associations and societies of teachers of dancing, and which is taught by every member of those bodies.

Some form of standardization became a necessity early in the twentieth century. After the First World War a new style of dancing swept over Britain. Gone were the established figures of the set and sequence dances, and in their place came the rag, one-step and early foxtrot. Confusion reigned in ballroom and restaurant. Dancers performed an astonishing variety of steps, many of them 'freaks', and most of them improvized. The waltz nearly died out during the war and the new generation of dancers knew nothing of it. People foxtrotted to waltz music, and the tango added to the general confusion. There was equal bewilderment in dancing schools and academies. Different teachers taught totally different versions of the same dance, and even of the same figure in any dance.

In May of 1920 the first of several informal conferences of dance teachers was called by Philip Richardson, the then Editor of *Dancing Times*. These conferences worked out and standardized steps for the one-step, waltz, foxtrot and tango and agreed on the elimination of freak steps, particularly the highly individualistic and sometimes dangerous dips and kicks. In 1921, the last of these informal conferences set up a committee which made certain minimum recommendations for the basic figures of foxtrot, waltz and tango and made a general recommendation as to style: 'In modern dancing the committee suggest that the knees must be kept together in passing and the feet parallel. They also repeat their suggestion that all eccentric steps be abolished and that dancers should do their best to progress always round the room.'

The same committee found that a wide divergence of opinion still existed about the waltz, but strongly urged that 'step, step together' should be the pattern – in other words, the 'modern waltz' as we know it today.

In the months and years following these recommendations a new style of dancing emerged. In place of the old foot positions (feet turned out, ballet-style) the parallel position was adopted with the feet pointing forward all the time. This fundamental change in style did not, of course, come about simply as a result of recommendations from conferences of dance teachers in 1920 and 1921. Even in the pre-war days of 1910 and 1911, dancers were finding that the turned-out positions of the feet, and

189

the continuous whirling of the fast rotary waltz were too artificial, and possibly too difficult, for their liking, hence the popularity of the Boston. These particular recommendations of the 1920s simply crystallized the general hankerings for a more natural way of dancing – more important than ever now that dancing was becoming available to ever wider sections of the public.

The Imperial Society of Teachers of Dancing (founded in 1904) formed a Ballroom Branch in 1924 which continued with the work of standardization. In 1929, at a further conference, which was highly representative of teachers of dancing, the basic steps of, *inter alia*, quickstep, valse and foxtrot were laid down and 'official speeds' were agreed on as follows:

Quickstep	54–56 bars per minute
Waltz	36–38 bars per minute
Foxtrot	38–42 bars per minute
Tango	30–32 bars per minute

A style of dancing based on natural movement had by this time become the accepted form of modern ballroom dancing. This has since been developed in various ways, but it still remains the basis of what is called in this country and in the U.S.A. the 'English style' (although in fact it is based on the smooth walking step of the Boston which came to us from America). This 'English style' is used for all international championships in modern ballroom dancing but, understandably, most other countries prefer to term it the 'international style'.

With ackowledgements to *Philip Richardson:* A History of Ballroom Dancing. *A. H. Franks:* The Modern Ballroom Dancer's Handbook.

Appendix G

THE TANGO: *Historical Development*

The origin of this dance has been the occasion of much research and speculation, and there are still differences of opinion on certain details. Piecing together the various theories, it seems likely that it is a hybrid dance deriving from three main sources: (i) the *Tangano*, a dance of the Africans transported as slaves to Cuba and Haiti in the early eighteenth century (Eros Nicola Siri, quoted by Franks: *Social Dance – A Short History*, p. 178); (ii) the *Habanera*, a Cuban dance of the nineteenth century (Curt Sachs: *World History of the Dance*, p. 445) and (iii) the *Milonga*, a dance of the poorer areas of Buenos Aires in the last two decades of the nineteenth century (Lisa Lekis: *Folk Dances of Latin America*, p. 174).

The Tangano was an African dance which was taken to Cuba and Haiti by Negroes captured as slaves in the early eighteenth century. The Habanera (meaning 'from the city of Havana') was a Cuban dance of the nineteenth century which developed originally from the music and rhythms of the slaves on the plantations. In the course of time both of these dances were taken to South America by Negroes migrating from Cuba to the River Plate area. Here the dances merged into one, and came to the notice of the local seamen and the visiting Argentine gauchos from the cattle-lands. Next the dance turned up, now showing considerable Spanish influence, in the drinking-shops and bordellos of Buenos Aires. It was danced (to the accompaniment of haunting, insidious melodies strummed on guitar and bandoneon) by gauchos, sailors and Italian immigrants, all competing for the favours of the half-Indian women habituées of the waterfront cafes. All the time it was becoming altered by the haphazard addition of movements and rhythms of other Spanish dances, notably the Milonga, a dance of the poorest areas of Buenos Aires in the 1880s. Before the turn of the century the negroid element had almost completely disappeared. The tango was now a sensuous, flamboyant and highly erotic dance, as yet known only in the lowest haunts of Buenos Aires and completely taboo in polite Argentine society.

As time passed, the tango became slightly more respectable, and along Calle Corrientes a number of bars grew up where small orchestras would play tango music for late-night customers. In time, although the dance was still fairly generally outlawed, the orchestras began to grow in size and number. Around 1910 some Parisian entertainment agents, on a visit to Buenos Aires, 'discovered' the music and dance, and promptly signed up several of the best orchestras to play in Paris.

191

Appendix G

The music was an immediate success in the French capital and other towns in France, but the dance had to be modified considerably before it could be accepted generally in public. It became slower and more measured, and the erotic elements were either discarded or toned down. In this way, the more respectable 'Argentine Tango' was born, and in its new form was re-exported back to Buenos Aires!

About the time of its 'discovery' by the Parisian agents in 1910, rumours of the tango reached the general public in London. After the summer of 1911, those who had seen it danced at Dinard, Deauville and other Casino towns began to ask for it in London, and 'tango teas' came into fashion. From then on, for nearly two seasons, London (in common with all the great cities in Europe) went tango mad. In 1913 and 1914 tango teas, publicized as 'Thés Tangos' were held in nearly every hotel and restaurant which had any floor space for dancing. Private tango teas became a prominent feature of many strata of social life, and the aspiring but inexperienced 'Thé dansant' hostess could learn, from Gladys Crozier's book, all she needed to know about how to give an 'Informal Tango Tea' in her own dainty drawing-room: a far cry, indeed, from the brothels of Buenos Aires.

The Press, meantime, was conducting a violent attack on the tango, publishing furious letters from readers protesting against its supposed indelicacies. Rumour had it that Queen Mary had banned the dance at court, but in the summer of 1914 at a ball given by the Grand Duke Michael at Kenwood, the Queen asked the exhibition dancers (Maurice and Florence Walton) if they would dance the tango for her, as she had never seen it. For nearly seven minutes, the exhibition dancers tango'd in front of the Queen and her assembled guests. At the end of the performance, the Queen's glowing praise showed that, far from being shocked, she was delighted by the dance.*

It took a long time, however, for the tango to gain general acceptance in the land of its origin. As late as 1914, the American Consul-General in Buenos Aires, Mr Richard Bartleman, devoted a special section to the tango in his annual report on conditions in the Argentine, stressing that it was not accepted in decent family circles. Not until the end of the First World War was it danced by respectable Argentinians, but, eventually, to know how to dance the tango became a measure of social success in Buenos Aires. In the course of time gramophone records were manufactured in thousands and the tango could be heard throughout the Argentine. Composers then began to write tangos with semi-symphonic preludes, and in the early 1920s, words were added to the music.

In the Argentine today the tango is being considerably undermined by modern influences. Statistics for the sale of gramophone records in Buenos Aires, published by Hugo Bambini, show that, whereas in 1953 tango records constituted 80% of the total, in 1963 that figure had fallen to 25%. The tango is being ousted by the 'beat' dances of the sixties. The Argentine Government, however, is putting up a determined fight on its behalf, and

* Recounted by Philip Richardson: *History of English Ballroom Dancing*.

in 1966 appointed a Government Committee to 'save the tango from oblivion'. As a result of that committee, the Cultural Board of the Ministry of Education has invited the co-operation of composers, authors, musical directors, record manufacturers and theatre proprietors to come together in a joint effort to revive and save the tango, in the city of its birth.

Returning to pre-war England, the tango that took London by storm in 1912 was described in detail by Gladys Crozier in her 40,000 word book *The Tango and how to dance it* published in England towards the end of 1913. The same service was performed for America some months later by the section on the tango in the Vernon Castles' book *Modern Dancing* published in 1914. The figures described in each book show considerable divergence, the Castle version being closer, in the opinion of A. H. Franks, to subsequent English development than the Crozier.

In England, the public craze for the tango evaporated in mid-1914, dispelled partly by the outbreak of war and partly by the coming of 'ragtime' – the new craze in music and dance. In the mid-1920s however, when England was 'dancing-mad', the tango enjoyed a second boom, under the name of the 'new French tango'. The craze spread from London to the provinces, and in the autumn of 1925 some pupils of West End dance-teachers were coming one hundred miles for their weekly tango lesson.

Throughout the twenties, the tango remained a leisurely dance, requiring cat-like grace rather than an abundance of energy. 'Imitate the sinuous grace of the tiger, mademoiselle' said the brilliant exhibition dancers, Los Alamanos, when asked for advice on how to perform the dance. During the thirties, however, the leading bands began to stress the beat until a much more staccato effect was obtained, and halfway through that decade there was a remarkable transformation in the general approach to the dance. Instead of dancing in a dreamy and leisurely way, dancers, particularly in competitions, now produced staccato movements of feet, hands and body which completely transformed the dance.

The modern tango, a staccato dance with a tempo of thirty-three bars a minute, bears little resemblance to the dance of 1912 or to the version which was standardized by the dance teachers' conferences of the 1920s. Yet it still retains that sinuous, cat-like glide which, together with the sensuous 'oversways', show it to be a relation – however distant – of that taboo dance of nineteenth century Buenos Aires.

Appendix H

Below is the programme of a London Old Time Dance Club for a dance held in January 1965. These are all sequence dances, mostly based on early versions of the waltz, tango, foxtrot and quickstep.

Programme

CHRYSANTHEMUM WALTZ

TRELAWNEY TANGO

FELICE FOXTROT

MAYFAIR QUICKSTEP

WHITE ROSE TANGO

MARINE FOURSTEP (PROG.)

ROSELANE WALTZ

BAMBI BLUES

TANGO SERIDA

MOONLIGHT SAUNTER

VARIETY FOXTROT

WALTZ COTILLON

IMPERIAL TWO-STEP (PROG.)

WEDGEWOOD BLUE GAVOTTE

TANGO MAGENTA

MILLBROOK FOXTROT

SHERRIE SAUNTER

HELENA QUICKSTEP

Appendix I

Jamaican Ska or Blue Beat

Introduction

Feet apart, bend trunk slightly forward. 1
Straighten trunk, flexing knees. 2
(Arms are behind back, hands clasped.)
Repeat several times.

Basic I

Touch L.F. to side without weight, bending trunk forward,
extending arms to side at shoulder height. 1
Close L.F. to R.F. flexing knees, straightening trunk and 2
crossing arms in front.
Reverse above and repeat as desired.
This step may be used in turning.

Basic II

Step sideways with L.F. arms out in front, bending trunk for- 1
ward.
Touch ball of R.F. back of L.F. pulling arms back with rowing 2
motion and bending trunk backward as flex knees.
Reverse and repeat as desired.
This step may be used turning.

Basic III

With feet apart transfer weight from one foot to the other as in
Basic II, with trunk bending and knees flexing but swing arms
up and down in front of body alternately; one arm is high as
other is low etc.

Heel Jump

Jump from both feet touching L. heel to side (without weight), 1
trunk bent slightly forward, both arms out to same side as heel.
Jump bringing both feet together, straighten trunk, bringing 2
arms close to body, elbows bent.
Reverse and repeat as desired.

Wash Wash

With feet apart, one foot forward, bend trunk slightly forward
and gradually bend knees deeply and use scrubbing motion
with hands.
Recover gradually.

O 195

Jockey

Feet apart, trunk bending forward, knees flexing as in previous figures, hold L. arm forward, snapping fingers as you circle arm to represent crop. R. hand slaps flank.

NOTE. There are many variations. Hip motion may be used. The above describes the man's part: the lady either does counterpart or uses the same foot as partner. It is danced in couples, facing each other, except when turning. There is no contact.

Appendix J

List of Tables 2 to 32

197

Appendix J

198

Appendix J

TABLE 2
Frequency of Dancing

Category * (Educational)	No. in sample	Every night of the week		Several times a week		Once a week		Once a fortnight		Once a month		Once every three months		Once every six months		Once a year or less		Total
		No.	%	No.	%	No.	%	No.	%	No.	%	No.	%	No.	%	No.	%	%
Secondary Tech. Schoolgirls	29	3	10·4	15	51·7	7	24·1	0	0	2	6·9	0	0	0	0	2	6·9	100
College of Further Education																		
Day Release Girls	53	0	0	20	37·7	14	26·4	4	7·6	6	11·3	5	9·4	4	7·6	0	0	100
Day Release Boys	54	1	1·9	8	14·8	8	14·8	6	11·2	9	16·6	6	11·2	7	12·9	9	16·6	100
College of Higher Education																		
Sec. Course Girls	55	1	1·8	5	9·2	17	30·9	8	14·6	14	25·4	6	10·9	2	3·6	2	3·6	100
Bus. Studies Girls	46	0	0	8	17·4	7	15·2	9	19·6	14	30·4	4	8·7	0	0	4	8·7	100
Bus. Studies Boys	42	0	0	7	16·7	14	33·3	7	16·7	4	9·5	6	14·2	2	4·8	2	4·8	100
Poly. Students	140	1	0·7	6	4·3	25	17·9	** 22	15·7	*** 32	22·9	18	12·8	† 16	11·4	†† 20	14·3	100
Whole Sample	419	6	1·4	69	16·5	92	22	56	13·4	81	19·3	45	10·7	31	7·4	39	9·3	100

* See Table 1 for details: ** 21 male, 1 female. *** 30 male, 2 females.
  † 15 male, 1 female. †† 18 male, 2 female.

199

TABLE 3

Frequency of Dancing

Summary of Important Aspects (compiled from Table 2)

Educational Category	Once a week or more		Once a year or less	
	MALE No. %	FEMALE No. %	MALE No. %	FEMALE No. %
Secondary Technical Schoolgirls		(25) 80·6		(2) 6·9
Day Release Boys	(17) 31·6		(9) 16·6	
Day Release Girls		(34) 64·0		(0) 0
Secretarial (F.T.) Course Girls		(23) 41·8		(2) 3·6
Business Studies (F.T.) Course Boys	(21) 50·0		(2) 4·8	
Business Studies (F.T.) Course Girls		(15) 32·5		(4) 8·7
Polytechnic Students	(32) 22·8	— —	(18) 13·0	(2) 33·1
Total: Male	(70) 30·0		(29) 13·0	
Total: Female		(97) 51·0		(10) 5·0
	M + F No. %		M + F No. %	
Total: Whole Sample	(167) 40		(39) 9·3	

TABLE 4
Polytechnic Students
Frequency of Dancing and Socio-Economic Class

Socio-Economic Classification	No. in Category	Once a fortnight or more		Once a year or less	
		No.	%	No.	%
I Upper Middle	7	5	71	1	1·4
II Middle	53	19	35·8	6	11
III Lower Middle	26	6	23	6	23
IV Skilled Working	34	14	41	5	14·7
V Unskilled Working	3	3	100	0	0
VI Casual or Nat. Assist.	Nil	—	—	—	—
Unclassified	17				
Total	140				

TABLE 5
Day Release and Business Studies Groups
Frequency of Dancing and Socio-Economic Class

	Working-class		Middle or lower-middle class	
	M No. %	F No. %	M No. %	F No. %
Once a week or more	17 31·6	34 64	21 50	15 32·5
Once a year or less	9 16·6	0 0	2 4·8	4 8·7
Number in Category	54	53	42	46

The percentages do not add up to *100* because for purposes of this Table the responses (4), (5), (6) and (7) to Question (1) were not included.

TABLE 6

Degree of Interest in Specified Dances

Secondary Technical Schoolgirls

Name of dance	% who dance it	% who put it as first preference	% who do not dance it but would like to	% who express no interest
JIVE	34·5	3·4	3·4	62
WALTZ	31·0	0	13·8	55·2
SAMBA	6·9	0	0	93·1
FOXTROT	6·9	0	0	93·1
ROCK	27·6	0	3·4	69
SLOW BLUES	37·9	0	10·4	51·7
TANGO	20·7	0	0	79·3
QUICKSTEP	6·9	0	0	93·1
SHAKE OR ANY BEAT DANCE	93·1	93·1	0	6·9
RUMBA	3·4	3·4	0	96·6
CHA-CHA	20·7	0	0	79·3
FOLK	37·9	0	13·8	48·3
OLD TIME	24·1	0	0	75·9
TWIST	44·8	0	6·9	48·3

TABLE 7

Degree of Interest in Specified Dances

Day Release Girls

Name of dance	% who dance it	% who put it as first preference	% who do not dance it but would like to	% who express no interest
JIVE	60·4	9·4	9·4	30·2
WALTZ	62·3	5·7	3·8	33·9
SAMBA	9·4	1·9	22·7	67·9
FOXTROT	11·2	0	13·3	75·5
ROCK	66	7·5	3·8	30·2
SLOW BLUES	79·2	13·2	0	20·8
TANGO	7·5	0	28·3	64·2
QUICKSTEP	37·8	5·7	15·1	47·1
SHAKE OR ANY BEAT DANCE	90·6	50·9	3·8	5·6
RUMBA	7·5	0	15·1	77·4
CHA-CHA	49	3·8	9·4	41·6
FOLK	28·3	0	7·6	64·1
OLD TIME	15·1	1·9	9·4	75·5
TWIST	54·7	0	1·9	43·4

Appendix J

TABLE 8

Degree of Interest in Specified Dances

Day Release Boys

Name of Dance	% who dance it	% who put it as first preference	% who do not dance it but would like to	% who express no interest
JIVE	63	7·4	9·2	27·8
WALTZ	59·3	7·4	11·1	29·6
SAMBA	1·9	0	18·5	79·6
FOXTROT	16·7	0	20·4	62·9
ROCK	66·7	7·4	1·9	31·4
SLOW BLUES	57·4	26	3·7	38·9
TANGO	3·7	0	22·2	74·1
QUICKSTEP	25·9	7·4	18·5	55·6
SHAKE OR ANY BEAT DANCE	63	22·2	7·4	29·6
RUMBA	3·7	0	16·7	79·6
CHA-CHA	37	1·9	11·1	51·9
FOLK	25·9	1·9	9·3	64·8
OLD TIME	7·4	0	5·6	87
TWIST	64·7	13	0	35·3

TABLE 9

Degree of Interest in Specified Dances
Secretarial Course Girls

Name of Dance	% who dance it	% who put it as first preference	% who do not dance it but would like to	% who express no interest
JIVE	65·5	12·7	3·6	30·9
WALTZ	67·3	7·3	3·6	29·1
SAMBA	16·4	3·6	18·2	65·4
FOXTROT	25·5	1·8	9·1	65·4
ROCK	38·2	1·8	0	61·8
SLOW BLUES	76·4	2·4	1·8	21·8
TANGO	16·4	0	23·6	60
QUICKSTEP	56·4	0	5·4	38·2
SHAKE OR ANY BEAT DANCE	90·9	38·2	0	9·1
RUMBA	9·1	0	18·2	72·7
CHA-CHA	58·2	5·4	7·3	34·5
FOLK	45·4	0	7·3	47·3
OLD TIME	12·7	0	7·3	80
TWIST	52·7	1·8	0	47·3

TABLE 10

Degree of Interest in Specified Dances

Business Studies Girls

Name of Dance	% who dance it	% who put it as first preference	% who do not dance it but would like to	% who express no interest
JIVE	69·6	2·2	4·3	26·1
WALTZ	63·0	2·2	2·2	34·8
SAMBA	21·8	0	4·3	73·9
FOXTROT	15·2	0	4·3	80·5
ROCK	45·6	0	0	54·4
SLOW BLUES	80·4	26·1	0	19·6
TANGO	17·4	2·2	17·4	65·2
QUICKSTEP	26·1	0	4·3	69·6
SHAKE OR ANY BEAT DANCE	89·1	60·9	0	10·9
RUMBA	13·0	0	6·5	80·5
CHA-CHA	58·7	2·2	8·7	32·6
FOLK	32·6	4·3	10·9	56·5
OLD TIME	8·7	0	0	91·3
TWIST	58·7	2·2	0	41·3

Appendix J

TABLE 11
Degree of Interest in Specified Dances
Business Studies Boys

Name of Dance	% who dance it	% who put it as first preference	% who do not dance it but would like to	% who express no interest
JIVE	59·5	4·8	2·4	38·1
WALTZ	54·8	4·8	2·4	42·8
SAMBA	4·8	0	7·1	88·1
FOXTROT	19·0	0	2·4	78·6
ROCK	42·8	2·4	0	57·2
SLOW BLUES	66·7	26·2	0	33·3
TANGO	0	0	7·1	92·9
QUICKSTEP	21·4	0	9·5	69·1
SHAKE OR ANY BEAT DANCE	78·6	45·2	0	21·4
RUMBA	7·1	0	4·8	88·1
CHA-CHA	40·5	0	4·8	54·7
FOLK	28·6	4·8	0	71·4
OLD TIME	16·7	0	0	83·3
TWIST	42·8	7·1	0	57·2

TABLE 12

Degree of Interest in Specified Dances

Polytechnical Students

Name of Dance	% who dance it	% who put it as first preference	% who do not dance it but would like to	% who express no interest
JIVE	52·1	19·3	8·6	39·3
WALTZ	73·6	16·4	6·4	20
SAMBA	15·7	0	17·8	66·5
FOXTROT	23·6	1·4	20·7	55·7
ROCK	48·6	21·4	1·4	50
SLOW BLUES	56·4	11·4	0·7	42·9
TANGO	15	0	25·7	59·3
QUICKSTEP	45	5·7	15·7	39·3
SHAKE OR ANY BEAT DANCE	63·5	17·1	0	36·5
RUMBA	21·4	11·4	12·2	76·4
CHA-CHA	52·9	5·7	7·8	39·3
FOLK	22·1	1·4	7·2	70·7
OLD TIME	17·1	0·7	2·9	80
TWIST	72·1	2·9	0	27·9

TABLE 13

Degree of Interest in Specific Dances
Summary compiled from Tables 6–12

Educational Category	The three dances (in order) most commonly danced		The dance shown most frequently as first preference		The dance most frequently shown as the one they do not do but would like to	
	Name of dance	% who dance it	Name of dance	% putting it first	Name of dance	%
Secondary Technical Schoolgirls	Shake/ Beat Twist Folk ⎱ Slow ⎰ Blues	93·1 44·8 37·9 37·9	Shake/ Beat	93·1	Folk Waltz	13·8 13·8
Day Release Boys	Rock Twist Jive ⎱ Shake/⎰ Beat	66·7 64·7 63 63	Slow Blues	26	Tango	22·2
Day Release Girls	Shake/ Beat Slow Blues Waltz	90·6 79·2 62·3	Shake/ Beat	50·9	Tango	28·3
Secretarial Course Girls	Shake/ Beat Slow Blues Waltz	90·9 76·4 67·3	Shake/ Beat	38·2	Tango	23·6
Business Studies Boys	Shake/ Beat Slow Blues Jive	78·6 80·4 69·6	Shake/ Beat	45·2	Quick-step	9·5

TABLE 13 *cont.*

Educational Category	The three dances (in order) most commonly danced		The dance shown most frequently as first preference		The dance most frequently shown as the one they do not do but would like to	
	Name of dance	*% who dance it*	*Name of dance*	*% putting it first*	*Name of dance*	*%*
Business Studies Girls	Shake/ Beat Slow Blues Jive	89·1 80·4 69·9	Shake/ Beat	60·9	Tango	17·4
Polytechnic Students	Waltz Twist Shake/ Beat	63·6 72·1 63·5	Rock	21·4	Tango	25·7

Appendix J

TABLE 14

Ballroom Dancing: Degree of Interest

(Information compiled from Tables 6–12)

Educational Category	WALTZ % who have no interest	FOXTROT % who have no interest	QUICK-STEP % who have no interest	TANGO % who have no interest
Secondary Technical Schoolgirls	55·2	93·1	93·1	79·3
Day Release Boys	29·6	62·9	55·6	74·1
Day Release Girls	33·9	75·5	47·1	64·2
Secretarial Course Girls	29·1	65·4	38·2	60
Business Studies Boys	42·8	78·6	69·1	92·9
Business Studies Girls	34·8	80·5	69·6	65·2
Polytechnic Students	20	55·7	39·3	59·3

NOTE: 'Have no interest' means (1) that they do not do the dance; and (2) that they express no wish to do it.

Appendix J

TABLE 14A
Ballroom Dances: Wish to Learn

Dance	Sec. Tech. Girls	Day Rel. Boys	Day Rel. Girls	Bus. St. Boys	Bus. St. Girls	Sec. Course Girls	Poly-technic Stdts.
	%	%	%	%	%	%	%
WALTZ	13·8	11·1	3·8	2·4	2·2	3·6	6·4
FOXTROT	0	20·4	13·3	2·4	4·3	9·1	20·7
QUICKSTEP	0	18·5	15·1	9·5	4·3	5·4	15·7
TANGO	0	22·2	28·3	7·1	17·4	23·6	25·7

TABLE 15
'Latin American' Social Dancing: Degrees of Interest
(Information compiled from Tables 6–12)

Educational Category	SAMBA % with no interest	RUMBA % with no interest	CHA-CHA % with no interest
Secondary Technical Schoolgirls	65·4	72·7	34·5
Day Release Boys	88·1	88·1	54·7
Day Release Girls	73·9	80·5	32·6
Secretarial Course Girls	65·4	72·7	34·5
Business Studies Boys	88·1	88·1	54·7
Business Studies Girls	73·9	80·5	34·5
Polytechnic Students	66·5	76·4	39·3

NOTE: 'Have no interest' means (1) that they do not dance it; and (2) that they express no wish to.

212

TABLE 16

Question 22
Modern 'Beat Dancing' – Educational Categories

Educational Category	% of group who dance beat	% of group who sometimes dance beat without partners
Secondary Technical Schoolgirls	93·1	72·3
Day Release Boys	63	48·0
Day Release Girls	90·6	64·1
Secretarial Course Girls	90·9	12·7
Business Studies Boys	78·6	26·2
Business Studies Girls	89·1	36·9
Polytechnic Students	63·5	13·5

TABLE 17
Modern Beat Dancing: Sex Differences

	No. in sample	Total who dance beat		Total who dance sometimes without partner	
		No.	%	No.	%
Male:					
Day Release	54	34		26	
Business Studies	42	33		11	
Total	96	67	69·8	37	38·5
Female:					
Day Release	53	51		34	
Business Studies	46	43		17	
Total	99	94	94·9	51	51·5

TABLE 18

Modern Beat Dancing: Class Differences

	No. in sample	Total who dance beat		Total who dance sometimes without partner	
		No.	%	No.	%
Working Class:					
Day Release Girls	53	51	90·6	34	64
Day Release Boys	54	34	63	26	48
Middle Class:					
Business Studies Boys	42	33	78·6	11	26·2
Business Studies Girls	46	43	89·1	17	37
Working class F	Summary		90·6		64
Middle class F			89·1		37
Working class M			63		48
Middle class M			78·6		26·2

TABLE 19

Beat Dancing: Age Differences

Age-group	No. in group	Those who sometimes dance without partner		Total who dance beat	
		No.	%	No.	%
13–15	29	21	72·4	27	93·1
16	38	20	52·6	34	81·5
17	58	28	48	49	84·5
18	83	27	32·5	74	89·2
19	54	12	22·2	41	75·9
20	54	15	27·8	48	88·9
21	39	6	15·4	31	79·5
22	21	2	9·5	16	76·2
23+	43	4	9·3	29	67·4

Rank Order Correlations

Age (order)	% partnerless dancing (correlated)	d	d²	% dancing beat (correlated)	d	d²
1	1	0	0	1	0	0
2	2	0	0	2	0	0
3	3	0	0	5	2	4
4	4	0	0	3	1	1
5	6	1	1	6	1	1
6	5	1	1	4	2	4
7	7	0	0	7	0	0
8	8	0	0	8	0	0
9	9	0	0	9	0	0
			2			10

Correlation of age and partnerless beat dancing   + 0·98
Correlation of age and beat dancing   + 0·92   Formula $\dfrac{1 - 6\Sigma d^2}{n(n^2 - 1)}$

TABLE 20

Age Group for whom Beat Dances Considered Unsuitable

Category	Over 20	Over 30	Over 40	Age is of no im- portance
	%	%	%	%
Secondary Technical Schoolgirls	13·8	34·5	3·4	48·3
Day Release Girls	7·5	37·8	20·8	34
Day Release Boys	12·9	25	16·6	42·5
Secretarial Course Girls	7·3	41·8	16·4	32·7
Business Studies Girls	15·2	41·3	15·2	26·1
Business Studies Boys	14·3	42·8	2·4	35·7
Polytechnic Students	9·28	24·3	17·1	43·6

N.B.: These percentages do not always add up to 100% since not everyone stated an opinion under this heading.

TABLE 21

Wish to Learn/Do Any New Dance

Educational Category	Wish to learn/do any new dance	
	Number	*%*
Secondary Technical Schoolgirls	17	58·6
Day Release Boys	29	53·7
Day Release Girls	34	64
Secretarial Course Girls	28	50
Business Studies Boys	10	23·8
Business Studies Girls	18	39·1
Polytechnic Students	82	58·6
Whole Sample	218	52

TABLE 22

Reasons for Going Dancing (in order of importance)

Category	Order of preference	A particular group is playing	To meet or be with the opposite sex	Dance is run by an organization you belong to	Your friends go	You enjoy dancing
		%	%	%	%	%
Secondary	1	6·9	48·3	0	34·5	10·3
Technical	2	17·3	3·4	3·4	27·6	48·2
Schoolgirls	3	27·6	20·7	13·8	24·1	17·3
	4	4·3	20·7	6·9	6·9	17·3
	5	6·9	6·9	69·0	0	6·9
Day Release	1	20·8	7·5	3·8	17·0	50·9
Girls	2	17·0	20·8	3·8	34·0	22·6
	3	18·8	17·0	18·5	32·0	13·2
	4	28·3	28·3	17·0	17·0	5·5
	5	9·4	24·5	52·8	0	5·5
Day Release	1	18·5	21·9	12·9	12·9	11·1
Boys	2	11·1	31·3	5·5	50·0	7·4
	3	21·9	24·1	7·4	14·8	14·8
	4	21·9	11·1	29·6	11·1	48·2
	5	21·9	5·5	35·3	3·7	11·1
Secretarial	1	5·4	27·3	5·4	1·8	40
Course Girls	2	10·9	25·4	5·4	20·0	27·3
	3	23·6	16·4	5·4	27·3	10·9
	4	21·8	10·9	25·4	23·6	1·8
	5	21·8	3·6	58·2	7·3	5·4
Business	1	23·9	19·6	6·5	21·7	23·9
Studies Girls	2	10·9	32·6	6·5	21·7	19·6
	3	19·6	10·9	10·9	32·6	21·7
	4	28·3	19·6	23·9	13·0	10·9
	5	8·7	13·0	47·8	6·5	19·6

N.B.: These percentages do not always add up to 100, since some reasons were left blank.

TABLE 22 *cont.*

Category	Order of pre-ference	A parti-cular group is playing	To meet or be with the opposite sex	Dance is run by an organ-ization you belong to	Your friends go	You enjoy dancing
		%	%	%	%	%
Business	1	9·5	45·2	11·9	16·7	14·3
Studies Boys	2	9·5	23·8	7·1	33·3	11·9
	3	14·3	11·9	11·9	23·8	28·6
	4	42·8	9·5	16·7	11·9	14·3
	5	14·3	0	42·8	4·8	23·8
Polytechnic	1	5·0	35·7	12·1	13·6	25·7
Students	2	7·9	21·4	12·1	28·6	12·8
	3	15·0	11·4	15·0	23·6	15·7
	4	20·0	12·8	24·3	10·0	16·4
	5	36·5	5·0	22·1	5·7	15·0

N.B.: These percentages do not always add up to 100, since some reasons were left blank.

TABLE 23
Summary of Table 22: Reasons for Going Dancing
The two reasons most frequently given first preference and the reason most frequently put last

Educational Category	The two reasons (in order) most frequently given first preference	% giving it as first preference	The reason most frequently put last	% putting it last
Secondary Technical Schoolgirls	(1) To meet or be with opposite sex	48·3	Dance is run by an organization you belong to	69
	(2) Your friends go	34·5		
Day Release Boys	(1) To meet or be with the opposite sex	21·9	Dance is run by an organization you belong to	35·3
	(2) A particular group is playing	20·8		
Day Release Girls	(1) You enjoy dancing	50·9	Dance is run by an organization you belong to	52·8
	(2) A particular group is playing	20·8		
Secretarial Course Girls	(1) You enjoy dancing	40	Dance is run by an organization you belong to	58·2
	(2) To meet or be with opposite sex	27·3		
Business Studies Boys	(1) To meet or be with opposite sex	45·2	Dance is run by an organization you belong to	42·8
	(2) Your friends go	16·7		
Business Studies Girls	(1) You enjoy dancing	23·9	Dance is run by an organization you belong to	47·8
	(2) A particular group is playing	23·9		
Polytechnic Students	(1) To meet or be with opposite sex	35·7	A particular group is playing	36·5
	(2) You enjoy dancing	25·7		

Appendix J

TABLE 24

Reasons for Enjoyment in Dancing

(in order of importance)

Category	Order of preference	The steps and movement	The presence of the opposite sex	The music and rhythm
		%	%	%
Secondary	1st	13·8	37·9	41·3
Technical	2nd	27·6	31·0	34·5
Schoolgirls	3rd	51·7	24·1	17·2
Day Release	1st	9·4	9·4	75·0
Girls	2nd	43·4	35·8	15·1
	3rd	51·0	49.0	3·8
Day Release	1st	12·9	29·6	48·2
Boys	2nd	14·8	42·7	33·4
	3rd	57·4	18·5	3·7
Secretarial	1st	9·1	27·3	54·5
Course Girls	2nd	20·0	40·0	25·4
	3rd	58·2	21·8	7·3
Business Studies	1st	2·2	19·6	73·9
Girls	2nd	28·3	47·8	17·4
	3rd	63·0	26·1	4·3
Business Studies	1st	14·3	45·2	35·7
Boys	2nd	21·4	30·9	47·6
	3rd	59·5	14·3	11·9
Polytechnic	1st	14·3	40·0	31·4
Students	2nd	16·4	24·3	38·6
	3rd	49·3	18·6	12·8

The percentages above relate to the percentages in each category giving first, second or third preference to each of the three reasons.

TABLE 25

Summary of Table 24: Reasons for Enjoyment in Dancing

The reason most commonly put first *and* last

Educational Category	The reason most frequently put first	%	The reason most frequently put last	%
Secondary Technical Schoolgirls	The music and rhythm	41·3	The steps and movement	51·7
Day Release Boys	The music and rhythm	48·2	The steps and movement	57·4
Day Release Girls	The music and rhythm	75·0	The steps and movement	51·0
Secretarial Course Girls	The music and rhythm	54·5	The steps and movement	58·2
Business Studies Boys	The presence of opposite sex	45·2	The steps and movement	59·5
Business Studies Girls	The music and rhythm	73·9	The steps and movement	63·0
Polytechnic Students	The presence of opposite sex	40·0	The steps and movement	49·3

TABLE 26

Secondary Technical Schoolgirls' Attitudes Expressed to
Beat and Ballroom Types of Dancing*

Reasons for liking beat	Reasons for disliking beat	Reasons for liking ballroom	Reasons for disliking ballroom
Rhythm of the music	Nil	I like to watch, but not to dance	I hate waltz
Rhythm		I like to watch only	They are old-fashioned, only old people do them
Own individual style and one can be less inhibited because there are no rules		I like waltz: it is the only ballroom dance I can do	They are old-fashioned
No specific rules		Because I have been doing them for so long and hope one day to be World Champion	They are too old for the younger generation
Loosens up the muscles			I don't no how to dance them
Loosens up the muscles			I don't know how to dance them
Loosens up the muscles			They are old-fashioned
They are modern			They are old-fashioned
They are modern			They are old-fashioned and a bore
They are modern			
They are modern			It is old-fashioned and boring
I like it			Alright for some people but boring for us
I like it			
I like it			Old fashioned and I like to be modern
I like it			

TABLE 26 *cont.*

Reasons for liking beat	*Reasons for disliking beat*	*Reasons for liking ballroom*	*Reasons for disliking ballroom*
I like it			Oldfashioned and I like to keep up with the modern dances
I like it			
They are nice			
They are nice			Oldfashioned and I like the modern dances
They are smashing			
There's a lot of movement and they are modern			Alright for some people but not for me
Movement and they are modern			It is square, man, square
They are modern and have a lot of movement			It's booring
They are real gear: the're fab			They are just for big squares, such as Mums and Dads
They are real gear: just great man			
I do			
I do			

Reasons most frequently mentioned for liking beat	*No. of times*	*Reasons most frequently mentioned for disliking ballroom*	*No. of times*
'Modern'	7	Old-fashioned and/or 'square'	12
'I like it,' 'I do'	7	Boring	5
'Movement' and 'loosens up muscles'	6		

* The schoolgirls' spelling has been retained !

TABLE 27

*College of Further Education: Day Release Girls' Attitudes
Expressed to Beat and Ballroom Forms of Dancing*

Reasons for Liking Beat

(1) You can dance on your own or in a crowd and when you feel like it and not have to wait to be asked – and similarly start and stop whenever you wish.

(2) Ideal for young teenage girls because they can dance in groups together omitting boys.

(3) One does not need a partner: a group of girls can do it together.

(4) Anyone can have a 'go': everyone can join in.

(5) One can create one's own variations without being tied to another person.

(6) One can do one's own steps or variations.

(7) It enables one to be creative and to relate the steps to the music.

(8) You can express how you feel when you dance modern.

(9) It is a way of expressing one's feelings in a free type of movement and rhythm.

(10) One can express one's rhythm in a happy free atmosphere.

(11) You are not restricted in the steps and movements; you can make up the steps, if you like, as you go along.

(12) You can dance your own way and just move to the music.

(13) You can really get into the feel of the dance.

(14) There is a sense of freedom to do any movements one would like.

(15) I can let myself go and dance how I like.

(16) I can do whatever steps I like that are in time with the music.

(17) One can dance freely to the rhythm and also develop one's own version of these dances.

(18) I find it very exciting for myself and all the other teenagers.

(19) When people dance in a crowd it seems to create an atmosphere of enjoyment.

(20) It makes you feel free to enjoy yourself.

(21) They are lively and fun to do.

(22) Enjoyment. Gives me a 'kick'.

(23) At a party they are lots of fun: they are lively.

(24) It is fun and they are quick; they are fast-moving, more enjoyable than slow dances.

(25) You can let yourself go and are unrestricted and you enjoy yourself.

(26) It is fun dancing them.

(27) They allow you to let yourself go.

(28) You can let yourself go – nobody really cares what they look like to other people watching.

(29) You can dance about and never do a wrong step so that way you don't feel silly.

(30) The steps are easy: anybody can do them.

(31) You just move around how you like.

TABLE 27 (*cont.*)

Reasons for Liking Beat (cont.)

(32)   There are no special steps to remember.
(33)   You can improvize: no one knows if you do the wrong steps – it does not throw you out of rhythm.
(34)   These dances are not hard to learn: one usually has to watch another person and in no time he or she can do the dance.
(35)   The modern generation can identify themselves with the music and feel inspired by it.
(36)   Modern and fashionable.
(37)   They are the 'in' things of the sixties.
(38)   You can adapt the dance to meet the latest movements going.
(39)   Makes a change from ballroom dancing.
(40)   More variety than in ballroom dancing.
(41)   The music is good: plenty of rhythm and movement.
(42)   The music is so lively.
(43)   You can dance to any record.
(44)   Suitable to a confined space.
(45)   Ideal for parties and small groups of friends.
(46)   Gets rid of surplus energy.
(47)   It is exercise: gets rid of energy.

SUMMARY

Type of Reason most frequently mentioned	*No. of times*	
Freedom:		
(a) linked with absence of need for partner (see (1) to (5) above)	5	
(b) linked with creative self-expression (see (6) to (17) above)	12	17
Fun: excitement: 'Letting Oneself Go' (see (18) to (28) above)		11
Ease of performance: No 'wrong' steps (see (29) to (34) above)		6
Modernity (see (35) to (38) above)		4

Reasons for Disliking Beat

(1) They are a waste of energy and look silly.

Reasons for Liking Ballroom

(1) The dances are fairly standardized and it is possible therefore to dance them in different places and with different people.
(2) There is a lot more to them than beat dances.
(3) Much more interesting.
(4) There are definite steps and variations which are fairly easy to learn.
(5) I feel a sense of achievement when dancing them.
(6) There is an art to them and when done properly give satisfaction.
(7) There are definite steps which I feel all teenagers should know.
(8) More boys would overcome shyness to ask a girl to dance if only they would learn them, instead of standing at the back of dance halls, idle.
(9) It is nice to be able to go to all types of dances and not feel out of it.
(10) Modern dances will forever change but these will stay the same.
(11) It looks nice to see a couple dancing together, with steps exactly the same.
(12) Elegant and ladylike. Smooth movement.
(13) Very nice if done properly.
(14) Graceful movement. The rhythm and systematic movements involved.
(15) Far more graceful on formal occasions where modern dances would look out of place.
(16) They are graceful and pleasing to watch.
(17) Every couple on the floor is doing practically the same movements.
(18) One can make conversation.
(19) Opportunity for conversation with one's partner.
(20) Quieter than 'beat'. They don't wear you out so quickly.
(21) They give you a chance to get near your partner.
(22) Much more intimate than dancing as one of a crowd.
(23) You can dance better with your partner.
(24) It closes the gap between old and young if you can dance 'their' dances with them.
(25) I think I will appreciate them more when I am older.
(26) You can have a lot of fun trying these dances and you can discover some of the reasons why elderly people enjoy them.
(27) They are something different now and again.
(28) They are a change from beat dances.
(29) There is more variety in the steps than if you were dancing a dance they do today.
(30) I enjoy them if they are done properly by people who can dance.
(31) I enjoy them.
(32) I prefer this type of dance because my fiancé can do them.

Appendix J

Reasons for Liking Ballroom (*cont.*)

Summary

Type of reason most frequently mentioned	No. of times
Interest and sense of achievement (see (1) to (9) above)	9
Pleasing to watch: graceful (see (11) to (17) above)	7
Opportunity to get to know partner (see (18) to (23) above)	6
'Closing gap' between young and old (see (24) to (26) above)	3
Variety (see (27) to (29) above)	3

Reasons for Disliking 'Ballroom'

(1) They are not my type.
(2) That's easy to answer – RUBBISH ! !
(3) They are out of date and do not appeal to me.
(4) I think it very boring for teenagers.
(5) They are too slow and old-fashioned.
(6) Because they are the same old steps and you have to be sure your feet are in the right place or you can look odd.
(7) I feel clumsy when doing these dances.
(8) Lessons usually have to be taken before one is perfect in the dance.

Summary

Type of reason most frequently mentioned	No. of times
Out of date, not for teenage generation (see (1) to (5) above)	5
Necessity for learning (see (6) to (8) above)	3

Appendix J

TABLE 28

College of Further Education
Day Release Boys' Attitude Expressed to Beat and Ballroom
Forms of Dancing

Reasons for Liking Beat

(1) They are easy to dance: no restriction to the movement and steps.
(2) One can do what one likes without keeping to any set movement.
(3) I can improvize and copy and nobody cares: it is so informal.
(4) Easy to do; they do not conform to a pattern.
(5) You can improvize to the music instead of having to *learn* definite steps.
(6) They give scope to the amateur.
(7) Sensation I derive out of moving to the beat and rhythm of the music.
(8) I can enjoy the music more by dancing and moving with the beat.
(9) The catchy rhythm of the dance and also the gay mood they add to any party.
(10) The good beat and rhythm.
(11) Because of the fast beat and rhythm.
(12) Enjoyment.
(13) You enjoy yourself and you meet more people.
(14) It gives me a chance to let off steam and enjoy myself.
(15) It's a way of letting off steam.
(16) They give you something out of life and then relax you.
(17) Great fun: I just like dancing them.
(18) They help to relieve the tension and boredom of everyday life.
(19) They have a lot of movement.
(20) A good energetic exercise.
(21) Energetic.
(22) Self-expression: fits in with present musical idiom.
(23) It allows you to express your feelings in a dance.
(24) If without a girl-friend you can still dance by yourself or with a crowd of boys.
(25) It is something to do at a party or dance.
(26) It is not so much the beat dances that I like but the atmosphere, girls and music that you get in these places.
(27) It is fashionable to do so.

Summary

Type of reason most frequently mentioned	No. of times
Fun: Enjoyment: Letting off steam (see (12) to (18) above)	7
Easy to Do: Informal (see (1) to (6) above)	6
The beat and rhythm (see (7) to (11) above)	5

Appendix J

Reasons for Disliking Beat

(1) You look a nit.
(2) They are ridiculous-looking dances.
(3) No set steps, just a jumble.
(4) Dances are very simple, and require no great hardship to learn.
(5) Noise too great so little talking is possible.
(6) You have no contact with your partner who could just be a puppet.

Reasons for Liking Ballroom

(1) You can get to know people on social occasions, e.g. weddings, firm' dances etc. if you know how to dance some of them.
(2) It is always handy to know how to do them later on in life.
(3) Not all dances – e.g. weddings – play all pop music and it is useful to dance these dances.
(4) It is useful to know these dances when at an important occasion, e.g. wedding, dinner and dance.
(5) I believe everyone should have a second form of dance to change to.
(6) You do not feel 'left out'.
(7) I like dancing and feel awkward if there are some I cannot do.
(8) I dance these at our football and cricket dances where a small band plays any music from Old Time to shake.
(9) They are for all ages.
(10) If you go to a dance in a different district it is quite probable the beat dances will be different, but the ballroom dances are the same wherever you go.
(11) The music is more tuneful and rhythmical to dance to.
(12) There is a fluid movement: the movements are interesting.
(13) Their grace.
(14) More enjoyment.
(15) It is relaxing.
(16) You can relax.
(17) They are smooth, elegant and very relaxing.
(18) A certain amount of skill is required as well as natural rhythm and very high standards are attainable by practice: a personal sense of achievement.
(19) There is more purpose in these dances.
(20) A person who can dance in ballroom style can say that he has accomplished something.
(21) One has a feeling of accomplishment at having learnt a dance that has been handed down over the years.
(22) Because I'm dancing with a girl.
(23) One has contact with one's partner.
(24) There is contact with the partner.
(25) It is easy to talk to people.
(26) I like all dances but not too much of the same.
(27) Make a change from the pop dances.
(28) It is a chance to dress properly – in a suit etc.

Reasons for Liking Ballroom (cont.)

Summary

Type of reason most frequently mentioned	No. of times
Usefulness on social occasions (see (1) to (10) above)	10
Enjoyment of movement and rhythm (see (11) to (17) above)	7
Sense of achievement (see (18) to (21) above)	4
Opportunity to get to know partner (see (22) to (25) above)	4

Reasons for Disliking Ballroom
(1) Set movements with little variation.
(2) They are conforming to society and we are told what to do – each step is laid down.

TABLE 29

College of Higher Education

Full-time Business Studies Course Girls' Attitudes Expressed to Beat and Ballroom Forms of Dancing

Reasons for Liking Beat
(1) There is freedom of movement and I like beat songs.
(2) The music creates a lively atmosphere.
(3) They have rhythm.
(4) The rhythm of the music is definite.
(5) Once I hear beat music I just can't sit down because it gives such a good atmosphere.
(6) Freedom of movement.
(7) They have some rhythm to them.
(8) Rhythm.
(9) I enjoy certain types of pop music which make me want to dance and the obvious dance is the 'beat' dances.
(10) Rhythm. Pleasant atmosphere.
(11) You can really dance with all of you and they are fun.
(12) It is active and sometimes you feel like living it up.
(13) They are great fun.
(14) Because they are a good way of getting rid of natural exuberance.
(15) They are lively and they get one going right up to a climax.

Reasons for Liking Beat (cont.)

(16) More life, fun, noise and altogether a great atmosphere.
(17) 'Cos they're sexy.
(18) They're fun.
(19) There are no rules of how they should be danced.
(20) Easy to do.
(21) They are more enjoyable and easy to do.
(22) They cheer you up and are easy to learn.
(23) No particular steps have to be learnt.
(24) They can be learnt quickly and are fairly easy.
(25) They are easy to learn and once you know them they are very enjoyable.
(26) They are not very hard to learn, so everyone can enjoy himself and be relaxed.
(27) They are easy to learn.
(28) You don't really have to know a particular step.
(29) They enable people to go without a boy and not look ridiculous.
(30) They lack conformism, one can develop a certain style of dancing, there is no partner to put one off.
(31) They are fashionable.
(32) They are the latest dances.
(33) Dancing helps the atmosphere and therefore one enjoys the occasion better.
(34) I like them.

Summary

Type of reasons most frequently mentioned	No. of times
Music, rhythm and movement (see (1) to (10) above)	10
Fun: Excitement: Letting oneself go (see (11) to (18) above)	8
Ease of performance: Little learning (see (19) to (28) above)	10

Reasons for Disliking Beat
(1) One looks and feels stupid dancing them.

Reasons for Liking Ballroom
(1) They are very graceful dances.
(2) Because it is graceful, attractive.
(3) They are graceful and rhythmic.

Reasons for Liking Ballroom (*cont.*)

(4) They are not so tiring as 'beat' dances and look much more elegant.
(5) They are so graceful and sophisticated.
(6) They remind me of the old days when there used to be the necessity to have a good partner; they are more romantic than nowadays.
(7) They are very relaxing and elegant.
(8) They are suitable when dancing with a member of the opposite sex.
(9) You are not so much on your own.
(10) They are more suitable when dancing with the opposite sex.
(11) They require skill.
(12) They have more meaning to them.
(13) It is nice for a change.

Summary

Type of reason most frequently mentioned	*No. of times*
Graceful, elegant, romantic etc. (see (1) to (7) above)	7
Presence of a partner (see (8) to (10) above)	3

Reasons for Disliking Ballroom

(1) They are for older people and young boys look so effeminate dancing them.
(2) They are square and stuffy and are for the over forties.
(3) More for old people.
(4) 'Square'. Only for Mum and Dad.
(5) Old fashioned and not many young people dance these any more.
(6) They are for the old people.
(7) They are difficult to learn and once you learn you can only do them with special partners.
(8) They are difficult to learn as people are wary of dancing because it is a skill.
(9) They are too complicated and I hate people treading on my feet.
(10) Difficult.
(11) You have to dance with no physical movement other than the feet.
(12) Too formal.
(13) I can't dance these dances and I prefer the people who like pop.
(14) I can't do them.
(15) Dead music.
(16) They're sexless.
(17) They are a bore.
(18) They are a drag.

Appendix J

Reasons for Disliking Ballroom (*cont.*)

Summary

Type of reason most frequently mentioned	No. of times
Out of date: not for teenage generation (see (1) to (6) above)	6
Necessity for learning, etc. (see (7) to (11) above)	5

TABLE 30

College of Higher Education
Full-time Business Studies Course Boys' Attitudes Expressed to
Beat and Ballroom Forms of Dancing

Reasons for Liking Beat

(1) It's good fun and I enjoy it.
(2) I enjoy the sensationalism.
(3) It allows one to 'go mad' to a limited extent, and to let off steam in a fairly safe way.
(4) It gives me the chance to work off excess energy.
(5) They give a way of expressing feelings in action, and letting off pent-up emotions.
(6) You let off steam, and meet the best of the females.
(7) They are lively and usually put one in a happy mood.
(8) It gets your feelings out of your system, and it's stimulating.
(9) It's great fun.
(10) Because of the rhythm.
(11) I like to dance to the rhythm of a record.
(12) I like dancing and listening to the music.
(13) I like beat music and to dance to it gives me even more pleasure.
(14) You can dance to the beat.
(15) Because I enjoy the rhythm of the beat and it is exercise at the same time.
(16) Beat and rhythm.
(17) It stimulates my emotions towards the opposite sex.
(18) It makes me feel very sexy towards the opposite sex.
(19) They are stimulating.
(20) Sexy; intimate.
(21) I like seeing girls' bosoms bounce.
(22) I can dance how I like.
(23) More freedom and movement in the dance.

234

Reasons for Liking Beat (cont.)

(24) They are informal, easy and uninhibited.
(25) Complete freedom of style and speed.
(26) It is only here for a short time and I intend to enjoy it while it lasts.
(27) I am freezing outside.
(28) They appeal to me and my friend, therefore I enjoy myself and I do not feel out of place.
(29) They are up to date.
(30) They are with it.

Summary

Type of reason most frequently mentioned	No. of times
Fun: Enjoyment; Letting off steam (see (1) to (9) above)	9
Beat and Rhythm (see (10) to (16) above)	7
Sex (see (17) to (21) above)	5
Easy to do: Informal: No rules (see (22) to (25) above)	4

Reasons for Disliking Beat

(1) I dislike the music.
(2) There is no physical contact.
(3) When you presumably become older, you cannot go to the firm's dance and do the shake.
(4) They consist of unnecessary sexual manifestations and barbaric gesticulations.

Reasons for Liking Ballroom

(1) They are a good thing to know.
(2) Only for the social necessity of being able to dance this sort of dance.
(3) When you are on holiday they do not go in for the modern dances, so to meet a member of the opposite sex I have to dance these.
(4) They are useful when you go to formal occasions such as marriage celebrations.
(5) They are partner dances.
(6) I find them relaxing, and you hold your partner.
(7) There is a chance to become closer to the partner.
(8) I enjoy the steps and movement, music and rhythm.
(9) They are dances, not 'displays'.

Reasons for Liking Ballroom (cont.)
(10) People enjoy doing them.
(11) It gives me a sense of achievement if I don't tread on my partner's feet.
(12) There is a set method.
(13) They are right for elderly people.
(14) They are the dances of the past and when danced, they bring back happy memories to mothers and fathers, grannies and grandfathers.

Summary

Type of reason most frequently mentioned	No. of times
Usefulness on social occasions (see (1) to (4) above)	4
Physical contact with partner (see (5) to (7) above)	3
Enjoyment of movement and rhythm (see (8) to (10) above)	3

Reasons for Disliking Ballroom
(1) They are boring.
(2) They are a drag.
(3) They are slow and uninteresting.
(4) They are boring.
(5) They seem boring.
(6) Old fashioned.
(7) Old fashioned.
(8) They are too formal.
(9) Too formal.
(10) They do not appeal to me.
(11) Do not enjoy them.
(12) I can't do them.
(13) I dislike the music.
(14) No real intimate relationship between partners.
(15) The type of people that go there are very unfriendly and keep to themselves.

Summary

Type of reason most frequently mentioned	No. of times
Boring, etc. (see (1) to (5) above)	5

Appendix J

TABLE 31

College of Higher Education
Full-time Secretarial Course Girls' Attitudes Expressed to
Beat and Ballroom Forms of Dancing

Reasons for Liking Beat

(1) Because of the rhythm, good music.
(2) They can be improvized and have great sense of rhythm.
(3) I like the rhythms and jumping around.
(4) I like jumping and wriggling about.
(5) The rhythm is marvellous and they are lively.
(6) I enjoy the movement and rhythm.
(7) Outlet for energies: rhythm.
(8) I love the rhythm.
(9) Because of the rhythm and the repetitive tunes.
(10) It enables you to let yourself go.
(11) They are exciting, one can meet other people from the same age group and different backgrounds.
(12) You can go wild and have a great time on your own (almost).
(13) They are rhythmatic – exciting and one can dance what one likes, within reason, and it makes one forget one's miseries.
(14) The repetitive rhythm is very inspiring and the actual vigorous movements allow for the release of tension and emotions.
(15) It is a lively dance, good exercise, and makes one feel young and gay.
(16) They make me happy and I like looking at longhaired groups playing. Fantastic.
(17) A means of escapism and the music is often very enjoyable.
(18) You can express your feelings more easily.
(19) Movements are free and not restricted by conventional steps.
(20) You can express yourself without restriction: can dance how you like.
(21) I feel more at home with these.
(22) I like to feel free to dance as I wish.
(23) They excite and arouse the emotions and bring an element of freedom – no longer restricted by social codes of behaviour.
(24) All young people – therefore not open to criticism from other age groups.
(25) The nature of modern dances enables the dancer to show his individuality in his movements.
(26) I can be in the company of my friends and yet they cannot impose themselves on me when dancing.
(27) You can dance how you like.
(28) I am an exhibitionist, and they are exciting but also very easy dances – no basic pattern to follow.
(29) It is a lively dance and one does not have to be a very good dancer to enjoy it.

Reasons for Liking Beat (cont.)

(30) Your partner doesn't necessarily have to be a good dancer for you to enjoy it.
(31) No fear of looking foolish if you do not know the steps. The atmosphere is also far less formal and you lose any inhibitions you may have about dancing.
(32) It is possible to do them without having to learn: one can improvize.

Summary

Type of reason most frequently mentioned	No. of times
Freedom including self-expression (see (15) to (28) above)	11
Music, rhythm and movement (see (1) to (9) above)	9
Fun; Excitement; Letting oneself go (see (10) to (17) above)	8
Ease of Performance: No wrong steps (see (29) to (32) above)	4

Reasons for Disliking Beat

(1) There is no skill attached and people look ungainly and silly.
(2) They require little or no skill.
(3) I don't think of to dance to jump around and shake.
(4) No definite pattern to the dancing and no particular rhythm.
(5) You do not dance with a person, only next to him.
(6) They allow no social contact and can be danced without a partner.
(7) I can't do them.
(8) I'm hopeless at dancing.
(9) They are too tiring.
(10) They change too quickly.

Summary

Type of reason most frequently mentioned	No. of times
No skill required (see (1) to (4) above)	4

Appendix J

Reasons for Liking Ballroom

(1) Rhythm and movement far greater than beat dances.
(2) They are elegant.
(3) They are graceful.
(4) Romantic, gentle and sophisticated. Graceful and, therefore, sexy too.
(5) The steps, movement, gracefulness.
(6) They are graceful and can be really enjoyable with the right partners.
(7) One can have fun. Gliding round the room with a good partner in the waltz or running round the room as in the quickstep is a wonderful feeling.
(8) Because I like the rhythm.
(9) You dance *with* a person.
(10) Movement together.
(11) You can dance with a partner.
(12) The presence of a partner.
(13) They allow contact with the opposite sex.
(14) Some skill is required.
(15) They are nice to dance and with a good partner many variations are possible.
(16) Because of the intricate steps.
(17) Sometimes I like to do more formal dancing.
(18) They are useful for community occasions or meetings of people who know each other well.
(19) For those who cannot let themselves go – it gives them an opportunity to dance without feeling self-conscious or ridiculous. There is safety in learned steps.

Summary

Type of reason most frequently mentioned	*No. of times*
Enjoyment of movement and rhythm (see (1) to (8) above)	8
The presence of a partner (see (9) to (13) above)	5
Skill required (see (14) to (16) above)	3

Reasons for Disliking Ballroom

(1) The rhythm is slow, unexciting.
(2) I do not like most of the bands who play the music.
(3) They are too slow.
(4) No rhythm.

Reasons for Disliking Ballroom (cont.)

(5) Boring.
(6) Too monotonous.
(7) They are boring.
(8) They're awfully boring.
(9) They are too inhibited and formal.
(10) Too regimented, stiff and exact.
(11) I cannot relax, or do not feel relaxed when dancing these.
(12) Most of these occasions are very formal.
(13) Few people in my age group do them: there is little satisfaction to be had from them.
(14) Few boys can dance them properly: they leave it to the girl to lead.
(15) They're 'out' and they make me mad and sick as well.
(16) I can't do them.
(17) The steps are too difficult for me.

Summary

Type of reason most frequently mentioned	No. of times
Dislike of music and rhythm (see (1) to (4) above)	4
Boring (see (5) to (8) above)	4
Stiff and formal (see (9) to (12) above)	4
Out of date: not for teenage generation (see (13) to (15) above)	3

TABLE 32

Polytechnic Students' Attitudes Expressed to Beat and Ballroom Forms of Dancing

Reasons for Liking Beat

(1) Escape valves to get rid of pent-up emotions.
(2) An outlet for emotions.
(3) Can pour all one's energy and tension out.
(4) Helps relieve tension.
(5) Physical exercise but also mentally relaxing.
(6) Relaxing.
(7) Releases pent-up energy: relaxation.
(8) They induce a spirit of enjoyment and happiness and make people relax.

Reasons for Liking Beat (cont.)

(9)   Can let one's hair down: experiment: exhibit: lose inhibitions.
(10) They make an occasion 'go'.
(11) Vibrant.
(12) Can let myself go.
(13) The fun, rhythm and excitement.
(14) Gets people in the right mood at a party.
(15) Simply enjoy doing them.
(16) A chance to let oneself go.
(17) Fun and part of the modern idiom.
(18) Gets me in the party spirit.
(19) I enjoy dancing them.
(20) Can let oneself go.
(21) Easy to do.
(22) No tedious lessons. Almost anyone can do them.
(23) Easy to perform: energy, not skill, is required.
(24) Easy steps: can dance with any girl.
(25) No stereotyped footwork. Flexibility of movements.
(26) They are easy.
(27) No learning or technicalities involved.
(28) No intricate steps – informal.
(29) Nobody notices if you can't dance.
(30) No worries about wrong steps; no one can judge how good a dancer you are because they don't know what or how you're trying to dance.
(31) No set steps, no embarrassment if partners do different steps.
(32) Little concentration needed to enjoy oneself.
(33) Steps are not fixed so person who is not good is not shown up.
(34) I do not need to learn any steps.
(35) Simple.
(36) Easy to copy: little to learn.
(37) Easy.
(38) Absolutely unconventional. Any body movement accepted.
(39) Can express feelings which the music stimulates.
(40) Expressive.
(41) Less formal and allow more freedom of movement and expression.
(42) Good for self-expression.
(43) Gives one a chance to express oneself in movement.
(44) Can express your appreciation of melody and rhythm: can dance as the mood of the music takes you.
(45) They allow unpretentious self-indulgence.
(46) Improvisation.
(47) One can jump about as one likes.
(48) Because of the freedom of movement.
(49) Improvisation.
(50) Free expression of how you feel at that moment.
(51) Rhythmic. Good exercise.
(52) It exercises the whole body.

Reasons for Liking Beat (cont.)

(53) Because of the music.
(54) Strong, quick and exciting movements.
(55) A chance to loosen up one's limbs.
(56) Movements natural and stimulated by a lively beat.
(57) Because of the loud beat music and the energetic nature of the dance.
(58) Imagination and sense of rhythm.
(59) Music is good and lively and exciting: it's also good exercise.
(60) They allow oneself to wallow in rhythm and to be soaked up to the eyeballs in 'music'.
(61) The rhythm.
(62) Good exercise.
(63) Good exercise.
(64) Form of display to the opposite sex.
(65) Physical stimulation.
(66) Because of the sexual undertones.
(67) Can meet opposite sex in informal way.
(68) Useful for meeting girls of own age.
(69) Opportunity to meet friends, including opposite sex.
(70) In this informal atmosphere, can more easily contact members of the opposite sex.
(71) To keep up with the times.
(72) For the young at heart.
(73) The atmosphere.
(74) Very informal. This mood sometimes appeals to me.
(75) Pleasant to dance and more interesting to watch than 'ballroom'.

Summary

Type of reason most frequently mentioned	No. of times
Ease of performance: no 'wrong' steps (see (21) to (27) above)	17
Freedom – including 'self-expression' (see (38) to (50) above)	13
Music: Rhythm: Movement: Exercise (see (51) to (63) above)	13
Fun: Excitement: Enjoyment: Letting oneself go (see (9) to (20) above)	12
Relief of tension (see (1) to (8) above)	8
Social and sexual (see (64) to (70) above)	7

Appendix J

Reasons for Disliking Beat

(1) No involvement with one's partner.
(2) No physical contact with partner hence dance them badly.
(3) Prefer close association with partner.
(4) Too far away from partner.
(5) No contact with partner to enhance the rhythm.
(6) Narcissistic and asocial. No possibility of talking etc.
(7) No skill or set pattern: just a shuffle.
(8) No rhythm or rhyme. All I hear is a few shouts or screams as though somebody is being strangled.
(9) No purpose or finesse. A muscle-searing experience.
(10) No steps. A man just makes a fool of himself.
(11) People dancing them look such bloody fools – enough to put me off.
(12) I am incapable of hurling myself around in such a fashion.
(13) Association with younger 'mods'. One looks ridiculous in public.
(14) I feel foolish doing them.
(15) You feel a fool doing it. (Don't mind others doing it.)
(16) Movements are clumsy and awkward (but I enjoy beat rhythms).
(17) Inelegant. To watch causes nausea.
(18) Complete lack of organization: reversion to animalia.
(19) I dislike the exhibitionism involved.
(20) More like a physical exercise than a dance: ungainly and at times provocative.
(21) They are monotonous.
(22) Solo dances are boring.
(23) Too tiring and dull.
(24) Because of the expense in erotic energy.
(25) A pointless waste of energy.
(26) I can't do them (but those who can look good).
(27) Moronic (but nice to watch).
(28) They don't click for me.
(29) I do not like the music: gives me a headache.
(30) I'm fat and ageing.*
(31) They give me a pain in the side.

Summary

Type of reason most frequently mentioned	No. of times
Lack of contact with partner (see (1) to (6) above)	6
Faer of looking ridiculous (see (11) to (25) above)	5
Inelegance etc. (see (16) to (23) above)	5
No skill required (see (7) to (10) above)	4

* Twenty-six years old !

Appendix J

Reasons for Liking Ballroom

(1) Makes talking to partner easy.
(2) The 'slowness' of the dances – more time to talk to partners.
(3) Can talk if one wants to.
(4) Close contact with partner.
(5) Close contact with partner.
(6) Close co-operation between partners.
(7) Physical contact with partners, discussion possible.
(8) Gives me a chance to lead the female for once.
(9) Can talk to my partner whether I know her or not.
(10) One may carry on a conversation while dancing.
(11) Enables me to dance *with* my partner – not detached from her.
(12) I enjoy dancing *with* a partner rather than *at* one.
(13) The music does not drown conversation.
(14) Exultant feelings accompanying performance of physical movements to a rhythm – movements being designed to harmonize with rhythm of the music.
(15) Beauty of the movements and footwork.
(16) The steps and movement.
(17) Great pleasure in moving in time and direction as led by partner.
(18) Graceful movements: melodious music.
(19) Much smoother expression of music and rhythm.
(20) Style of movement and style of music.
(21) Can move all over the dance floor: not confined to particular area.
(22) The movement – and ability to move around the floor gracefully.
(23) This is real dancing with movements that mean something and not just a gangling shuffle.
(24) Definite steps are involved: you are *really* dancing with a partner.
(25) They have rhythm.
(26) Pleasant sensation.
(27) The music.
(28) Latin American rhythm.
(29) The steps involve skill.
(30) Require thought, concentration and practice. Most rewarding and look great when performed well.
(31) Sense of achievement as more difficult to do well.
(32) Satisfaction in completion of complicated manoeuvres which carry a couple gracefully from one end of the floor to the other.
(33) Set technique which I like, but still scope for improvisation.
(34) I enjoy mastering the steps and get a tremendous 'lift' when dancing them.
(35) Control and timing.
(36) Well-defined and one knows at every point what to do next.
(37) The skill.
(38) Useful socially – e.g. can pile on the charm and impress the boss's wife.
(39) They show dignity and confidence.
(40) Useful social attributes.

Reasons for Liking Ballroom (cont.)

(41) Useful on social occasions.
(42) Helpful for formal dances and parties and you have to behave yourself properly.
(43) Necessary for functions later on in life.
(44) 'Better' type of girl – more mature and probably middle class rather than upper working class.
(45) More relaxing and the company one meets is usually more mature (intellectually).
(46) They make a change and enable one to meet a different kind of person.
(47) The opposite sex dress in more traditional style.
(48) A lot of grace (I wish I could dance them).
(49) They are graceful and can create an enjoyable evening.
(50) They are graceful.
(51) They are graceful and elegant.
(52) The steps are graceful.
(53) Attractive and graceful to watch if good.
(54) I'm a romantic, at heart.
(55) The music is soft and the atmosphere more romantic.
(56) I'm a romantic.
(57) More sophisticated and the surroundings are more luxurious.
(58) More sophisticated.
(59) The atmosphere.
(60) They introduce an element of glamour and elegance into my life – which I find peculiarly refreshing.
(61) They are always here.
(62) Don't know why.
(63) The enjoyment.
(64) Good fun if you know what you are doing.
(65) Relaxing and provide a good social evening.
(66) More relaxing and light.
(67) One does not get so warm.

Summary

Type of reason most frequently mentioned	No. of times
Enjoyment of music, movement, rhythm (see (14) to (28) above)	15
Contact with partner and possibility of conversation (see (1) to (13) above)	13
Skill and sense of achievement (see (29) to (38) above)	9
The general atmosphere (romantic, sophisticated etc.) (see (54 to (60) above)	7
Usefulness on social occasions (see (38) to (43) above)	6
Graceful (see (48) to (53) above)	6

Reasons for Disliking Ballroom
(1) They are too hard to learn.
(2) Too complicated.
(3) Too complicated and intricate.
(4) They are difficult to perform.
(5) I know very few of the steps.
(6) There is more emphasis on skill than enjoyment.
(7) I dislike formality in dancing.
(8) They are too formal.
(9) Too inhibiting and formal.
(10) They look pompous.
(11) I resent the 'suavity' of those (in my own age-group) who practise this type of dance.
(12) The atmosphere is very dull.
(13) I dislike the type of music.
(14) The music is provided by an antiquated, unmusical hard-working band. The pulse and harmony of modern music is lacking.
(15) They are too slow: no rhythm in the movement.
(16) They are conventional and rhythm is limited to the lower part of the body.
(17) They have repetitive steps and little opportunity for experiment.
(18) Little skill is needed and all you need is an attractive or intelligent (or both) partner to pass the time away.
(19) My girl-friend does not like them.
(20) Dancing is an effeminate pastime.
(21) They are a pointless waste of energy.

Summary

Type of reason most frequently mentioned	*No. of times*
Necessity for learning etc. (see (1) to (6) above)	6
Stiff; formal; dull etc. (see (7) to (12) above)	6

Appendix K

(1) How often, on an average, do you dance?	Answers
(This includes all occasions – for example: at home, at parties, at clubs and at 'dances'). Put a ring round the number which most nearly applies to you.	1. Every night of the week. 2. Several times a week. 3. Once a week. 4. Once a fortnight. 5. Once a month. 6. Once every three months. 7. Once every six months. 8. Once a year, or less.

(2) Read through the list of dances in col. (i)	Dance (i)	Preference (ii)
(a) Cross out all those which you do not dance.	JIVE (to jazz)	
	WALTZ	
(b) For those dances not crossed out, please indicate your preference by putting in col. (ii), 1st for the most preferred and so on to the least preferred.	SAMBA	
	FOXTROT	
	ROCK	
	SLOW BLUES	
	TANGO	
	QUICKSTEP	

R*

	SHAKE OR ANY MODERN BEAT DANCES	
	RUMBA	
	CHA-CHA	
	FOLK (Country, Scottish, Finn-jenka, Zorba's dance, etc.)	
	OLD TIME	
	TWIST	
(3) Are there any dances crossed out in Question (2) which you would like to dance? (a) Put a ring round the word which applies. (b) If YES, please indicate which by writing the names in col. (ii)	(i) YES/NO	(ii)
(4) If you dance the beat dances, do you ever do so without any partner at all – that is, just as one of a crowd? (a) Put a ring round the word which applies. (b) Leave blank if you do not dance these.	(i) YES/NO	(ii)
(5) If you go dancing, do you go because – Please indicate the order of importance of these reasons by putting 1st, 2nd, 3rd, 4th, 5th, in column (ii): 1st for the most important, 5th for the least important.	(i) A particular group is playing? You want to meet or be with the opposite sex?	(ii)

	The dance is run by an organization you belong to?	
	Your friends go?	
	You enjoy dancing?	
(6) In my view, enjoyment in dancing comes mainly from – Please indicate the order of importance of these reasons by putting 1st, 2nd, 3rd, in col. (ii), 1st for the most important, 3rd for the least important. Leave blank if you do *not* enjoy dancing.	(i)	(ii)
	The steps and movement.	
	The presence of the opposite sex.	
	The music and rhythm.	

(7) In my view, the shake and other beat dances are not suitable for people who are –

   Put a ring round the number which applies.

    1. Over twenty.

    2. Over thirty.

    3. Over forty.

OR 4. Age is of no importance here.

(8) I like the 'beat' dances such as the shake etc. because –

   OR

   I dislike the 'beat' dances such as shake etc. because –

   (a) Please complete one of the above statements.

   (b) Leave blank if you do not care one way or the other.

(9) I like 'traditional' ballroom dances (such as foxtrot, waltz, quickstep) because – *OR* I dislike 'traditional' ballroom dances (such as foxtrot, waltz, quickstep) because – (a) please complete one of the above statements. (b) leave blank if you do not care one way or the other.	
(10) For statistical and record purposes would you be kind enough to supply the following information?	NAME
	AGE
	OCCUPATION*
	FATHER'S OCCUPATION

* If student, please state faculty.

Appendix L

FORM B.   Six sample questions –

Do you like plenty of excitement and bustle around you?

Have you often lost sleep over your worries?

Do you often make up your mind too late?

Do you sometimes laugh at a dirty joke?

Do you feel uncomfortable in anything but everyday clothes?

Do you get very bad headaches?

Total number of questions: 57.

Notes

NOTES TO CHAPTER I (pp. 1 to 5)

[1] See principally R. DAHRENDORF, 'Towards a theory of social conflict' in *Social Change* by A. & E. Etzioni. (1964).

R. P. DORE, 'Function and Cause'. *American Sociological Review*. December 1961.

G. C. HOMANS, 'Bringing Men Back In'. *American Sociological Review*. December 1964.

D. LOCKWOOD, 'Social Integration and System Integration in *Explorations in Social Change*. Ed. Zollschan & Hirsch. (1964).

[2] R. FLETCHER, 'Functionalism as a Social Theory', *Sociological Review*, July 1956. N.B. The view that although functionalism is not, strictly speaking, a theory it is nevertheless exceedingly useful, as a conceptual scheme would presumably be conceded even by many of its critics. For example, Homans (op. cit.) is against the use of the word 'theory' rather than the usefulness of the approach: '. . . Analysis is not explanation, and a conceptual scheme is not a theory . . . The trouble with their [the functionalists] theory was not that it was wrong but that it was not a theory . . .'

[3] For example, T. PARSONS, *The Social System, passim*.

PARSONS AND SMELSER, *Economy and Society*, pp. 46–51.

HARE, BORGATTA AND BALES, *Small groups: studies in social interaction*, pp. 127–31.

[4] A. RADCLIFFE-BROWN, 'On the concept of function in social science'. *American Anthropologist* 1935.

[5] E. DÜRKHEIM, *The Rules of Sociological Method*, p. 110.

[6] *Ibid.*, p. 111.

[7] G. M. TREVELYAN, *English Social History*, Introduction pp. x–xi.

[8] A. H. FRANKS, *Social Dance: A Short History*, p. 76.

NOTES TO CHAPTER II (pp. 9 to 17)

[1] R. VOSS, *Der Tanz und seine Geshichte*. Berlin 1896. pp. 3–15.

[2] A. E. CRAWLEY, Article on 'Processions and Dances' in *Encyclopaedia of Religion and Ethics*.

[3] SUSANNE K. LANGER, *Feeling and Form*, pp. 167–87.

[4] WOLFGANG KÖHLER, *Psychologische Forschung*. I. pp. 33–5.

[5] CURT SACHS, *World History of the Dance*, p. 11.

[6] For example, A. E. CRAWLEY, *op. cit.*

HAVELOCK ELLIS, *The Dance of Life*.

[7] J. MACLAREN, *My Crowded Solitude*, p. 55.

[8] BELA MITTELMANN, Foreword to *Dance in psychotherapy* by E. Rosen, p. xi.

[9] W. WUNDT, *Völkerpsychologie*, Bd. 1 Teil 1. p. 277.

Notes

[10] CURT SACHS, *op. cit.*, p. 5.

[11] C. HOSE AND W. MCDOUGALL, *Pagan Tribes of Borneo*, Vol. 11, pp. 156–7.

[12] A. WERNER, *Native Tribes of British Central Africa*, pp. 126–7.

[13] A. RADCLIFFE-BROWN, *The Andaman Islanders*, p. 128.

[14] W. D. HAMBLY, *Tribal Dancing and Social Development*, p. 26.

[15] Quoted by W. Hambly, *op. cit.*, p. 26.

[16] REV. CANON J. ROSCOE, *The Bagesu*, pp. 16, 70.

[17] W. HAMBLY, *op. cit.*, p. 129.

[18] A. C. HADDON, *Head Hunters – Black, White and Brown*, p. 187.

[19] W. HAMBLY, *op. cit.*, p. 80.

[20] W. HAMBLY, *op. cit.*, p. 215.

[21] GEOFFREY GORER, *Africa Dances*, pp. 321–2.

[22] SIR JAMES FRAZER, 'Spirits of the Corn and the Wild', in *The Golden Bough*, Pt. V, p. 186.

[23] C. HOSE in Preface to *Tribal Dancing and Social Development*, W. Hambly, p. 7.

[24] W. H. R. RIVERS, *The Todas*, p. 377.

[25] C. G. SELIGMAN, *The Veddahs of Ceylon*, p. 132.

[26] A. L. HASKELL, *The Story of Dance*, p. 22.

[27] M. MEAD, 'Coming of Age in Samoa', in *From the South Seas*, pp. 223–4.

[28] *Ibid.*, pp. 110–21.

[29] M. MEAD, 'Sex and Temperament in three Primitive Societies', in *From the South Seas*, pp. 57–8 *et passim*.

NOTES TO CHAPTER III (pp. 18 to 27)

[1] CURT SACHS, *World History of the Dance*, p. 20.

[2] *Ibid.*, pp. 12–13.

[3] *Ibid.*, p. 18.

[4] J. F. C. HECKER, MD, *Epidemics of the Middle Ages*. Book II, p. 2.

[6] *Limburg Chronicle*, published C. D. Vogel, 1828, p. 71.

[7] *Journal de Paris* 1785. 'Dans la ville y eut des dansans, tant grands que petits onze cents'. Quoted by Hecker, p. 10.

[8] On this point the *Limburg Chronicle* is more explicit than Hecker cares to be: '. . . und fand man da zu Cölln mehr dann hundert Frauen und Dienstmägde, die nicht eheliche Männer hatten. Die wurden alle in der Täntzerey Kinder-tragend . . .'

[9] J. F. C. HECKER, *op. cit.*, pp. 10–11.

[10] J. of Königshoven, quoted by Hecker, p. 14.

[11] J. F. C. HECKER, *op. cit.*, p. 59.

[12] *Ibid.*, pp. 65–6.

[13] *Ibid.*, pp. 80–1.

[14] *Ibid.*, pp. 90–7. Much of the information here was derived by Hecker from Epiphan. Ferdinand. Venet. 1621 fol. Hist. LXXXI. Ferdinando was a physician in Messapia at the beginning of the seventeenth century, was himself an eye-witness of the 'mania' and collected a large number of statements from sufferers.

Notes

[15] Dorland's *Medical Dictionary*, 14th ed., reprinted March 1967.

[16] *Ibid.*

[17] *Ibid.*

[18] J. F. C. HECKER, *op. cit.*, pp. 27–9. The dance curse is the theme taken up by Hans Christian Andersen in the fairy tale *The Red Shoes.*

[19] BECKMANN, *History of the Principality of Anhalt*, Zerbst, 1710, cited by Hecker, p. 28.
There is a strong echo of this in Göthe's *Rattenfänger* or *Pied Piper of Hamelin:*

> Und wären Knaben noch so trutzig
> Und wären Mädchen noch so stutzig
> In meine Saiten greif' ich ein
> Sie müssen alle hinterdrein.

[20] R. MERTON, *Social Theory and Social Structure*, p. 53.

[21] J. M. CLARK, *The Dance of Death in the Middle Ages and the Renaissance*, p. 23. Various encyclopaedias give the date of the first appearance of the representation of the Dance of Death as the year 1312, on the cloister walls of Klingenthal, Kleinbasel, Switzerland. This must be a perpetuation of a mistake made originally by an eighteenth century master baker named Büchel who misread the date on the wall as 1312. Büchel subsequently corrected his error and made clear that the date was 1512, and that in any event this date referred to a renovation and not to the original painting (the date of which is uncertain but is thought to be early fifteenth century). See J. M. Clark, pp. 64–5.

[22] Wolan wolan jr herren vnd knecht
> Spryngt her by võ allé geschlecht
> Wie jung wie alt wie schon od krusz
> Jr muszent alle in disz dantz husz.

Typographischer Totentanz mit 42 Holzschnitten. (Mainz, bei Jacob Meydenbach). One copy is in the British Museum.
English translation of this verse in Curt Sachs, *World History of the Dance*, p. 259.

[23] There are two types of choral dance, the complex (or 'place-changing' variety) with which we are not concerned here, and the simple. In the simple choral the dancer keeps his original place. 'Whether the dancers move in a circle, in a straight line, in figure eights, they remain in line and are led by the dance leader like sheep by the oldest wether' Curt Sachs, *World History of the Dance*, p. 142.

NOTES TO CHAPTER IV (pp. 31 to 38)

[1] G. M. TREVELYAN, *English Social History*, pp. 95–6.

[2] GLYNNE WICKHAM, *Early English Stages 1300–1660*, p. 16 *et passim.*

[3] *Ibid.*, p. 17.

[4] JACQUES BRETEL, *Le Tournoi de Chauvency*, ed. Maurice Delbouille, 1932 (Liege–Paris).
11. 1343 to 1359.
A fuller extract from the original French, ed. P. I. J. Delmotte (Valenciennes 1835) is quoted by Glynne Wickham, *op. cit.*, pp. 361–2, note 16, but lines 1355 and 1359 are misquoted, respectively, as 'Qui dont veist dances venir' and 'N'i a celui qui ne fes joie' (a rendering which appears to be untranslatable).

[5] GLYNNE WICKHAM, *op. cit.*, p. 21.

[6] MS LANSDOWNE 285, f.10 quoted by Glynne Wickham, *op. cit.*, p. 22.

[7] W. W. SKEAT, *The Flower and the Leaf, Chaucerian and other Pieces* (1897), pp. 361 to 379.

[8] HARL. MS 247, f.122. Original text is quoted in E. K. Chambers: *Medieval Stage*, p. 394. This text is paraphrased by John Stowe, in his *Survey of London* 1603, but Stowe fails to bring out clearly the segregation between the mummers and the Royal party.

[9] MELUSINE WOOD, *Historical Dances (twelfth to nineteenth century)*, pp. 11, 12. Technical details of how to dance the branle and the estampie are given by Melusine Wood, *op. cit.*, pp. 20–36.

[10] *Ibid.*, p. 11.

[11] THOMAS WARTON, *The History of English Poetry* (1774), Vol. I, p. 113.

[12] TREVISA HIGDEN (Rolls), VII. 123. 1387.

[13] GOWER, *Confessio Amantis*, III, 365, 1394.

[14] DOUGLAS KENNEDY (*English Folk-Dancing: Today and Yesterday*) states that the English were renowned for their skill in this dance and gained for themselves the attribute 'Angli-carolant'. This, however, is not substantiated by any historical evidence and Violet Alford (correspondence with the author) is of the opinion that 'Angli-carolant' is probably a mistake for 'Angli-jubilant', an expression which occurs in the Latin version of a contemporary French proverb: 'Galli cantant, Angli jubilant, Hispani plangunt, Germani ulutant, Itali caprizant'. This is translated by Chappell (*Popular Music of the Olden Time*, Vol. I, Introd. IX, c.1880) as 'The French pipe, the English carol (rejoice or sing, merrily), the Spaniards wail, the Germans howl, the Italians caper'. It seems reasonably clear that this does not refer to the 'carole' as a dance.

[15] MS HARLEY 978. Reference in Melusine Wood, *op. cit.*, p. 13.

[16] The Pastons were making this improvement in their manor-houses in the reign of Henry VI. H. S. Bennett: *The Pastons and their England*, p. 92.

[17] G. M. TREVELYAN, *op. cit.*, p. 16.

[18] *Ibid.*, p. 26.

[19] GLYNNE WICKHAM, *op. cit.*, p. 181.

[20] G. M. TREVELYAN, *op. cit.*, pp. 57–8.

[21] MELUSINE WOOD, *More Historical Dances*, p. 110.

[22] A full technical account of the Morris dance with a detailed description of the Headington, Ilmington, Tideswell and other dances is given in *The Morris Book* by Cecil J. Sharp and H. C. Micilwaine.

[23] CURT SACHS, *World History of the Dance*, p. 336.

[24] DOUGLAS KENNEDY, *English Folk-Dancing: Today and Yesterday*, pp. 48–50.

NOTES TO CHAPTER V (pp. 39 to 43)

[1] College of Arms Ms 1st M.13, ff. 53 and 53b. Reference in Glynne Wickham, *Early English Stages, 1300–1660*, p. 209.

[2] *Ibid.*, f. 53b. Reference in Glynne Wickham, *op. cit.*, p. 209.

[3] Halls Chronicle, p. 526. Reference in Glynne Wickham, *op. cit.*, p. 218.

Notes

[4] E. K. CHAMBERS, *The Elizabethan Stage*, pp. 149–50.

[5] E. K. CHAMBERS, *Ibid.*, pp. 154–5.

[6] Original in the Bodleian Library, Oxford.

[7] MELUSINE WOOD, *Historical Dances*, pp. 40–1.

[8] *Ibid.*, p. 39.

[9] Original is in the Royal Library of Brussels. Ms 9085.

[10] A. H. FRANKS, *Social Dance: A Short History*, p. 33.

[11] *Ibid.*, p. 34.

[12] The word 'branle' (derived from the French 'branler' – to swing from side to side) is sometimes used for a step or – as here – for a movement where the dancers sway from left to right alternately, and sometimes for a round, linked dance in which this swaying movement is made. In England, the word was sometimes rendered as 'brawl'.

[13] For a complete and detailed description of the French Basse Danse see Thoinot Arbeau's *Orchésographie*, and for clear present-day instructions on how to dance it see Mabel Dolmetsch: 'Dances of England and France 1450 to 1600, pp. 18 to 48.

[14] SIR THOMAS ELYOT, *The Boke named the Governour* (Everyman edition), p. 97.

[15] MELUSINE WOOD, *op. cit.*, p. 94.

[16] ARBEAU, *Orchésographie*, pp. 57–8.

[17] R. ST. JOHNSTON, *History of Dancing*, p. 134.

[18] SURREY, *Poems*, Clarendon Series, p. 25.

[19] G. M. TREVELYAN, *op. cit.*, p. 134.
One example of Henry VIII's compositions entitled 'The Kynge's Balade' or 'Passetyme with Good Companye' with music for lute appears in Harley Ms (B.M.). The first verse is as follows:

> Passetyme with good company
> I love and shall until I die
> Grudge who will, but none deny
> So God be pleased this life will I
> For my pastance, hunt, sing and dance
> My heart is set, all goodly sport
> To my comfort, who shall me let.

[20] JOHN STOW, *A Survey of London*, ed. Kingsford, p. 95.

[21] GLYNNE WICKHAM, *op. cit.*, p. 225.

NOTES TO CHAPTER VI (pp. 44 to 52)

[1] SIR JOHN DAVIES, 'Orchestra', Stanzas LXIII and LXIV.

[2] Ring dances differ from 'Rounds' in that they imply some object in the middle – e.g. a tree or a maypole – towards which the dancers advance. The three best known ring dances at this time were: Sellenger's Round, Gathering Peascods, and Jenny Pluck Pears. (M. Wood, *More Historical Dances*, p. 96).

[3] The word 'measure' was used first for a version of the English Basse Danse, and later for the Pavane and Almayn. (M. Dolmetsch, *Dances of England and France 1450–1600*, pp. 49, 51).

Notes

[4] For a detailed description of galliards, La Voltas and courantoes see Arbeau's *Orchésographie*, and for more manageable and present-day instructions on how to dance see M. Dolmetsch, *Dances of England and France 1450–1600*, pp. 102–43.)

[5] MELUSINE WOOD, The *Dancing Times*, June 1935, p. 266.

[6] VON WEDEL, *Queen Elizabeth and some Foreigners* (1585), p. 338.

[7] E. K. CHAMBERS, *The Elizabethan Stage*, p. 96.

[8] CURT SACHS, *World History of the Dance*, pp. 374–7.

[9] *Ibid.*, pp. 361–3.

[10] A. H. FRANKS, *Social Dance: A Short History*, p. 61.

[11] M. DOLMETSCH, *Dances of England and France 1450–1600*, p. 144. (This work contains detailed instructions for this dance.)

[12] J. NICHOLS, *Progresses of Queen Elizabeth*, Vol. II ('The Queene's Entertainement at Cowdrey'), p. 6.

[13] Sidney Papers II, p. 155.

[14] In spite of this long history, the first literary reference to 'country-dancing' appears to be that in the play 'Misogonus' c.1560 (Authorship uncertain. Ms in collection of Duke of Devonshire).

> Trifle not the tyme then say what shall we have
> What countrye dauncis do you here frequent . . .
> (Act 11, Sc. 4)

See Journal of the E.F.D.S.S. Vol. IX No. 3. J. P. Cunningham.

[15] THOMAS NASHE, *The Works of Thomas Nash*, Vol. III, p. 122.

[16] For example, 'Rogero' in Webbe: *Discourse of English Poetrie*, 1586; 'Rogero' and 'Turkeylony' in Gesson, *School of Abuse*, 1579; 'All the Flowers of the Broom' in Breton's *Works of a young Wit*, 1577; 'Peggy Ramsey' in Shakespeare's *Twelfth Night* (II, iii, 81).

[17] Ms Bodleian Douce 280, Rawl. Poet 163 and B. M. Harl. 367 (Turkeyloney). Ms Bodleian Douce 280 (Basilena).
M. WOOD gives both instructions and music for these two dances in *More Historical Dances*, p. 96.

[18] E. M. W. TILLYARD, *The Elizabethan World Picture*, pp. 94–6.

[19] *Ibid.*, pp. 77–80.

[20] SHAKESPEARE, *Henry V*, Act III, Sc. 5.

[21] MELUSINE WOOD, *More Historical Dances*, p. 96.

[22] C. R. BASKERVILL, *The Elizabethan Jig*. This is an authoritative study of every aspect, particularly of the stage jig.

[23] DANCKERT, *Die Geschichte der Gigue* (1924), Chap. 1.

[24] C. R. BASKERVILL, *op. cit.*, p. 6.

[25] Seventeenth-century Ballad 'The Young-Man's Ramble', *Pepys Collection* (III, 47).

[26] C. R. BASKERVILL, *op. cit.*, p. 359.

[27] Sixteenth-century poem by Chester, *Poems by Salisbury and Chester*, ed. Brown, pp. 19–20.

Notes

[28] In its final form, however, the French Basse Danse had a springing step (*Pas de Brébant*) at the end. (M. Wood, *op. cit.*, p. 37.)

[29] G. M. TREVELYAN, *English Social History*, p. 139.

[30] HAKLUYT, *The Principall Navigations Voiages and Discoveries of the English Nation* (1589).

[31] G. M. TREVELYAN, *op. cit.*, p. 139.

[32] *Ibid.*, p. 162.

NOTES TO CHAPTER VII (pp. 53 to 58)

[1] REGINALD ST JOHNSTON, *History of Dancing*, p. 59.

[2] MILTON's *Comus* was performed in 1634 for the family of Lord Bridgewater.

[3] A. H. FRANKS, *Social Dance: A Short History*, p. 75.

[4] A round, linked dance with a swaying movement. See Note [12], Chap. V.

[5] MELUSINE WOOD, *Historical Dances (Twelfth to Nineteenth Century)*, p. 119.

[6] A. H. FRANKS, *op. cit.*, p. 77.

[7] MELUSINE WOOD, *op. cit.*, p. 119.
NOTE: All through the early history of courtly social dancing it was customary for the gentleman to kiss his partner at the conclusion of a dance, and he would have been considered lacking in manners had he not done so. Hence, in *Henry VIII*, Shakespeare makes the king say, with reference to dancing: 'I were unmannerly to take you out, and not to kiss you'.

[8] MELUSINE WOOD, *op. cit.*, p. 119.

[9] *Ibid.*, p. 119.

[10] E. A. B. BARNARD, *A Seventeenth Century Country Gentleman*, pp. 18–19, 43, 57.

[11] O. CROMWELL, *The Writings and Speeches of Oliver Cromwell*, ed. W. C. Abbott, Vol. IV, pp. 661–2.

[12] The sarabande was a passionate and unbridled dance known in sixteenth-century Spain. It was introduced into France in the seventeenth century and Charles would certainly have learnt it there. Very little is known about how it was danced in France and other countries (except that it had gliding steps and was in triple time) but, as a courtly dance, it would undoubtedly have shed its cruder features. (Curt Sachs, *History of the Dance*, p. 370.)

[13] EDMONDSTOUNE DUNCAN, Article on 'King's Music' in *Monthly Musical Record*, 1902. Reprinted in Preface to *Kings' Music. Vocal Pieces*, Edmondstoune Duncan, Augener's Edition, No. 8926.

[14] SAMUEL PEPYS, *The Diary of Samuel Pepys*, ed. H. B. Wheatley, Vol. II, pp. 430–1.

[15] SAMUEL PEPYS, *op. cit.*, Vol. II, p. 398.
2 November 1662.
    'This day I bought the book of country-dances against my wife's woman Gosnell comes, who dances finely; and there meeting Mr Playford he did give me his Latin songs of Mr. Deering's, which he lately printed . . .'

[16] DOUGLAS KENNEDY, *English Folk Dancing: Today and Yesterday*, p. 84.

[17] G. M. TREVELYAN, *English Social History*, p. 206.

[18] *Ibid.*, p. 281.

Notes

NOTES TO CHAPTER VIII (pp. 59 to 65)

[1] G. M. TREVELYAN, *English Social History*, p. 338.

[2] MELUSINE WOOD, *Historical Dances (Twelfth–Eighteenth Century)*, p. 145.

[3] SOAME JENNYNS, *Poems on Several Occasions*, (1729), 'The Art of Dancin g' Canto II, p. 24.

> To her [France] we all our Noble Dances owe,
> The spritely Rigadoon and Louvre slow,
> The Boree and Courant, unpractis'd long
> Th'immortal minuet and the sweet Bretagne.

[4] MELUSINE WOOD, *op. cit.*, p. 145.

[5] CURT SACHS, *World History of the Dance*, p. 406.

[6] *Ibid.*, p. 405.

[7] REGINALD ST JOHNSTON, *History of Dancing*, p. 142.

[8] MELUSINE WOOD, *op. cit.*, p. 145.
An idea of the standard young ladies were supposed to attain before leaving school can be obtained from Pemberton: *An Essay for the Further Improvement of Dancing:* 1711.

[9] C. M. FANSHAWE, *Memorials of Miss Catherine Maria Fanshawe*, pp. 23–8. 'Elegy on the Abrogation of the Birthnight Ball, and consequent final subversion of the Minuet'.

[10] MELUSINE WOOD, *op. cit.*, p. 102.

[11] *Ibid.*, p. 103.

[12] *Ibid.*, p. 103.

[13] That the cotillon was also well known in Scotland is clear from the following lines from Burns' 'Tam O Shanter' (1791):

> Warlocks and witches in a dance
> Nae cotillion brent new frae France
> But hornpipes, jigs, strathspeys and reels
> Put life and mettle in their heels.

[14] CURT SACHS, *op. cit.*, p. 422.

[15] MELUSINE WOOD, *More Historical Dances*, p. 132.

[16] CURT SACHS, *op. cit.*, p. 414.

[17] P. J. S. RICHARDSON, *The Social Dances of the Nineteenth Century*, p. 32.

[18] BRYAN LITTLE, *Bath Portrait*, p. 34.

[19] P. J. S. RICHARDSON, *op. cit.*, p. 23.

[20] Quoted by P. J. S. Richardson, *op. cit.*, p. 25.

[21] Quoted by P. J. S. Richardson, *op. cit.*, p. 41.

[22] G. M. TREVELYAN, *op. cit.*, p. 397.

[23] A. H. FRANKS, *Social Dance: A Short History*, p. 41.

NOTES TO CHAPTER IX (pp. 66 to 79)

[1] P. J. S. RICHARDSON, *The Social Dances of the Nineteenth Century*, p. 52.

[2] *Ibid.*, p. 57.

[3] MRS LILLY GROVE, *Dancing* (The Badminton Library of Sports and Pastimes) (1895), p. 408.

Notes

[4] G. YATES, *The Ball or A Glance at Almack's* (1829), pp. 16–17.

[5] P. J. S. RICHARDSON, *op. cit.*, p. 59.

[6] CAPTAIN GRONOW, *Reminiscences and Recollections*. (Ed.) John Raymond, p. 44.

[7] REGINALD ST JOHNSTON, *History of Dancing*, p. 143.

[8] P. J. S. RICHARDSON, *op. cit.*, p. 61.

[9] ARTHUR FRANKS, *Social Dance: A Short History*, p. 142.

[10] P. J. S. RICHARDSON, *op. cit.*, p. 59.

[11] CURT SACHS, *op. cit.*, p. 429.
PAUL NETTL, 'The Waltz' in *Chujoy*: Dance Encyclopaedia.

[12] MELUSINE WOOD, *More Historical Dances*, p. 133.

[13] P. J. S. RICHARDSON, *op. cit.*, p. 63.

[14] BYRON, The Waltz: An Apostrophic hymn, 11, 233–5.

[15] BYRON, *English Bards and Scotch Reviewers*, 11, 660–8.

> . . . .
> Now round the room the circling dow'gers sweep,
> Now in loose waltz the thin-clad daughters leap;
> The first in lengthen'd line majestic swim
> The last display the free unfetter'd limb!
> Those for Hibernia's lusty sons repair
> With art the charms which nature could not spare;
> Those after husbands wing their eager flight
> Nor leave much mystery for the nuptial night.

[16] HENDRIK VAN LOON, *The Arts of Mankind*, p. 534.
Note, too, the famous sally of Charles-Joseph, Prince de Ligne: '*Le congrès ne marche pas, il danse*'.

[17] *The Times*, Monday, 15 July:
> On Friday night the Prince Regent gave a grand ball and supper at Carlton House to a numerous party. After supper dancing was resumed, which was kept up till a late hour on Saturday morning. The dancing consisted only of waltzing and cotillons, in which none of the Royal Family joined. The Queen sat in her State Chair accompanied by the Prince Regent, who was close in his attendance upon his Royal Mother all the night.

[18] A. H. FRANKS, *op. cit.*, p. 130.

[19] In 1815 at the Congress of Vienna people wished to see a minuet danced and only with difficulty could a couple be found who remembered the movements. (M. Wood, *More Historical Dances*, p. 133.)

[20] *Modern Etiquette in Public and Private:* A New and Revised Edition. Published Frederick Warne & Co. 1895, pp. 112, 120, 121.

[21] A. H. FRANKS, *op. cit.*, p. 133.

[22] CAPTAIN GRONOW, *op. cit.*, p. 44.

[23] P. J. S. RICHARDSON, *op. cit.*, p. 29.

[24] CAPTAIN GRONOW, *op. cit.*, p. 49.

[25] P. J. S. RICHARDSON, *op. cit.*, p. 52.

[26] *Ibid.*, p. 53.

[27] *Ibid.*, p. 69.

Notes

[28] J. S. POLLOCK, *La Terpsichore Moderne: La Gallopade.*

[29] Some authorities, for example PAUL NETTL in the *Story of Dance Music* consider that the word 'polka' derives from 'pulka' meaning a half-step.

[30] DR ARTHUR MICHEL, Dance Magazine 1944, quoted in Chujoy, Anatole *Dance Encyclopaedia*, p. 379.

[31] P. J. S. RICHARDSON, *op. cit.*, p. 82.

[32] *The Times*, 14 March 1844.

[33] ALLEN DODSWORTH, *Dancing and its Relations to Education and Social Life*, p. 17.

[34] This information is contained in a small book (see also Note 35) compiled with the help of Coulon, but not written by him. It is usually referred to as Coulon, *Polka.*

[35] COULON, *Polka*, p. 24.

[36] P. J. S. RICHARDSON, *op. cit.*, p. 89.

[37] *Illustrated London News*, 11 May 1844.

[38] See page 76.

[39] THOMAS WILSON, *The Art of Dancing*, 1852, *passim.*

[40] P. J. S. RICHARDSON, *op. cit.*, p. 108.

[41] COULON, *Polka.*

[42] THOMAS WILSON, *op. cit.*, p. 99.

[43] P. J. S. RICHARDSON, *op. cit.*, p. 102.

[44] ANON, Routledge's *Ballroom Companion*, p. 61.

[45] R. ST JOHNSTON, *History of Dancing*, p. 154.

[46] HEINRICH HEINE, *Heine's Gesammelte Werke*, Vol. 7, p. 192.
Was die Bälle der vornehmen Welt noch langweiliger macht, als sie von Gott und Rechts wegen sein dürften, ist die dort herreschende Mode, dass man nur zum Schein tanzt, dass man die vorgeschriebenen Figuren nur gehend executiert, dass man ganz gleichgültig, fast verdriesslich die Fusse bewegt. Keiner will mehr den anderen amusieren, und dieser Egoismus beurkundigt sich auch im Tanze der heutigen Gesellschaft.

[47] CELLARIUS, *Fashionable Dancing*, p. 10.

[48] P. J. S. RICHARDSON, *op. cit.*, p. 93.

[49] *Ibid.*, p. 109.

[50] W. H. HOLDEN, *They Startled Grandfather*, p. 36.

[51] *Ibid.*, p. 36.

[52] P. J. S. RICHARDSON, *op. cit.*, p. 113.

[53] *Ibid.*, p. 118.

[54] S. DANNETT AND F. RACHEL, *Down Memory Lane*, p. 63.

[55] P. J. S. RICHARDSON, *op. cit.*, p. 119.

[56] *Ibid.*, p. 120.

[57] TROY AND MARGARET KINNEY, *The Dance*, p. 269.

[58] JOHN STUART MILL, *The Subjection of Women*, p. 29.

Notes

NOTES TO CHAPTER X (pp. 80 to 87)

[1] A. H. FRANKS, *Social Dance: A Short History*, p. 186.

[2] P. J. S. RICHARDSON, *History of English Ballroom Dancing*, p. 13.

[3] In a 'sequence dance' (never to be found on the programme of a 'smart' function) the various movements have to be taken in a specified order. Each movement is made up of a definite number of steps arranged to occupy a certain number of bars. As a result, the same step is being danced by all couples simultaneously. This permits a greater number of dancers to be on the floor at the same time, and makes the dance easy to teach to many people at the same session.

[4] R. ST JOHNSTON, *History of Dancing*, p. 78.

[5] A. H. FRANKS, *op. cit.*, pp. 164–5. See also Appendix F.

[6] *Ibid.*, p. 165.

[7] A. H. FRANKS, *op. cit.*, pp. 179–80.

[8] LISA LEKIS, *Folk Dances of Latin America*, p. 202.

[9] S. DANNETT AND F. RACHEL, *Down Memory Lane*, p. 63.

[10] A. H. FRANKS, *op. cit.*, p. 166.

[11] S. DANNETT AND F. RACHEL, *op. cit.*, p. 66.

[12] P. J. S. RICHARDSON, *op. cit.*, p. 29.

[13] IRENE AND VERNON CASTLE, *Modern Dancing*, 1914, p. 43.

[14] *Ibid.*, p. 44.

[15] A. H. FRANKS, *op. cit.*, p. 176.

[16] A. H. FRANKS, *op. cit.*, p. 183.

[17] *Ibid.*, p. 183.

[18] STANLEY NELSON, Addenda 'Dance Bands' to *History of English Ballroom Dancing* by P. J. S. Richardson, p. 136.

[19] P. J. S. RICHARDSON, *op. cit.*, p. 37.

[20] P. J. S. RICHARDSON, *op. cit.*, p. 38.

[21] P. J. S. RICHARDSON, *op. cit.*, p. 38.

[22] A. H. FRANKS, *op. cit.*, p. 187.

[23] STANLEY NELSON, *op. cit.*, pp. 135–6.

[24] STANLEY JACKSON, *The Savoy – Romance of a Great Hotel*, p. 107.

[25] R. GRAVES AND A. HODGE, *The Long Weekend: A Social History of Great Britain 1918–1939*, p. 42.

NOTES TO CHAPTER XI (pp. 88 to 96)

[1] R. GRAVES AND A. HODGE, *The Long Weekend: A Social History of Great Britain, 1918–19*, p. 42.

[2] R. BENNETT, *A Picture of the Twenties*, p. 48.

[3] *The Times*, 2 January 1920.

[4] R. GRAVES AND A. HODGE, *op. cit.*, p. 119.

[5] *Daily Mail*, 16 October 1926.

[6] G. KURATH AND N. CHILKOVSKY, 'Jazz Choreology' in *Men and Cultures*, ed. A. Wallace, p. 153.

[7] JOHN MONTGOMERY, *The Twenties: An Informal Short History*, p. 191.

[8] J. COLLIER AND I. LANG, *Just the Other Day*, pp. 171–3.

[9] *Ibid.*, pp. 171–3.

[10] JOHN MONTGOMERY, *op. cit.*, p. 191.

[11] J. COLLIER AND I. LANG, *op. cit.*, p. 173.

[12] J. B. NICHOLS, *The Sweet and Twenties*, p. 192.

[13] P. J. S. RICHARDSON, *History of English Ballroom Dancing*, p. 64.

[14] S. DANNETT AND F. RACHEL, *Down Memory Lane*, p. 122.

[15] CURT SACHS, *World History of the Dance*, p. 445.

[16] R. BENNETT, *op. cit.*, p. 66.

[17] J. COLLIER AND I. LANG, *op. cit.*, pp. 159–60.

[18] A. H. FRANKS, *Social Dance: A Short History*, p. 187.

[19] ALLEN HUTT, *The Post-War History of the British Working-Class*, p. 64.

[20] W. BEVERIDGE, *Full Employment in a Free Society*, p. 47.

[21] Percentage unemployment rate of insured population was 10·7 (W. Beveridge, *op. cit.*, p. 47).

[22] A. S. J. TESSIMOND, Latter-Day Oracles: 'Dance Band' in *A Treasury of Modern Poetry*, ed. Megroz, p. 222.

NOTES TO CHAPTER XII (pp. 97 to 100)

[1] W. BEVERIDGE, *Full Employment in a Free Society*, p. 47.

[2] S. DANNETT AND F. RACHEL, *Down Memory Lane*, p. 129.

[3] P. J. S. RICHARDSON, *History of English Ballroom Dancing*, p. 113.

[4] The 'Lindy Hop' made its first appearance in the U.S.A. in the late twenties and was called the 'Lindbergh Hop' to commemorate Lindbergh's flight across the Atlantic in 1927. It was lost in the 'Jazz Age' but reappeared in the thirties to be taken over by the 'swing' enthusiasts. It is thus a product of ragtime, jazz and blues as well as swing music. (Dannett & Rachel, p. 136.)

[5] FRANK BORROWS, *Theory and Technique of Latin American Dancing*, p. 6.

[6] *Ibid.*, p. 173.

[7] GROVE's *Dictionary of Music and Musicians*, ed. Eric Blom, p. 215.

[8] PERCY SCHOLES, *The Oxford Companion to Music*, 9th edn., p. 906.

[9] LISA LEKIS, *Folk Dances of Latin America*, p. 229.

[10] L. SCRIVENER, ed., *The Complete Ballroom Dancer*, p. 112. Part II: PIERRE, 'Latin-American Dancing'.

[11] LISA LEKIS, *Folk Dances of Latin America*, p. 228.

[12] *The Times*, 14 March 1966.

Notes

NOTES TO CHAPTER XIII (pp. 101 to 106)

[1] L. SCRIVENER, ed., *The Complete Ballroom Dancer*, p. 234.

[2] DOUGLAS KENNEDY, *The Dance Observer*, New York, March 1940, p. 36, 'Folk-Dance: England'.

[3] Example of a typical 'call':
> Rope your cow and brand your calf
> Swing your honey an hour and a half
> You swing her and she'll swing you
> Promenade home two by two.

[4] In 1946 3,000 city dwellers assembled on the Mall in New York's Central Park to 'square dance' to the music of Ed. Durlacher and the Top Hands. Dannet & Rachel, *Down Memory Lane*, p. 178.

[5] FRANK BORROWS, *Theory and Technique of Latin-American Dancing* (1961 ed.), p. 6.

[6] *Ibid.*, p. 6.

[7] *Ibid.*, p. 3.

[8] L. SCRIVENER (ed.), *op. cit.*, Part II, p. 113.

[9] The new sound in the late forties was one which stressed more adventurous cross-rhythmic patterns and accents for the drums, and a whole new range of harmonic progressions for the horns. In America, Charlie Parker, Dizzy Gillespie, Miles Davis and Thelonious Monk replaced the school of Louis Armstrong, and in Britain, too, the jazz scene was irrevocably changed. See D. Jewell, 'Sound of the Forties' in *Sunday Times Magazine*, 3 January, 1965.

[10] See, *inter alia*, REX HARRIS, *Jazz*.
E. BORNEMANN, 'The Roots of Jazz' in *Jazz*, ed. Hentoff & McCarthy.
S. FINKELSTEIN, *Jazz – a People's Music*.
R. BLESH, *Shining Trumpets*.

[11] LISA LEKIS, *Dancing Gods, passim*.

[12] *Ibid.*, p. 29.

NOTES TO CHAPTER XIV (pp. 107 to 109)

[1] S. DANNETT AND F. RACHEL, *Down Memory Lane*, p. 170.

[2] FRANK BORROWS, *Theory and Technique of Latin American Dancing*, p. 4.

[3] *Ibid.*, p. 4.

[4] *Ibid.*, p. 238.

[5] L. SCRIVENER (ed.), *The Complete Ballroom Dancer*, p. 104.

[6] FRANK BORROWS, *op. cit.*, p. 174.

[7] *Ibid.*, p. 9.

[8] CARR-SAUNDERS, CARADOG JONES AND MOSER, *A Survey of Social Conditions in England and Wales*, p. 9.

[9] *Ibid.*, p. 15.

Notes

[1] For example 'The Girl from Ipanema' (Garota de Ipanema).

[2] In the ballrooms of Brazil, however, the Bossa Nova has almost completely ousted the samba, which is now rather looked down on as a 'low status' dance. (Information supplied by the Cultural Attaché to the Brazilian Embassy, August 1965).

[3] FRANK BORROWS, *Theory and Technique of Latin American Dancing*, p. 174.

[4] GRAHAM TURNER, *Encounter*, June 1962. 'Inside the Twist'.

[5] *Ibid.*

[6] *Ibid.*

[7] *Ibid.*

[8] Correspondence (May 1963) between the author and the Asst. Press Secretary to the Queen.

[9] *New Melody Express*, 13 September 1963 (Derek Johnson). 'Rhythm and blues is at last beginning to register over here . . .'
New Melody Express, 31 December, 1963. 'Rhythm and blues is enjoying more interest in Britain . . .'

[10] During slavery in Jamaica all that had survived of African religion was a cult known in the island as Myalism. This came from the surviving fragments of former African secret societies. Its central ceremony was a death-and-resurrection dance. Towards the end of slavery this cult fused with the fundamentalist Baptist Christianity of negro American slave missionaries, brought over to the island by their loyalist masters after the American revolution. The fashion produced a new religion in Jamaica – what is now known as Pocomania.
(H. O. L. Patterson. Ph.D. Thesis. 'The Sociology of Slavery', 1965, London.)

[11] 'The Dance Invasion' by Orlando Patterson in *New Society*, 15 September 1966.

[12] Quoted by *New Musical Express*, March 1964.

[13] C. HAMBLETT AND J. DEVERSON, *Generation X*, p. 13. (Quotation from Peter Laccohee in June 1964.)

[14] See Appendix I for detailed description as given by the Official Board of Ballroom Dancing.

[15] 'The Dance Invasion', Orlando Patterson, *New Society*, 15 September 1966.

[16] Extract from letter written to author.

[17] A. NAHER, 'A physiological explanation of unusual behaviour in ceremonies involving drums'. *Human Biology*, 34:2, 1962, pp. 151–60.
A. NAHER, 'Auditory driving observed with scalp electrodes in normal subjects'. *E.E.G. and Clinical Neurophysics*, 13, 1961, pp. 449–51.
I. OSWALD, 'Falling asleep during intense rhythmic stimulation'. *British Medical Journal*, i, 14 May 1960, pp. 1450–5.
(I am indebted to Graham Reed, Lecturer in Clinical Psychology at the University of Manchester, for these sources.)

[18] In this connection, it is interesting to consider Eisenstadt's hypothesis that age groups, youth movements, etc., do not exist in all societies but arise only under very specific conditions. In modern societies, for example, a 'lack of any

clear definition of the roles of youth by adults necessarily makes youth groups one of the most important channels through which change takes place and sometimes develops them into channels of outright rebellion and deviance.' EISENSTADT, *From Generation to Generation*, p. 323.

[19] Ernst Kris uses the expression 'The language of the body is replaced by the language of words' in pointing out that spontaneous free expression of emotion in physical form is greatly inhibited by training and social custom, and that the acquisition of speech reduces physical expressiveness. ERNST KRIS, *Psycho-analytic Explorations in Art*, p. 223.

NOTES TO CHAPTER XVI (pp. 120 to 132)

[1] *The Times*, 5 December 1962.

[2] *New Society*, 4 October 1962.
G. ROWNTREE, 'New Facts on Teenage Marriage'.

[3] Britain, An Official Handbook 1967.

NOTES TO CHAPTER XVII (pp. 135 to 136)

[1] JOHN HENRY CARDINAL NEWMAN, *The Idea of a University*, Discourse VI, ed. C. F. Harrold, p. 120.
Newman is here talking of the distinction between 'acquisition' and 'philosophy'.

NOTES TO CHAPTER XVIII (pp. 137 to 171)

[1] For example, M. STEWART: 'The Leisure Activities of School children', W.E.A. 1948; M. STEWART: 'The Leisure Activities of School children', W.E.A. 1960; L. T. WILKINS: The Adolescent in Britain, 1955; T. VENESS: School Leavers – Their aspirations and expectations; Report of the Central Advisory Council for Education, Vol. II (Surveys).

[2] M. STEWART, 'The Leisure Activities of School children', W.E.A. 1948.

[3] M. STEWART, 'The Leisure Activities of School children', W.E.A., 1960.

[4] M. STEWART, 'The Leisure Activities of School children', W.E.A., 1960, p. 20. See also p. 19, and Table 13 which shows that in comparison with other pursuits dancing plays a far more important part (than in 1948) in the leisure hours of both grammar and modern school pupils.

[5] T. VENESS, *School Leavers – Their aspirations and expectations*, p. 118. See also page 244, note 23.

[6] L. T. WILKINS, *The Adolescent in Britain*, 1955.

[7] 15 to 18: Report of the Central Advisory Council for Education – England, Vol. II (Surveys), pp. 96 and 97.

[8] 15 to 18: Report of the Central Advisory Council for Education – England, Vol. II (Surveys), p. 96.

[9] E. M. AND M. EPPEL, *Adolescents and Morality*, Foreword, p. x.

[10] 15 to 18: Report of the Central Advisory Council for Education – England, Vol. II (Surveys), p. 95.

[11] CURT SACHS, *World History of the Dance*, p. 25.

[12] In this connection it is of interest that M. Schofield finds an association between frequency of dancing and sex experience for boys and girls. The association is not a causal relationship and operates in a different way for each sex. Thus, girls who went dancing with 'steady' boy-friends were more likely to be experienced than those who went with other people, but Schofield had already established that girls with steady boy-friends were more experienced, whether they went to dances or not. With boys, sex experience was not associated with those who went dancing with their girl-friends (as compared with mixed groups or with other boys) but was associated with the number of times they went dancing. It was also however associated in equally significant fashion with the number of times they went to the cinema and, in general, was linked with their degree of 'outgoingness' and gregariousness.
M. SCHOFIELD, *The Sexual Behaviour of Young People*, pp. 171–2, 227.

NOTES TO CHAPTER XIX (pp. 172 to 174)

[1] EISENSTADT, *From Generation to Generation*, Chap. I and *passim*.

[2] See also R. BENEDICT, 'Continuities and Discontinuities in Culture Conditioning' in *Psychiatry I*, 1938, pp. 161–7.

[3] See the discussion in W. H. J. SPROTT, *Science & Social Action*, pp. 46–7.

[4] The theory of alienation is discussed at some length by T. PARSONS, *The Social System*, Chap. VII.

[5] If the theory is correct that this solution is an alternative to the 'deviant' solutions, one would expect the rise of beat clubs and groups in any particular area to coincide with a decline in neurotic illness, delinquency and 'embittered rebellion'. COLIN FLETCHER, writing in *New Society* (20 February 1964) does in fact point out that in Merseyside the advent of beat music totally changed the character of two violent gangs: the guitar came to replace the cosh. His views, however, were subsequently questioned in a letter from the Chief Constable, Liverpool, who expressed the opinion that the beat groups were the product of the non-violent rather than the violent Liverpool gangs.

[6] The fact that the world of pop and beat is to a considerable extent associated with drug-taking shows, however, that the borderline between deviant and non-deviant solutions may be fairly tenuous.

INDEX TO WORKS CITED

The numbers following each reference give the pages in the text on which that reference is cited, or discussed.

ARBEAU, T. *Orchesography*, 1588 (Translated C. W. Beaumont). C. W. Beaumont, 1925. *39, 42, 44–46, 257 n., 258 n.*

BARNARD, E. A. B. *A Seventeenth Century Country Gentleman*. Heffer and Sons Ltd., 1944. *55*

BASKERVILL, C. R. *The Elizabethan Jig*. Univ. of Chicago Press, 1929. *50*

BENNETT, H. S. *The Pastons and their England*. Cambridge Univ. Press, 1932. *256 n.*

BENNETT, R. *A Picture of the Twenties*. Vista Books, 1961. *88, 92*

BEVERIDGE, W. *Full Employment in a Free Society*. Allen & Unwin, 1944. *94, 97, 264 n.*

BLESH, R. *Shining Trumpets*. Cassell & Co., 1958. *104*

BORROWS, F. *Theory and Technique of Latin American Dancing*. Miller, 1961. *98, 102, 107, 108, 110*

BRETEL, J. *Le Tournoi de Chauvency*. Ed: Maurice Delbouille, 1932. In Bodleian Library Oxford. *31*

Britain: An Official Handbook H.M.S.O., 1967. *131*

BYRON, LORD. *Byron's Poems*. Everyman's Library, 1963. *68, 261 n.*

CARR-SAUNDERS, JONES and MOSER *Social Conditions in England and Wales*. O.U.P., 1958. *109*

CASTLE, IRENE and VERNON *Modern Dancing 1914*. In British Museum. *84, 193*

CELLARIUS, H. *Fashionable Dancing 1847*. In British Museum. *76*

CHAMBERS, E. K. *The Elizabethan Stage*. Oxford Univ. Press, 1923. *39, 40, 45*

CHAMBERS, E. K. *The Medieval Stage*. Clarendon Press, 1953. *32, 256 n.*

CHAPPELL *Music of the Olden Time c. 1880*. Chappell & Co., In British Museum. *256 n.*

CHUJOY, A. *Dance Encyclopaedia*. A. S. Barnes & Co. Inc., 1949. *68, 72*

CLARK, J. M. *The Dance of Death in the Middle Ages*. Jackson, Son & Co., 1950. *25*

COLLIER and LANG *Just the Other Day*. Hamilton, 1932. *90, 92*

COPELAND, R. *Manner of dancynge of bace Dances after the use of France*. In Bodleian Library, Oxford. *40, 41, 120, 181*

COULON *The Polka 1844*. In library of Royal Academy of Dancing. *73, 74, 75*

CRAWLEY, A. E. 'Processions and Dances' in *Encyclopaedia of Religion and Ethics*. *9, 10*

Index to Works Cited

CROMWELL, O. *The Writings and Speeches of Oliver Cromwell*, Vol. IV, Ed. W. C. Abbott. Harvard Univ. Press, 1947. *55*

Crowther Report '15 to 18. Report of the Central Advisory Council for Education—England' Vol. II (Surveys). H.M.S.O., 1960. *137, 138, 142, 146, 147*

DANNETT, S. and RACHEL, F. *Down Memory Lane*. Greenberg, 1954. *77, 83, 91, 97, 107, 265 n.*

DAVIES, SIR JOHN *Orchestra, or a Poem of Dancing, 1596*, Ed. E. M. W. Tillyard. Chatto & Windus, 1945. *44, 45*

DODSWORTH, A. *Dancing and its Relations to Education and Social Life, 1885*. In library of Royal Academy of Dancing, Harper & Brothers. *73*

DOLMETSCH, M. *Dances of England and France 1450–1600*. Routledge & Kegan Paul, 1949. *47, 258 n.*

DÜRKHEIM, E. *The Rules of Sociological Method*. Free Press, N.Y., 1950. *4*

DWYER, N. *Dance the Twist*. Britannia Books, 1962. *112, 113*

EISENSTADT, S. N. *From Generation to Generation*. Free Press Glencoe, 1964. *72, 266–7 n.*

ELLIS, HAVELOCK *The Dance of Life*. Constable & Co., 1923. *10*

ELYOT, SIR THOMAS *The Boke named the Governour*. Everyman's Library, 1907. *41, 42*

EPPEL, E. M. and M. *Adolescents and Morality*. Routledge & Kegan Paul, 1966. *142*

ETZIONI, A. and E. *Social Change*. Basic Books, N.Y., 1964. *2*

FANSHAWE, C. M. *Memorials of Miss Catherine Maria Fanshawe*. Privately printed. In British Museum. *59, 60, 61*

FINKELSTEIN, S. *Jazz—A People's Music*. Citadel Press, N.Y., 1948. *104*

FRANKS, A. H. *Social Dance: A Short History*. Routledge & Kegan Paul, 1963. *5, 40, 41, 54, 65, 67, 70, 75, 82, 86, 93, 193*

FRANKS, A. H. *The Modern Ballroom Dancer's Handbook*. Pitman, 1963. *190*

FRAZER, SIR J. *The Golden Bough*, Macmillan, 1915. *15* (an abridged version entitled *Magic and Religion* was published in 1944 for 'The Thinkers' Library'. Watts & Co).

GORER, G. *Africa Dances*. Faber & Faber, 1935. *12, 15*

GRAVES and HODGE *A Social History of Great Britain 1918–1939*. Faber & Faber, 1961. *87, 88*

GRONOW, CAPTAIN *The Reminiscences and Recollections of Captain Gronow*, Ed. J. Raymond. Bodley Head, 1964. *67, 71, 72*

GROVE, G. *Dictionary of Music and Musicians*, Ed. Eric Blom. Macmillan, 1936. *67, 99*

GROVE, MRS. LILY *Dancing*. The Badminton Library of Sports and pastimes, 1895. *67*

HADDON, A. C. *Head-Hunters—Black, White and Brown*, Methuen, 1932. *14* (an abridged version was published in 1932 for 'The Thinkers' Library', Watts & Co.).

HAMBLETT, C. and DEVERSON, J. *Generation X*. Tandem Books, 1964. *114*

HAMBLY, W. *Tribal Dancing and Social Development*. Witherby, 1926. *12, 13, 14, 15, 16*

Index to Works Cited

HARE, BORGATTA and BALES *Small groups: studies in social interaction.* Knopf, 1955. *2–3*

HARRIS, REX *Jazz.* Penguin Books, 1952. *104*

HASKELL, A. L. *The Story of Dance.* Rathbone Books, 1960. *16*

HECKER, J. F. C. *Epidemics of the Middle Ages* (Translated B. G. Babington, 1835). In British Museum. *19–22, 25*

HEINE, H. *Heine's Gesammelte Werke.* Gustav Karpeles, Berlin, 1877. *76, 262 n.*

HENTOFF and MCCARTHY (Ed) *The Roots of Jazz.* Rinehart & Co., 1959. *104*

HOLDEN, W. H. *They Startled Grandfather.* British Technical and General Press, 1950. *77*

HOSE, C. and MCDOUGALL, W. *Pagan Tribes of Borneo.* Macmillan, 1912. *12*

HUTT, A. *The Postwar History of the British Working Class.* Gollancz, 1937. *94*

JACKSON, S. *The Savoy: Romance of a Great Hotel.* Muller, 1964. *86*

JENNYNS, SOAME *Poems on Several Occasions* 'The Art of Dancing', 1725. In British Museum. *59*

JOHNSTON, R. ST. *History of Dancing.* Simpkin, Marshall, Kent, 1906. *43, 53, 60, 67, 76, 122*

KENNEDY, D. *English Folk Dancing: Today and Yesterday.* G. Bell & Sons Ltd., 1964. *38, 56, 256 n.*

KINNEY, TROY and MARGARET *The Dance.* Tudor Publishing Co., 1935. *78*

KÖHLER, W. *Psychologische Forschung.* Leipzig, 1925. *4*

KRIS, ERNST *Psycho-analytic Explorations in Art.* International Univ. Press, N.Y., 1952. *267 n.*

KURATH and CHILKOVSKY "Jazz Choreology" in *Men and Cultures*, Ed. A. Wallace. Congrès Internationale des Sciences Anthropologiques et Ethnologiques, Philadelphia, 1956. *89*

LANGER, S. K. *Feeling and Form.* Routledge & Kegan Paul, 1953. *9*

LANGDON-DAVIES, J. *Dancing Catalans.* Jonathon Cape, 1929. *125*

LEKIS, LISA *Dancing Gods.* Scarecrow Press, 1960. *104, 105*

LEKIS, LISA *Folk Dances of Latin America.* Scarecrow Press, 1958. *82, 99*

LITTLE, B. *Bath Portrait.* Burleigh Press, 1961. *63*

LOON, VAN H. *The Arts of Mankind.* Harrap & Co., 1938. *69*

MACLAREN, J. *My Crowded Solitude.* Angus & Robertson, 1956. *10*

MEAD, M. *From the South Seas.* Morrow & Co., 1939. *17*

MEGROZ, R. L. *A Treasury of Modern Poetry.* Pitman, 1936. *88, 96*

MERTON, R. *Social Theory and Social Structure.* Free Press, Glencoe, 1963, *25*

MONTGOMERY, J. *The Twenties: An Informal Short History.* Unwin, 1957. *90*

MILL, JOHN STUART *The Subjection of Women*, Ed Stanton Coit, Longmans, Green & Co., 1906. *79, 124*

NASHE, THOS. *The Works of Thos. Nashe*, Ed R. B. McKerrow 'Have with you to Saffron Walden'. A. H. Bullen, 1904. *47, 48*

NETTL, PAUL *The Story of Dance Music.* Philosophical Library Inc., 1947. *72*

NICHOLS, J. *Progresses of Queen Elizabeth.* Published 1788. In British Museum. *47*

NICHOLS, J. B. *The Sweet and Twenties.* Weidenfeld & Nicolson, 1958. *91*

PARSONS, T. *The Social System*. Tavistock Publications, 1952. *2–3, 172, 174*

PARSONS, T. and SMELSER *Economy and Society*. Routledge & Kegan Paul, 1956. *2–3*

PATTERSON, H. O. L. *The Sociology of Slavery*. MacGibbon & Kee, 1967. *114*

PEMBERTON, E. *Dancing Master: An Essay for the Further Improvement of Dancing*, 1711. In British Museum. *260 n.*

PEPYS, SAMUEL *The Diary of Samuel Pepys*, Ed H. B. Wheatley. G. Bell & Sons Ltd., 1893. *53, 55, 56, 57*

PLAYFORD, JOHN *The English Dancing Master*, 1651. In British Museum. *56, 57*

POLLOCK, J. S. *La Terpsichore Moderne*, c. 1830. In library of Royal Academy of Dancing. *72*

RADCLIFFE-BROWN, A. *The Andaman Islanders*. C.U.P., 1933. *3, 13*

RICHARDSON, P. J. S. *History of English Ballroom Dancing*. Herbert Jenkins, 1946. *85, 86, 91, 98, 189, 190*

RICHARDSON, P. J. S. *The Social Dances of the Nineteenth Century*. Herbert Jenkins, 1960. *62, 63, 64, 66, 67, 68, 71, 72, 74, 75, 76, 77, 78, 84, 187, 188*

RIVERS, W. H. R. *The Todas*. Macmillan & Co., 1906. *16*

ROSCOE, REV. CANON J. *The Bagesu and other Tribes of the Uganda Protectorate*. C.U.P., 1924. *13*

ROSEN, E. *Dance in Psychotherapy*. Columbia Univ., 1957. *11*

SACHS, CURT *World History of the Dance*. W. W. Norton & Co., 1937. *10, 11, 18, 19, 26, 37, 45, 46, 60, 62, 68, 91, 168*

SCHOFIELD, M. *The Sexual Behaviour of Young People*. Longmans, Green & Co., 1965. *268 n.*

SCHOLES, PERCY *Oxford Companion to Music*. O.U.P., 1938. *99*

SCRIVENER, L. (Ed) *The Complete Ballroom Dancer*. Evans Bros., 1957. *99, 101, 102, 103, 108*

SELIGMANN, C. G. *The Veddahs of Ceylon*. Cambridge Archaeological and Ethnological Series, Macmillan & Co., 1906. *16*

SHARP, CECIL J. and MICILWAINE, H. C. *The Morris Book*. Novello & Co. Ltd., 1912. In British Museum. *256 n.*

SKEAT, W. W. *Chaucerian and Other Pieces*. Oxford Univ. Press, Reprinted, 1935. *32*

SPROTT, W. J. H. *Science and Social Action*. Watts, 1954. *172*

STEWART, M. *The Leisure Activities of School Children*. W.E.A., 1948. *137*

STEWART, M. *The Leisure Activities of School Children*. W.E.A., 1960. *137*

STOW, JOHN *Survey of London 1603*. Ed Kingsford, 1908. *43, 256 n.*

SURREY *Poems*, Ed Emrys Jones. Clarendon: Medieval & Tudor Series, 1964. *43*

TILLYARD, E. M. W. *The Elizabethan World Picture*. Chatto & Windus, 1958. *48, 49*

TREVELYAN, G. M. *English Social History*. Longmans, Green & Co., 1944. *4, 31, 35, 36, 43, 51, 57, 58, 61, 64*

VENESS, T. *School leavers—their aspirations and expectations*. Methuen, 1962. *137, 144*

Index to Works Cited

VOSS, R. *Der Tanz und seine Geschichte*. Berlin, 1869. *9*

WARTON, T. *History of English Poetry*, 1781. In British Museum. *34*

VON WEDEL *Queen Elizabeth and some Foreigners*, 1585. Ed Victor von Kearwill. In British Museum. *45*

WERNER, A. *The Natives of British Central Africa*. Constable, 1906. *13*

WICKHAM, GLYNNE *Early English Stages 1300–1600*. Routledge & Kegan Paul, 1959. *31, 32, 36, 39, 43*

WILSON, THOS. *The Art of Dancing*, 1852. In British Museum. *75*

WILKINS, L. T. *The Adolescent in Britain*, 1955. Unpublished. *137, 138, 147*

WOOD, M. *Historical Dances (12th–19th century)*. C. W. Beaumont, 1952 for Imperial Society of Teachers of Dancing. *33, 34, 40, 42, 44, 54, 59, 60, 61*

WOOD, M. *More Historical Dances*. C. W. Beaumont, 1956 for Imperial Society of Teachers of Dancing. *37, 49, 51, 62, 68, 258 n., 261 n.*

WUNDT, W. *Völkerpsychologie*. Leipzig, 1920. *11*

YATES, G. *The Ball or A Glance at Almacks*, 1829. In British Museum. *67*

ZOLLSCHAN and HIRSCH (Eds) *Explorations in Social Change*. Routledge & Kegan Paul, 1964. *2*

(No Author) *Modern Etiquette in Public and Private*. Frederick Warne & Co., 1895. *70*

(No Author) *Routledge's Ballroom Guide*. Routledge, Warne & Routledge, 1864. *75*

JOURNALS AND PERIODICALS

American Anthroplogist, 1935. *3*

American Sociological Review, December, 1961. *2*
  December, 1956, *2*

British Medical Journal, 14 May, 1960. *115*

The Daily Mail, 13 February, 1922, 28 October, 1925 and 16 October, 1926. *89*

The Dancing Times, March, 1911. *84*
  June, 1935. *44*

The Dance Observer, N.Y., March, 1940. *102*

E.E.G. and Clinical Neurophysics, 13, 1961. *115*

Encounter, June, 1962. *111–13*

Human Biology, 34: 2, 1962. *115*

Illustrated London News, April, 1844, May, 1844. *74*

Journal of the English Folk Dance and Song Society, Vol. IX, No. 3. *258 n.*

Limburg Chronicle, 1828. *20*

Monthly Musical Record, 1902. *55*

New Melody Express, 13 September, 1963, 31 December, 1963. *113*

New Musical Express, March, 1964. *114*

New Society, 4 October, 1962. *131*
  20 February, 1964. *268 n.*
  23 December, 1965. *104, 105*
  15 September, 1966. *114*

273

INDEX

275

The International Library of

Sociology

and Social Reconstruction

Edited by W. J. H. SPROTT
Founded by KARL MANNHEIM

ROUTLEDGE & KEGAN PAUL
BROADWAY HOUSE, CARTER LANE, LONDON, E.C.4

CONTENTS

PRINTED IN GREAT BRITAIN BY HEADLEY BROTHERS LTD
109 KINGSWAY LONDON W C 2 AND ASHFORD KENT

GENERAL SOCIOLOGY

Brown, Robert. Explanation in Social Science. *208 pp. 1963. (2nd Impression 1964.) 25s.*

Gibson, Quentin. The Logic of Social Enquiry. *240 pp. 1960. (3rd Impression 1968.) 24s.*

Homans, George C. Sentiments and Activities: Essays in Social Science. *336 pp. 1962. 32s.*

Isajiw, Wsevelod W. Causation and Functionalism in Sociology. *165 pp. 1968. 25s.*

Johnson, Harry M. Sociology: a Systematic Introduction. *Foreword by Robert K. Merton. 710 pp. 1961. (5th Impression 1968.) 42s.*

Mannheim, Karl. Essays on Sociology and Social Psychology. *Edited by Paul Keckskemeti. With Editorial Note by Adolph Lowe. 344 pp. 1953. (2nd Impression 1966.) 32s.*

Systematic Sociology: An Introduction to the Study of Society. *Edited by J. S. Erös and Professor W. A. C. Stewart. 220 pp. 1957. (3rd Impression 1967.) 24s.*

Martindale, Don. The Nature and Types of Sociological Theory. *292 pp. 1961. (3rd Impression 1967.) 35s.*

Maus, Heinz. A Short History of Sociology. *234 pp. 1962. (2nd Impression 1965.) 28s.*

Myrdal, Gunnar. Value in Social Theory: A Collection of Essays on Methodology. *Edited by Paul Streeten. 332 pp. 1958. (3rd Impression 1968.) 35s.*

Ogburn, William F., and **Nimkoff, Meyer F.** A Handbook of Sociology. *Preface by Karl Mannheim. 656 pp. 46 figures. 35 tables. 5th edition (revised) 1964. 45s.*

Parsons, Talcott, and **Smelser, Neil J.** Economy and Society: A Study in the Integration of Economic and Social Theory. *362 pp. 1956. (4th Impression 1967.) 35s.*

Rex, John. Key Problems of Sociological Theory. *220 pp. 1961. (4th Impression 1968.) 25s.*

Stark, Werner. The Fundamental Forms of Social Thought. *280 pp. 1962. 32s.*

FOREIGN CLASSICS OF SOCIOLOGY

Durkheim, Emile. Suicide. A Study in Sociology. *Edited and with an Introduction by George Simpson. 404 pp. 1952. (4th Impression 1968.) 35s.*

Professional Ethics and Civic Morals. *Translated by Cornelia Brookfield. 288 pp. 1957. 30s.*

Gerth, H. H., and **Mills, C. Wright.** From Max Weber: Essays in Sociology. *502 pp. 1948. (6th Impression 1967.) 35s.*

Tönnies, Ferdinand. Community and Association. (*Gemeinschaft und Gesellschaft.*) *Translated and Supplemented by Charles P. Loomis. Foreword by Pitirim A. Sorokin. 334 pp. 1955. 28s.*

SOCIAL STRUCTURE

Andreski, Stanislav. Military Organization and Society. *Foreword by Professor A. R. Radcliffe-Brown. 226 pp. 1 folder. 1954. Revised Edition 1968. 35s.*

Cole, G. D. H. Studies in Class Structure. *220 pp. 1955. (3rd Impression 1964.) 21s. Paper 10s. 6d.*

Coontz, Sydney H. Population Theories and the Economic Interpretation. *202 pp. 1957. (3rd Impression 1968.) 28s.*

Coser, Lewis. The Functions of Social Conflict. *204 pp. 1956. (3rd Impression 1968.) 25s.*

Dickie-Clark, H. F. Marginal Situation: A Sociological Study of a Coloured Group. *240 pp. 11 tables. 1966. 40s.*

Glass, D. V. (Ed.). Social Mobility in Britain. *Contributions by J. Berent, T. Bottomore, R. C. Chambers, J. Floud, D. V. Glass, J. R. Hall, H. T. Himmelweit, R. K. Kelsall, F. M. Martin, C. A. Moser, R. Mukherjee, and W. Ziegel. 420 pp. 1954. (4th Impression 1967.) 45s.*

Jones, Garth N. Planned Organizational Change: An Exploratory Study Using an Empirical Approach. *About 268 pp. 1969. 40s.*

Kelsall, R. K. Higher Civil Servants in Britain: From 1870 to the Present Day. *268 pp. 31 tables. 1955. (2nd Impression 1966.) 25s.*

König, René. The Community. *232 pp. Illustrated. 1968. 35s.*

Lawton, Denis. Social Class, Language and Education. *192 pp. 1968. (2nd Impression 1968.) 25s.*

McLeish, John. The Theory of Social Change: Four Views Considered. *About 128 pp. 1969. 21s.*

Marsh, David C. The Changing Social Structure in England and Wales, 1871-1961. *1958. 272 pp. 2nd edition (revised) 1966. (2nd Impression 1967.) 35s.*

Mouzelis, Nicos. Organization and Bureaucracy. An Analysis of Modern Theories. *240 pp. 1967. (2nd Impression 1968.) 28s.*

Ossowski, Stanislaw. Class Structure in the Social Consciousness. *210 pp. 1963. (2nd Impression 1967.) 25s.*

SOCIOLOGY AND POLITICS

Barbu, Zevedei. Democracy and Dictatorship: Their Psychology and Patterns of Life. *300 pp. 1956. 28s.*

Crick, Bernard. The American Science of Politics: Its Origins and Conditions. *284 pp. 1959. 32s.*

Hertz, Frederick. Nationality in History and Politics: A Psychology and Sociology of National Sentiment and Nationalism. *432 pp. 1944. (5th Impression 1966.) 42s.*

Kornhauser, William. The Politics of Mass Society. *272 pp. 20 tables. 1960. (3rd Impression 1968.) 28s.*

Laidler, Harry W. History of Socialism. Social-Economic Movements: An Historical and Comparative Survey of Socialism, Communism, Co-operation, Utopianism; and other Systems of Reform and Reconstruction. *New edition. 992 pp. 1968. 90s.*

Lasswell, Harold D. Analysis of Political Behaviour. An Empirical Approach. *324 pp. 1947. (4th Impression 1966.) 35s.*

Mannheim, Karl. Freedom, Power and Democratic Planning. *Edited by Hans Gerth and Ernest K. Bramstedt. 424 pp. 1951. (3rd Impression 1968.) 42s.*

Mansur, Fatma. Process of Independence. *Foreword by A. H. Hanson. 208 pp. 1962. 25s.*

Martin, David A. Pacificism: an Historical and Sociological Study. *262 pp. 1965. 30s.*

Myrdal, Gunnar. The Political Element in the Development of Economic Theory. *Translated from the German by Paul Streeten. 282 pp. 1953. (4th Impression 1965.) 25s.*

Polanyi, Michael. F.R.S. The Logic of Liberty: Reflections and Rejoinders. *228 pp. 1951. 18s.*

Verney, Douglas V. The Analysis of Political Systems. *264 pp. 1959. (3rd Impression 1966.) 28s.*

Wootton, Graham. The Politics of Influence: British Ex-Servicemen, Cabinet Decisions and Cultural Changes, 1917 to 1957. *316 pp. 1963. 30s.*
Workers, Unions and the State. *188 pp. 1966. (2nd Impression 1967.) 25s.*

FOREIGN AFFAIRS: THEIR SOCIAL, POLITICAL AND ECONOMIC FOUNDATIONS

Baer, Gabriel. Population and Society in the Arab East. *Translated by Hanna Szöke. 288 pp. 10 maps. 1964. 40s.*

Bonné, Alfred. State and Economics in the Middle East: A Society in Transition. *482 pp. 2nd (revised) edition 1955. (2nd Impression 1960.) 40s.*
Studies in Economic Development: with special reference to Conditions in the Under-developed Areas of Western Asia and India. *322 pp. 84 tables. 2nd edition 1960. 32s.*

Mayer, J. P. Political Thought in France from the Revolution to the Fifth Republic. *164 pp. 3rd edition (revised) 1961. 16s.*

CRIMINOLOGY

Ancel, Marc. Social Defence: A Modern Approach to Criminal Problems. *Foreword by Leon Radzinowicz. 240 pp. 1965. 32s.*

Cloward, Richard A., and **Ohlin, Lloyd E.** Delinquency and Opportunity: A Theory of Delinquent Gangs. *248 pp. 1961. 25s.*

5

Downes, David M. The Delinquent Solution. A Study in Subcultural Theory. *296 pp. 1966. 42s.*

Dunlop, A. B., and **McCabe, S.** Young Men in Detention Centres. *192 pp. 1965. 28s.*

Friedländer, Kate. The Psycho-Analytical Approach to Juvenile Delinquency: Theory, Case Studies, Treatment. *320 pp. 1947. (6th Impression 1967). 40s.*

Glueck, Sheldon and **Eleanor.** Family Environment and Delinquency. *With the statistical assistance of Rose W. Kneznek. 340 pp. 1962. (2nd Impression 1966.) 40s.*

Mannheim, Hermann. Comparative Criminology: a Text Book. *Two volumes. 442 pp. and 380 pp. 1965. (2nd Impression with corrections 1966.) 42s. a volume.*

Morris, Terence. The Criminal Area: A Study in Social Ecology. *Foreword by Hermann Mannheim. 232 pp. 25 tables. 4 maps. 1957. (2nd Impression 1966.) 28s.*

Morris, Terence and **Pauline,** assisted by **Barbara Barer.** Pentonville: A Sociological Study of an English Prison. *416 pp. 16 plates. 1963. 50s.*

Spencer, John C. Crime and the Services. *Foreword by Hermann Mannheim. 336 pp. 1954. 28s.*

Trasler, Gordon. The Explanation of Criminality. *144 pp. 1962. (2nd Impression 1967.) 20s.*

SOCIAL PSYCHOLOGY

Barbu, Zevedei. Problems of Historical Psychology. *248 pp. 1960. 25s.*

Blackburn, Julian. Psychology and the Social Pattern. *184 pp. 1945. (7th Impression 1964.) 16s.*

Fleming, C. M. Adolescence: Its Social Psychology: With an Introduction to recent findings from the fields of Anthropology, Physiology, Medicine, Psychometrics and Sociometry. *288 pp. 2nd edition (revised) 1963. (3rd Impression 1967.) 25s. Paper 12s. 6d.*

The Social Psychology of Education: An Introduction and Guide to Its Study. *136 pp. 2nd edition (revised) 1959. (4th Impression 1967.) 14s. Paper 7s. 6d.*

Homans, George C. The Human Group. *Foreword by Bernard DeVoto. Introduction by Robert K. Merton. 526 pp. 1951. (7th Impression 1968.) 35s.*

Social Behaviour: its Elementary Forms. *416 pp. 1961. (3rd Impression 1968.) 35s.*

Klein, Josephine. The Study of Groups. *226 pp. 31 figures. 5 tables. 1956. (5th Impression 1967.) 21s. Paper 9s. 6d.*

Linton, Ralph. The Cultural Background of Personality. *132 pp. 1947. (7th Impression 1968.) 18s.*

Mayo, Elton. The Social Problems of an Industrial Civilization. With an appendix on the Political Problem. *180 pp. 1949. (5th Impression 1966.) 25s.*

Ottaway, A. K. C. Learning Through Group Experience. *176 pp. 1966. (2nd Impression 1968.) 25s.*

Ridder, J. C. de. The Personality of the Urban African in South Africa. A Thematic Apperception Test Study. *196 pp. 12 plates. 1961. 25s.*

Rose, Arnold M. (Ed.). Human Behaviour and Social Processes: an Interactionist Approach. *Contributions by Arnold M. Rose, Ralph H. Turner, Anselm Strauss, Everett C. Hughes, E. Franklin Frazier, Howard S. Becker, et al. 696 pp. 1962. (2nd Impression 1968.) 70s.*

Smelser, Neil J. Theory of Collective Behaviour. *448 pp. 1962. (2nd Impression 1967.) 45s.*

Stephenson, Geoffrey M. The Development of Conscience. *128 pp. 1966. 25s.*

Young, Kimball. Handbook of Social Psychology. *658 pp. 16 figures. 10 tables. 2nd edition (revised) 1957. (3rd Impression 1963.) 40s.*

SOCIOLOGY OF THE FAMILY

Banks, J. A. Prosperity and Parenthood: A study of Family Planning among The Victorian Middle Classes. *262 pp. 1954. (3rd Impression 1968.) 28s.*

Bell, Colin R. Middle Class Families: Social and Geographical Mobility. *224 pp. 1969. 35s.*

Burton, Lindy. Vulnerable Children. *272 pp. 1968. 35s.*

Gavron, Hannah. The Captive Wife: Conflicts of Housebound Mothers. *190 pp. 1966. (2nd Impression 1966.) 25s.*

Klein, Josephine. Samples from English Cultures. *1965. (2nd Impression 1967.)*
  1. Three Preliminary Studies and Aspects of Adult Life in England. *447 pp. 50s.*
  2. Child-Rearing Practices and Index. *247 pp. 35s.*

Klein, Viola. Britain's Married Women Workers. *180 pp. 1965. (2nd Impression 1968.) 28s.*

McWhinnie, Alexina M. Adopted Children. How They Grow Up. *304 pp. 1967. (2nd Impression 1968.) 42s.*

Myrdal, Alva and Klein, Viola. Women's Two Roles: Home and Work. *238 pp. 27 tables. 1956. Revised Edition 1967. 30s. Paper 15s.*

Parsons, Talcott and Bales, Robert F. Family: Socialization and Interaction Process. *In collaboration with James Olds, Morris Zelditch and Philip E. Slater. 456 pp. 50 figures and tables. 1956. (3rd Impression 1968.) 45s.*

Schücking, L. L. The Puritan Family. *Translated from the German by Brian Battershaw. 212 pp. 1969. About 42s.*

THE SOCIAL SERVICES

Forder, R. A. (Ed.). Penelope Hall's Social Services of Modern England. *288 pp. 1969. 35s.*

George, Victor. Social Security: Beveridge and After. *258 pp. 1968. 35s.*

Goetschius, George W. Working with Community Groups. *256 pp. 1969. 35s.*

Goetschius, George W. and **Tash, Joan.** Working with Unattached Youth. *416 pp. 1967. (2nd Impression 1968.) 40s.*

Hall, M. P., and **Howes, I. V.** The Church in Social Work. A Study of Moral Welfare Work undertaken by the Church of England. *320 pp. 1965. 35s.*

Heywood, Jean S. Children in Care: the Development of the Service for the Deprived Child. *264 pp. 2nd edition (revised) 1965. (2nd Impression 1966.) 32s.*

An Introduction to Teaching Casework Skills. *190 pp. 1964. 28s.*

Jones, Kathleen. Lunacy, Law and Conscience, 1744-1845: the Social History of the Care of the Insane. *268 pp. 1955. 25s.*

Mental Health and Social Policy, 1845-1959. *264 pp. 1960. (2nd Impression 1967.) 32s.*

Jones, Kathleen and **Sidebotham, Roy.** Mental Hospitals at Work. *220 pp. 1962. 30s.*

Kastell, Jean. Casework in Child Care. *Foreword by M. Brooke Willis. 320 pp. 1962. 35s.*

Morris, Pauline. Put Away: A Sociological Study of Institutions for the Mentally Retarded. *Approx. 288 pp. 1969. About 50s.*

Nokes, P. L. The Professional Task in Welfare Practice. *152 pp. 1967. 28s.*

Rooff, Madeline. Voluntary Societies and Social Policy. *350 pp. 15 tables. 1957. 35s.*

Timms, Noel. Psychiatric Social Work in Great Britain (1939-1962). *280 pp. 1964. 32s.*

Social Casework: Principles and Practice. *256 pp. 1964. (2nd Impression 1966.) 25s. Paper 15s.*

Trasler, Gordon. In Place of Parents: A Study in Foster Care. *272 pp. 1960. (2nd Impression 1966.) 30s.*

Young, A. F., and **Ashton, E. T.** British Social Work in the Nineteenth Century. *288 pp. 1956. (2nd Impression 1963.) 28s.*

Young, A. F. Social Services in British Industry. *272 pp. 1968. 40s.*

SOCIOLOGY OF EDUCATION

Banks, Olive. Parity and Prestige in English Secondary Education: a Study in Educational Sociology. *272 pp. 1955. (2nd Impression 1963.) 32s.*

Bentwich, Joseph. Education in Israel. *224 pp. 8 pp. plates. 1965. 24s.*

Blyth, W. A. L. English Primary Education. A Sociological Description. *1965. Revised edition 1967.*

1. Schools. *232 pp. 30s. Paper 12s. 6d.*
2. Background. *168 pp. 25s. Paper 10s. 6d.*

Collier, K. G. The Social Purposes of Education: Personal and Social Values in Education. *268 pp. 1959. (3rd Impression 1965.) 21s.*

Dale, R. R., and **Griffith, S.** Down Stream: Failure in the Grammar School. *108 pp. 1965. 20s.*

Dore, R. P. Education in Tokugawa Japan. *356 pp. 9 pp. plates. 1965. 35s.*

Edmonds, E. L. The School Inspector. *Foreword by Sir William Alexander. 214 pp. 1962. 28s.*

Evans, K. M. Sociometry and Education. *158 pp. 1962. (2nd Impression 1966.) 18s.*

Foster, P. J. Education and Social Change in Ghana. *336 pp. 3 maps. 1965. (2nd Impression 1967.) 36s.*

Fraser, W. R. Education and Society in Modern France. *150 pp. 1963. (2nd Impression 1968.) 25s.*

Hans, Nicholas. New Trends in Education in the Eighteenth Century. *278 pp. 19 tables. 1951. (2nd Impression 1966.) 30s.*
  Comparative Education: A Study of Educational Factors and Traditions. *360 pp. 3rd (revised) edition 1958. (4th Impression 1967.) 25s. Paper 12s. 6d.*

Hargreaves, David. Social Relations in a Secondary School. *240 pp. 1967. (2nd Impression 1968.) 32s.*

Holmes, Brian. Problems in Education. A Comparative Approach. *336 pp. 1965. (2nd Impression 1967.) 32s.*

Mannheim, Karl and **Stewart, W. A. C.** An Introduction to the Sociology of Education. *206 pp. 1962. (2nd Impression 1965.) 21s.*

Morris, Raymond N. The Sixth Form and College Entrance. *231 pp. 1969. 40s.*

Musgrove, F. Youth and the Social Order. *176 pp. 1964. (2nd Impression 1968.) 25s. Paper 12s.*

Ortega y Gasset, José. Mission of the University. *Translated with an Introduction by Howard Lee Nostrand. 86 pp. 1946. (3rd Impression 1963.) 15s.*

Ottaway, A. K. C. Education and Society: An Introduction to the Sociology of Education. *With an Introduction by W. O. Lester Smith. 212 pp. Second edition (revised). 1962. (5th Impression 1968.) 18s. Paper 10s. 6d.*

Peers, Robert. Adult Education: A Comparative Study. *398 pp. 2nd edition 1959. (2nd Impression 1966.) 42s.*

Pritchard, D. G. Education and the Handicapped: 1760 to 1960. *258 pp. 1963. (2nd Impression 1966.) 35s.*

Richardson, Helen. Adolescent Girls in Approved Schools. *Approx. 360 pp. 1969. About 42s.*

Simon, Brian and **Joan** (Eds.). Educational Psychology in the U.S.S.R. *Introduction by Brian and Joan Simon. Translation by Joan Simon. Papers by D. N. Bogoiavlenski and N. A. Menchinskaia, D. B. Elkonin, E. A. Fleshner, Z. I. Kalmykova, G. S. Kostiuk, V. A. Krutetski, A. N. Leontiev, A. R. Luria, E. A. Milerian, R. G. Natadze, B. M. Teplov, L. S. Vygotski, L. V. Zankov. 296 pp. 1963. 40s.*

SOCIOLOGY OF CULTURE

Eppel, E. M., and **M.** Adolescents and Morality: A Study of some Moral Values and Dilemmas of Working Adolescents in the Context of a changing Climate of Opinion. *Foreword by W. J. H. Sprott. 268 pp. 39 tables. 1966. 30s.*

Fromm, Erich. The Fear of Freedom. *286 pp. 1942. (8th Impression 1960.) 25s. Paper 10s.*
The Sane Society. *400 pp. 1956. (4th Impression 1968.) 28s. Paper 14s.*

Mannheim, Karl. Diagnosis of Our Time: Wartime Essays of a Sociologist. *208 pp. 1943. (8th Impression 1966.) 21s.*
Essays on the Sociology of Culture. *Edited by Ernst Mannheim in co-operation with Paul Kecskemeti. Editorial Note by Adolph Lowe. 280 pp. 1956. (3rd Impression 1967.) 28s.*

Weber, Alfred. Farewell to European History: or The Conquest of Nihilism. *Translated from the German by R. F. C. Hull. 224 pp. 1947. 18s.*

SOCIOLOGY OF RELIGION

Argyle, Michael. Religious Behaviour. *224 pp. 8 figures. 41 tables. 1958. (4th Impression 1968.) 25s.*

Nelson, G. K. Spiritualism and Society. *313 pp. 1969. 42s.*

Stark, Werner. The Sociology of Religion. A Study of Christendom.
Volume I. Established Religion. *248 pp. 1966. 35s.*
Volume II. Sectarian Religion. *368 pp. 1967. 40s.*
Volume III. The Universal Church. *464 pp. 1967. 45s.*

Watt, W. Montgomery. Islam and the Integration of Society. *320 pp. 1961. (3rd Impression 1966.) 35s.*

SOCIOLOGY OF ART AND LITERATURE

Beljame, Alexandre. Men of Letters and the English Public in the Eighteenth Century: 1660-1744, Dryden, Addison, Pope. *Edited with an Introduction and Notes by Bonamy Dobrée. Translated by E. O. Lorimer. 532 pp. 1948. 32s.*

Misch, Georg. A History of Autobiography in Antiquity. *Translated by E. W. Dickes. 2 Volumes. Vol. 1, 364 pp., Vol. 2, 372 pp. 1950. 45s. the set.*

Schücking, L. L. The Sociology of Literary Taste. *112 pp. 2nd (revised) edition 1966. 18s.*

Silbermann, Alphons. The Sociology of Music. *Translated from the German by Corbet Stewart. 222 pp. 1963. 32s.*

SOCIOLOGY OF KNOWLEDGE

Mannheim, Karl. Essays on the Sociology of Knowledge. *Edited by Paul Kecskemeti. Editorial note by Adolph Lowe. 352 pp. 1952. (4th Impression 1967.) 35s.*

Stark, W. America: Ideal and Reality. The United States of 1776 in Contemporary Philosophy. *136 pp. 1947. 12s.*

The Sociology of Knowledge: An Essay in Aid of a Deeper Understanding of the History of Ideas. *384 pp. 1958. (3rd Impression 1967.) 36s.*

Montesquieu: Pioneer of the Sociology of Knowledge. *244 pp. 1960. 25s.*

URBAN SOCIOLOGY

Anderson, Nels. The Urban Community: A World Perspective. *532 pp. 1960. 35s.*

Ashworth, William. The Genesis of Modern British Town Planning: A Study in Economic and Social History of the Nineteenth and Twentieth Centuries. *288 pp. 1954. (3rd Impression 1968.) 32s.*

Bracey, Howard. Neighbours: On New Estates and Subdivisions in England and U.S.A. *220 pp. 1964. 28s.*

Cullingworth, J. B. Housing Needs and Planning Policy: A Restatement of the Problems of Housing Need and "Overspill" in England and Wales. *232 pp. 44 tables. 8 maps. 1960. (2nd Impression 1966.) 28s.*

Dickinson, Robert E. City and Region: A Geographical Interpretation. *608 pp. 125 figures. 1964. (5th Impression 1967.) 60s.*

The West European City: A Geographical Interpretation. *600 pp. 129 maps. 29 plates. 2nd edition 1962. (3rd Impression 1968.) 55s.*

The City Region in Western Europe. *320 pp. Maps. 1967. 30s. Paper 14s.*

Jackson, Brian. Working Class Community: Some General Notions raised by a Series of Studies in Northern England. *192 pp. 1968. (2nd Impression 1968.) 25s.*

Jennings, Hilda. Societies in the Making: a Study of Development and Redevelopment within a County Borough. *Foreword by D. A. Clark. 286 pp. 1962. (2nd Impression 1967.) 32s.*

Kerr, Madeline. The People of Ship Street. *240 pp. 1958. 28s.*

Mann, P. H. An Approach to Urban Sociology. *240 pp. 1965. (2nd Impression 1968.) 30s.*

Morris, R. N., and **Mogey, J.** The Sociology of Housing. Studies at Berinsfield. *232 pp. 4 pp. plates. 1965. 42s.*

Rosser, C., and **Harris, C.** The Family and Social Change. A Study of Family and Kinship in a South Wales Town. *352 pp. 8 maps. 1965. (2nd Impression 1968.) 45s.*

RURAL SOCIOLOGY

Chambers, R. J. H. Settlement Schemes in Africa: A Selective Study. *Approx. 268 pp. 1969. About 50s.*

Haswell, M. R. The Economics of Development in Village India. *120 pp. 1967. 21s.*

11

Littlejohn, James. Westrigg: the Sociology of a Cheviot Parish. *172 pp. 5 figures. 1963. 25s.*

Williams, W. M. The Country Craftsman: A Study of Some Rural Crafts and the Rural Industries Organization in England. *248 pp. 9 figures. 1958. 25s.* (*Dartington Hall Studies in Rural Sociology*.)

The Sociology of an English Village: Gosforth. *272 pp. 12 figures. 13 tables. 1956.* (*3rd Impression 1964.*) *25s.*

SOCIOLOGY OF MIGRATION

Humphreys, Alexander J. New Dubliners: Urbanization and the Irish Family. *Foreword by George C. Homans. 304 pp. 1966. 40s.*

SOCIOLOGY OF INDUSTRY AND DISTRIBUTION

Anderson, Nels. Work and Leisure. *280 pp. 1961. 28s.*

Blau, Peter M., and Scott, W. Richard. Formal Organizations: a Comparative approach. *Introduction and Additional Bibliography by J. H. Smith. 326 pp. 1963.* (*4th Impression 1969.*) *35s. Paper 15s.*

Eldridge, J. E. T. Industrial Disputes. Essays in the Sociology of Industrial Relations. *288 pp. 1968. 40s.*

Hollowell, Peter G. The Lorry Driver. *272 pp. 1968. 42s.*

Jefferys, Margot, with the assistance of Winifred Moss. Mobility in the Labour Market: Employment Changes in Battersea and Dagenham. *Preface by Barbara Wootton. 186 pp. 51 tables. 1954. 15s.*

Levy, A. B. Private Corporations and Their Control. *Two Volumes. Vol. 1, 464 pp., Vol. 2, 432 pp. 1950. 80s. the set.*

Liepmann, Kate. Apprenticeship: An Enquiry into its Adequacy under Modern Conditions. *Foreword by H. D. Dickinson. 232 pp. 6 tables. 1960.* (*2nd Impression 1960.*) *23s.*

Millerson, Geoffrey. The Qualifying Associations: a Study in Professionalization. *320 pp. 1964. 42s.*

Smelser, Neil J. Social Change in the Industrial Revolution: An Application of Theory to the Lancashire Cotton Industry, 1770-1840. *468 pp. 12 figures. 14 tables. 1959.* (*2nd Impression 1960.*) *50s.*

Williams, Gertrude. Recruitment to Skilled Trades. *240 pp. 1957. 23s.*

Young, A. F. Industrial Injuries Insurance: an Examination of British Policy. *192 pp. 1964. 30s.*

ANTHROPOLOGY

Ammar, Hamed. Growing up in an Egyptian Village: Silwa, Province of Aswan. *336 pp. 1954.* (*2nd Impression 1966.*) *35s.*

Crook, David and Isabel. Revolution in a Chinese Village: Ten Mile Inn. *230 pp. 8 plates. 1 map. 1959.* (*2nd Impression 1968.*) *21s.*

The First Years of Yangyi Commune. *302 pp. 12 plates. 1966. 42s.*

Dickie-Clark, H. F. The Marginal Situation. A Sociological Study of a Coloured Group. *236 pp. 1966. 40s.*

Dube, S. C. Indian Village. *Foreword by Morris Edward Opler. 276 pp. 4 plates. 1955. (5th Impression 1965.) 25s.*
India's Changing Villages: Human Factors in Community Development. *260 pp. 8 plates. 1 map. 1958. (3rd Impression 1963.) 25s.*

Firth, Raymond. Malay Fishermen. Their Peasant Economy. *420 pp. 17 pp. plates. 2nd edition revised and enlarged 1966. (2nd Impression 1968.) 55s.*

Gulliver, P. H. The Family Herds. A Study of two Pastoral Tribes in East Africa, The Jie and Turkana. *304 pp. 4 plates. 19 figures. 1955. (2nd Impression with new preface and bibliography 1966.) 35s.*
Social Control in an African Society: a Study of the Arusha, Agricultural Masai of Northern Tanganyika. *320 pp. 8 plates. 10 figures. 1963. (2nd Impression 1968.) 42s.*

Ishwaran, K. Shivapur. A South Indian Village. *216 pp. 1968. 35s.*
Tradition and Economy in Village India: An Interactionist Approach. *Foreword by Conrad Arensburg. 176 pp. 1966. (2nd Impression 1968.) 25s.*

Jarvie, Ian C. The Revolution in Anthropology. *268 pp. 1964. (2nd Impression 1967.) 40s.*

Jarvie, Ian C. and Agassi, Joseph. Hong Kong. A Society in Transition. *396 pp. Illustrated with plates and maps. 1968. 56s.*

Little, Kenneth L. Mende of Sierra Leone. *308 pp. and folder. 1951. Revised edition 1967. 63s.*

Lowie, Professor Robert H. Social Organization. *494 pp. 1950. (4th Impression 1966.) 50s.*

Mayer, Adrian C. Caste and Kinship in Central India: A Village and its Region. *328 pp. 16 plates. 15 figures. 16 tables. 1960. (2nd Impression 1965.) 35s.*
Peasants in the Pacific: A Study of Fiji Indian Rural Society. *232 pp. 16 plates. 10 figures. 14 tables. 1961. 35s.*

Smith, Raymond T. The Negro Family in British Guiana: Family Structure and Social Status in the Villages. *With a Foreword by Meyer Fortes. 314 pp. 8 plates. 1 figure. 4 maps. 1956. (2nd Impression 1965.) 35s.*

DOCUMENTARY

Meek, Dorothea L. (Ed.). Soviet Youth: Some Achievements and Problems. *Excerpts from the Soviet Press, translated by the editor. 280 pp. 1957. 28s.*

Schlesinger, Rudolf (Ed.). Changing Attitudes in Soviet Russia.

2. The Nationalities Problem and Soviet Administration. Selected Readings on the Development of Soviet Nationalities Policies. *Introduced by the editor. Translated by W. W. Gottlieb. 324 pp. 1956. 30s.*

Reports of the Institute of Community Studies

(*Demy 8vo.*)

Cartwright, Ann. Human Relations and Hospital Care. *272 pp. 1964. 30s.*

Patients and their Doctors. A Study of General Practice. *304 pp. 1967. 40s.*

Jackson, Brian. Streaming: an Education System in Miniature. *168 pp. 1964.* (*2nd Impression 1966.*) *21s. Paper 10s.*

Jackson, Brian and **Marsden, Dennis.** Education and the Working Class: Some General Themes raised by a Study of 88 Working-class Children in a Northern Industrial City. *268 pp. 2 folders. 1962.* (*4th Impression 1968.*) *32s.*

Marris, Peter. Widows and their Families. *Foreword by Dr. John Bowlby. 184 pp. 18 tables. Statistical Summary. 1958. 18s.*

Family and Social Change in an African City. A Study of Rehousing in Lagos. *196 pp. 1 map. 4 plates. 53 tables. 1961.* (*2nd Impression 1966.*) *30s.*

The Experience of Higher Education. *232 pp. 27 tables. 1964. 25s.*

Marris, Peter and **Rein, Martin.** Dilemmas of Social Reform. Poverty and Community Action in the United States. *256 pp. 1967. 35s.*

Mills, Enid. Living with Mental Illness: a Study in East London. *Foreword by Morris Carstairs. 196 pp. 1962. 28s.*

Runciman, W. G. Relative Deprivation and Social Justice. A Study of Attitudes to Social Inequality in Twentieth Century England. *352 pp. 1966.* (*2nd Impression 1967.*) *40s.*

Townsend, Peter. The Family Life of Old People: An Inquiry in East London. *Foreword by J. H. Sheldon. 300 pp. 3 figures. 63 tables. 1957.* (*3rd Impression 1967.*) *30s.*

Willmott, Peter. Adolescent Boys in East London. *230 pp. 1966. 30s.*

The Evolution of a Community: a study of Dagenham after forty years. *168 pp. 2 maps. 1963. 21s.*

Willmott, Peter and **Young, Michael.** Family and Class in a London Suburb. *202 pp. 47 tables. 1960.* (*4th Impression 1968.*) *25s.*

Young, Michael. Innovation and Research in Education. *192 pp. 1965. 25s. Paper 12s. 6d.*

Young, Michael and **McGeeney, Patrick.** Learning Begins at Home. A Study of a Junior School and its Parents. *About 128 pp. 1968. 21s. Paper 14s.*

Young, Michael and **Willmott, Peter.** Family and Kinship in East London. *Foreword by Richard M. Titmuss. 252 pp. 39 tables. 1957.* (*3rd Impression 1965.*) *28s.*

The British Journal of Sociology. *Edited by Terence P. Morris. Vol. 1, No. 1, March 1950 and Quarterly. Roy. 8vo., £3 annually, 15s. a number, post free. (Vols. 1-18, £8 each. Individual parts £2 10s.*

All prices are net and subject to alteration without notice

15

1268 H.B.